1 9 9 5

GREENBERG'S
POCKET PRICE GUIDE
LIONEL TRAINS
1 9 0 1 - 1 9 9 5

Founded by Bruce C. Greenberg, Ph.D.

✓ W9-AMP-045

any
dling,
f the
ticles

1027

ISBN: 0-89778-396-4

Lionel ® and American Flyer are the registered trademarks of Lionel Trains, Inc., Chesterfield, Michigan.

INTRODUCTION

This **Pocket Price Guide** lists all major Lionel items numerically for the years 1901-1942 and 1945-1995 (there was no Lionel production during World War II). Announced product releases for 1995 were obtained from Lionel's 1994 Stocking Stuffers/1995 Spring Releases catalog, which was available in July, 1994. This is a preliminary list of planned production, and these 1995 items are subject to change. Subsequent additions to the 1995 product line will be reported in the 1996 edition of this pocket guide.

The values quoted in this guide are for the most common variety of each item. Some rare variations are worth considerably more, and a few of the more important ones are cited. For more detailed information about variations, please consult these comprehensive guides: *Greenberg's Guide to Lionel Trains: 1901-1942, Volumes I, II,* and *III; Greenberg's Guide to Lionel Trains: 1945-1969, Volumes I, II, III, IV, V,* and *VI; Greenberg's Guide to Lionel Trains: 1970-1991, Volumes I and II; and Greenberg's Guide to Lionel Paper and Collectibles.*

Dates cited in this guide are cataloged dates. If there is no catalog date, production dates are listed, if known. Lionel Trains are frequently marked with "Built" or "New" dates. These dates often reflect the dates that Lionel's artists picked up from prototype photographs or the date when the artists prepared their drawings. These dates may or may not have any relation to catalog dates or actual production dates. In some cases, Lionel numbered cars with a number different from the catalog number. In these cases we also list this number, enclosed in parentheses, and refer the reader to the published catalog number for the price.

In recent years, reproductions of Prewar and Postwar Lionel trains and train parts have become a major concern for collectors. Today it is difficult to find a Prewar or Postwar Lionel item that has not had parts reproduced or remanufactured for it. Collectors need to be aware of this—while many reproductions are marked or exhibit distinct differences from the original to indicate that they are indeed reproductions, many others are virtually identical to the originals. In some reported cases reproduction markings have been removed. Very close and careful study of an item is advised before making a purchase.

Also, collectors should be aware that counterfeit reproductions of some popular Lionel Postwar items do appear from time to time in the marketplace. These counterfeits often are extremely difficult to detect. If you have any doubts at all about an item's authenticity, you should seek the assistance of a knowledgeable and reputable collector.

We have provided several columns for items listed in Sections 1, 2, 3, 4, and 6. The first two columns give the current market values for each piece. In the Prewar and Postwar sections, values are denoted by Good and Excellent. In both Modern Era sections, the Large Scale section, and the Catalog section, values are given for Excellent and New. The "Color" column in the Prewar and Postwar sections is for noting colors, markings, or other distinguishing characteristics. The "Cond" column is for noting the condition of the piece. The "$" column is for recording your cost in acquiring the item.

We are constantly striving to improve **Greenberg's Pocket Price Guide**. If you find any missing items or detect any misinformation, please, by all means, write to us at the address listed on the Contents page. If you have recommendations for improving a listing, we would also like to hear from you. But please keep in mind that listings for a pocket guide in this compact size and format must always be brief.

R01065 81097

HOW VALUES WERE DETERMINED

The values presented in this Pocket Price Guide are meant to serve only as a *guide* to collectors. They are an averaged reflection of prices for items bought and sold across the country, and are intended to assist the collector in making informed decisions concerning purchases and sales.

Values listed herein are based on values obtained at train meets held throughout the nation during the Spring and Summer of 1994, and from private transactions reported by members of our nationwide review panel. Values in your area may be consistent with values published in this guide, or higher or lower, depending upon the relative availability, scarcity, or desirability of a particular item. General economic conditions in your area may also affect values. Even regional preferences for specific road names may be a factor.

If you are selling a train to an individual who is planning to resell it—a retailer, for example—you will NOT obtain the values reported in this book. Rather, you may expect to receive about 50 percent of these prices. For your item to be of interest to such a buyer, it must be purchased for considerably less than the price listed here. But, if you are dealing one-to-one with another private collector, values may be expected to be more consistent with this guide.

Our studies of train values indicate that mail order and retail store prices are generally higher than prices found at train meets due to the cost and effort of running a retail establishment or producing and distributing a price list, as well as packing and shipping trains.

WE STRONGLY RECOMMEND THAT NOVICE COLLECTORS SEEK THE ADVICE AND ASSISTANCE OF FRIENDS OR ASSOCIATES WHO HAVE EXPERIENCE IN BUYING, SELLING, AND TRADING TRAINS.

NEW FEATURES IN THIS EDITION

We have instituted several typographic changes in this edition designed to make the entries more readable. We hope you'll like this improvement!

This new edition also lists Lionel production from 1970 to 1995 (which we define as Modern Era) in two subsections. The first Modern Era section covers 1970-1986, when Lionel Electric Trains were manufactured by various subsidiaries of General Mills—most notably Model Products Corporation (MPC) and the Fundimensions toy division. The second Modern Era section lists items manufactured by Richard Kughn's Lionel Trains, Inc. (LTI), from 1987 through pre-announced 1995 production. The enormous volume of production since 1970—and especially since 1987— made it both logical and necessary to better define the distinct entities that have manufactured Lionel Trains in this period. Changes in Lionel's product numbering system from four digits to five digits contributed to the practicality of this restructuring. Our forthcoming comprehensive books detailing Modern Era Lionel production will follow this revised structure, and we are confident this will assist collectors in more easily identifying and accurately dating items of interest.

We are very grateful to Todd Wagner for his efforts in compiling, organizing, and confirming the extensive Modern Era lists. Todd's abiding interest in Lionel Trains, combined with his knowledge of the product and meticulous approach to toy train research, have helped to make this the most comprehensive record to date of Modern Era production. Special thanks, too, to Sherrie Weitzman, Steve Saxton, and Melissa Seifert, at Lionel Trains, Inc., for the valuable assistance they provided in verifying item numbers, production dates, and descriptions.

This 15th edition also involved the participation of many other people who generously gave of their time and knowledge. We appreciate their contributions to this publication, and to our enjoyment of the hobby.

—**Allan W. Miller, Editor**

DEFINITIONS

This Pocket Price Guide lists prices for Prewar and Postwar Trains as GOOD and EXCELLENT. Modern Era (1970-1995) Trains, Large Scale Trains, and catalogs are priced EXCELLENT and NEW. Prices for restored pieces fall between Good and Excellent, depending on the item. New pieces bring a substantial premium over Excellent pieces. Fair pieces bring substantially less than Good and Excellent pieces.

In the toy train field there is a great deal of concern with exterior appearance and less concern with operation. If operation is important to you, ask the seller if the train runs. If the seller indicates that he does not know whether the equipment operates, you should test it. Most train meets provide test tracks for this purpose.

Trains and related items are usually classified by condition relating to appearance. The following definitions apply for this guide:

- **FAIR**—well-scratched, chipped, dented, rusted, or warped condition.
- **GOOD**—scratched, small dents, and dirty.
- **VERY GOOD**—few scratches, no dents, rust or warpage; very clean.
- **EXCELLENT**—minute scratches or nicks; no dents or rust; exceptionally clean.
- **LIKE NEW**—free of blemishes, nicks or scratches; original condition throughout, with vibrant colors; only faint signs of handling or use; price includes original box.
- **NEW**—brand new, absolutely unmarred, all original and unused, in original packaging with all paperwork provided by the manufacturer.
- **RESTORED**—professionally refurbished and refinished with a color that approximates the original finish. Trim and ornamentation are present and in Like New condition. The finish appears in Like New condition.

- **CP (Current Production)** means that the item is now being advertised, manufactured, or is currently available from retail stores.
- **REPRODUCTION**—a product intended to closely resemble the original item. It may or may not be marked as such, but should be so marked. Reproductions are currently available for many desirable Prewar and Postwar items.
- **NRS (No Recorded Sales)** means that we do not know the current market value of the item. The item may be very scarce and bring a substantial premium over items in its general class, or it may be relatively common but unnoticed. Usually NRS listings occur when an older and previously unknown item is first reported, although we are still discovering relatively common variations that have not been previously reported. If you have confirmable information about the value of an NRS item, please write to us.
- **NM (Not Manufactured)** means that the item may have been cataloged or other wise advertised, but it was not produced.
- **(#)** Numbers that have been put in parentheses by us do not appear on the actual items.
- **No Number** means item may have lettering, but lacks an item number.
- **(no letters)** means no lettering or number appears on the item.
- ***** means excellent reproductions have been made.
- **[#]** means decorations which make this item unique were not done by Lionel.

CONTENTS

This handy reference is divided into seven major sections: Prewar 1901-1942, Postwar 1945-1960, Modern Era (MPC) 1970-1986, Modern Era (LTI) 1987-1995, Special Production, Large Scale, and Catalogs. In the first four sections and in the Large Scale section, production is listed numerically, using the item's catalog number. In the Prewar section, equipment is further described by Gauge—Standard, O, OO, or 2-7/8. The Gauge type is within the parentheses.

Steam locomotives in all sections include value with tender, even if tenders are not listed in detail. Be advised that the value of steam locomotives, particularly those of the Prewar period, may be significantly affected by the type of tender the item came with. For detailed information on tenders, consult the relevant comprehensive guides.

If you cannot find an item, or believe an item has been erroneously described or priced, please let us know by writing to:

Editor—Lionel Pocket Guide (10-8290)
Books Division
Kalmbach Publishing Co.
P. O. Box 1612
21027 Crossroads Circle
Waukesha, WI 53187-1612

NOTE: Values listed are for the most common variation. Many Prewar items have numerous known variations. Please consult the comprehensive Prewar Guides for complete descriptions.

		Good	Exc	Color	Cond	$
001	Steam 4-6-4 (OO), *38-42*	170	380			
1	Bild-A-Motor, *28-31*	60	150			
1	Trolley (Std.), *06-14*	1300	3500			
1/111	Trolley Trailer (Std.), *06-14*	1000	3000			
002	Steam 4-6-4 (OO), *39-42*	140	300			
2	Bild-A-Motor, *28-31*	70	170			
2	Countershafting, *04-11*		NRS			
2	Trolley (Std.), *06-16**	1200	2500			
2/200	Trolley Trailer (Std.), *06-16*	1000	2000			
003	Steam 4-6-4 (OO), *39-42*	165	400			
3	Trolley (Std.), *06-13*	1400	3500			
3/300	Trolley Trailer (Std.), *06-13*	1300	3000			
004	Steam 4-6-4 (OO), *39-42*	160	300			
4	Electric 0-4-0 (O), *28-32**	500	900			
4	Trolley (Std.), *06-12*	3000	5500			
4U	#4 Kit form (O), *28-29*	1000	1500			
5	Electric (2-7/8") (see 100)					
5	Steam 0-4-0, no tender, Early (Std.), *06-07*	1000	1600			
5	Steam 0-4-0, w/ tender, Early Special (Std.), *06-09*	1200	1800			
5	Steam 0-4-0, no tender, Later (Std.), *10-11*	700	1300			
5	Steam 0-4-0, w/ tender, Later Special (Std.), *10-11*	800	1500			
5/51	Steam 0-4-0, w/ tender, Latest (Std.), *12-23*	750	1000			
6	Steam 4-4-0 (Std.), *06-23*	800	1200			
6	Steam 0-4-0 Special (Std.), *08-09*	2000	3500			
7	Steam 4-4-0 (Std.), *10-23**	1800	2800			
8	Electric 0-4-0 (Std.), *25-32*	140	250			
8	Trolley (Std.), *08-14**	3000	6000			

PREWAR (1901-1942)

		Good	Exc	Color	Cond	$
8E	Electric 0-4-0 (Std.), *26-32*	150	250	___	___	___
9	Electric 0-4-0 (Std.), *29**	1200	2200	___	___	___
9	Trolley (Std.), *09*	3000	6000	___	___	___
9E	Electric 0-4-0 (Std.), *28-35**	600	1200	___	___	___
9U	Electric 0-4-0 Kit (Std.), *28-29*	1200	3500	___	___	___
9	Motor Car (Std.), *09-12*		NRS	___	___	___
10	Electric 0-4-0 (Std.), *25-29**	95	175	___	___	___
10	Interurban (Std.), *10-16*	1000	2000	___	___	___
10E	Electric 0-4-0 (Std.), *26-30*	95	175	___	___	___
011	Switches, pair (O), *33-37*	20	45	___	___	___
11	Flatcar, Early (Std.), *06-11*	150	300	___	___	___
11	Flatcar, Later (Std.), *11-16*	50	100	___	___	___
11	Flatcar, Latest (Std.), *16-18*	50	100	___	___	___
11	Flatcar, Lionel Corp. (Std.), *18-26*	40	80	___	___	___
012	Switches, pair (O), *27-33*	18	38	___	___	___
12	Gondola, Early (Std.), *06-11*	500	700	___	___	___
12	Gondola, Later (Std), *11-16*	50	100	___	___	___
12	Gondola, Latest (Std.), *16-18*	40	80	___	___	___
12	Gondola, Lionel Corp. (Std.), *18-26*	50	80	___	___	___
013	(2) 012 Switches and 439 Panel Board	70	170	___	___	___
13	Cattle Car, Early (Std.), *06-11*	200	400	___	___	___
13	Cattle Car, Later (Std.), *11-16*	150	300	___	___	___
13	Cattle Car, Latest (Std.), *16-18*	50	100	___	___	___
13	Cattle Car, Lionel Corp. (Std.), *18-26*	50	100	___	___	___
0014	Boxcar (OO), *38-42*	30	80	___	___	___
14	Boxcar, Early (Std.), *06-11*	*175*	350	___	___	___
14	Boxcar, Later (Std.), *11-16*	60	100	___	___	___
14	Boxcar, Latest (Std.), *16-18*	60	100	___	___	___
14	Boxcar, Lionel Corp. (Std.), *18-26*	50	75	___	___	___
0015	Tank Car (OO), *38-42*	30	70	___	___	___
15	Oil Car, Early (Std.), *06-11*	50	100	___	___	___
15	Oil Car, Later (Std.), *11-16*	50	100	___	___	___
15	Oil Car, Latest (Std.), *16-18*	50	100	___	___	___
15	Oil Car, Lionel Corp. (Std.), *18-26*	50	100	___	___	___
0016	Hopper Car (OO), *38-42*	48	100	___	___	___
16	Ballast (Dump) Car, Early (Std.), *06-26*	200	400	___	___	___
16	Ballast (Dump) Car,					

		Good	Exc	Color	Cond	$
	Later (Std.), *11-16*	90	175	___	___	___
16	Ballast (Dump) Car,					
	Latest (Std.), *16-18*	90	175	___	___	___
16	Ballast (Dump) Car,					
	Lionel Corp. (Std.), *18-26*	90	175	___	___	___
0017	Caboose (OO), *38-42*	30	65	___	___	___
17	Caboose, Early (Std.), *06-11*	175	350	___	___	___
17	Caboose, Later (Std.), *11-16*	60	120	___	___	___
17	Caboose, Latest (Std.), *16-18*	70	150	___	___	___
17	Caboose, Lionel Corp. (Std.), *18-26*	40	80	___	___	___
18	Pullman (Std.), *08*	800	1800	___	___	___
18	Pullman (Std.), *11-13*		NRS	___	___	___
18	Pullman (Std.), *13-15*	200	300	___	___	___
18	Pullman (Std.), *15-18*	200	300	___	___	___
18	Pullman (Std.), *18-22*	80	150	___	___	___
18	Pullman (Std.), *23-26*	275	600	___	___	___
19	Combine (Std.), *08*	800	1800	___	___	___
19	Combine (Std.), *11-13*		NRS	___	___	___
19	Combine (Std.), *13-15*	200	300	___	___	___
19	Combine (Std.), *15-18*	200	300	___	___	___
19	Combine (Std.), *18-22*	80	150	___	___	___
19	Combine (Std.), *23-26*	275	600	___	___	___
020	90° Crossover (O), *15-42*	2	6	___	___	___
020X	45° Crossover (O), *17-42*	3	9	___	___	___
20	90° Crossover (Std.),	4	10	___	___	___
20	Direct Current Reducer, *06*	—	300	___	___	___
20X	45° Crossover (Std.), *28-32*	5	10	___	___	___
021	Switches, pair (O), *15-37*	15	45	___	___	___
21	Switches, pair (Std.), *15-25*	40	95	___	___	___
21	90° Crossover (Std.), *06*	10	20	___	___	___
022	Switches, pair, Remote (O), *38-42*	35	70	___	___	___
22	Switches, pair (Std.), *06-25*	40	70	___	___	___
023	Bumper (O), *15-33*	10	25	___	___	___
23	Bumper (Std.), *06-23*	20	35	___	___	___
0024	PRR Boxcar (OO), *39-42*	35	70	___	___	___
24	Railway Station (Std.), *06*		NRS	___	___	___
025	Bumper (O), *28-42*	10	22	___	___	___
0025	Tank Car (OO), *39-42*	30	70	___	___	___
25	Open Station (Std.), *06*		NRS	___	___	___

PREWAR (1901-1942)		Good	Exc	Color	Cond	$
25	Bumper (Std.), *27-42*	20	45	___	___	___
26	Passenger Bridge (Std.), *06*		NRS	___	___	___
0027	Caboose (OO), *39-42*	30	70	___	___	___
27	Lighting Set, *11-23*	15	35	___	___	___
27	Station (Std.), *09-12*		NRS	___	___	___
28	Double Station w/ dome, *09-12*		NRS	___	___	___
29	Day Coach (Std.), *07-22*	1500	3000	___	___	___
29	(See #3 Trolley)					
31	Combine (Std.), *21-25*	60	85	___	___	___
32	Mail Car (Std.), *21-25*	60	85	___	___	___
32	Miniature Figures, *09-18*	75	140	___	___	___
33	Electric 0-6-0, Early (Std.), *13*	250	600	___	___	___
33	Electric 0-4-0, Later (Std.), *13-24*	60	125	___	___	___
34	Electric 0-6-0, Early (Std.), *12*	450	900	___	___	___
34	Electric 0-4-0 (Std.), *13*	175	400	___	___	___
35	Blvd. Lamp, 6 1/8" high, *40-42*	25	55	___	___	___
35	Pullman (Std.), *12-13*	125	200	___	___	___
35	Pullman (Std.), *14-16*	40	60	___	___	___
35	Pullman (Std.), *15-18*	50	80	___	___	___
35	Pullman (Std.), *18-23*	25	40	___	___	___
35	Pullman (Std.), *24*	30	50	___	___	___
35	Pullman (Std.), *25-26*	30	50	___	___	___
36	Observation (Std.), *12-13*	125	200	___	___	___
36	Observation (Std.), *14-16*	40	60	___	___	___
36	Observation (Std.), *15-18*	50	80	___	___	___
36	Observation (Std.), *18-23*	25	40	___	___	___
36	Observation (Std.), *24*	30	50	___	___	___
36	Observation (Std.), *25-26*	30	50	___	___	___
38	Electric 0-4-0 (Std.), *13-24*	95	150	___	___	___
40	(See #4 Trolley)					
41	Accessory Contactor, *37-42*	1	3	___	___	___
042	Switches, pair (O), *38-42*	22	55	___	___	___
42	Electric 0-4-4-0, square hood, Early (Std.), *12**	900	1800	___	___	___
42	Electric 0-4-4-0, round hood, Later (Std.), *13-23*	225	450	___	___	___
043/43	Bild-A-Motor Gear Set, *29*		NRS	___	___	___
43	Boat, Runabout, *33-36, 39-41*	370	530	___	___	___
0044	Boxcar (OO), *39-42*	25	60	___	___	___

		Good	Exc	Color	Cond	$
0044K	Boxcar Kit (OO), *39-42*	60	130			
44	Boat, Speedster, *35-36*	370	650			
0045	Tank Car (OO), *39-42*	30	75			
0045K	Tank Car Kit (OO), *39-42*	60	135			
45/045/45N	Automatic Gateman, *35-42*	30	80			
0046	Hopper Car (OO), *39-42*	40	75			
0046K	Hopper Car Kit (OO), *39-42*	50	100			
46	Crossing Gate, *39-42*	28	80			
0047	Caboose (OO), *39-42*	30	65			
0047K	Caboose Kit (OO), *39-42*	60	130			
47	Crossing Gate, *39-42*	45	125			
48W	Whistle Station, *37-42*	25	70			
49	Lionel Airport, *37-39*	100	290			
50	Airplane, *36-39*	90	240			
50	Electric 0-4-0 (Std.), *24*	95	175			
50	Cardboard Train, Cars, Accessory (O), *43**	200	350			
51	Steam 0-4-0, 5 Late eight-wheel (Std.), *12-23*	650	1000			
51	Lionel Airport, *36, 38*	70	210			
52	Lamp Post, *33-41*	45	95			
53	Electric 0-4-4-0, Early (Std.), *12-14*	1000	2500			
53	Electric 0-4-0, Later (Std.), *15-19*	450	800			
53	Electric 0-4-0, Latest (Std.), *20-21*	150	400			
53	Lamp Post, *31-42*	35	75			
53	Electric 0-6-6-0, Early (Std.), *11*		NRS			
54	Electric 0-4-4-0, Early (Std.), *12**	2500	4000			
54	Electric 0-4-4-0, Late (Std.), *13-23*	1800	2800			
54	Lamp Post, *29-35*	40	85			
55	Airplane w/ stand, *37-39*	160	485			
56	Lamp Post, removable lens and cap, *24-42*	30	85			
57	Lamp Post w/ street names, *22-42*	45	95			
58	Lamp Post, 7-3/8" high, *22-42*	25	55			
59	Lamp Post, 8-3/4" high, *20-36*	40	95			
60/060	Telegraph Post (Std./O), *29-42*	7	18			
60	Electric 0-4-0, F.A.O.S. (Std.), *15 u*		NRS			
61	Electric 0-4-4-0, F.A.O.S. (Std.), *15 u*		NRS			

		Good	Exc	Color	Cond	$
61	Lamp Post, one globe, *14-36*	45	85	___	___	___
62	Electric 0-4-0, F.A.O.S. (Std.), *24-32 u*		NRS	___	___	___
62	Semaphore, *20-32*	18	45	___	___	___
63	Lamp Post, two globes, *33-42*	120	220	___	___	___
63	Semaphore, *15-21*	18	45	___	___	___
64	Lamp Post, *40-42*	20	60	___	___	___
64	Semaphore, 6-3/4" high, *15-21*	20	60	___	___	___
65	Semaphore, one-arm, *15-26*	20	60	___	___	___
65	Whistle Contoller, *35*	3	6	___	___	___
66	Semaphore, two-arm, *15-26*	28	65	___	___	___
66	Whistle Controller, *36-39*	2	5	___	___	___
67	Lamp Post, *15-32*	70	120	___	___	___
67	Whistle Controller, *36-39*	2	18	___	___	___
68/068	Crossing Sign, *25-42*	10	12	___	___	___
69/069/69N	Electric Warning Signal, *21-42*	20	60	___	___	___
70	Outfit: (2) 62s (1) 59 (1) 68	50	120	___	___	___
071	(6) 060 Telegraph Poles (Std.), *24-42*	70	145	___	___	___
71	(6) 60 Telegraph Poles (Std.)	70	145	___	___	___
0072	Switches, pair (OO), *38-42*	130	225	___	___	___
0074	Boxcar (OO), *39-42*	30	75	___	___	___
0075	Tank Car (OO), *39-42*	40	100	___	___	___
076/76	Block Signal, *23-28*	25	70	___	___	___
76	Warning Bell and Shack, *39-42*	80	180	___	___	___
0077	Caboose (OO), *39-42*	30	60	___	___	___
77/077/77N	Automatic Crossing Gate, *23-39*	25	50	___	___	___
78/078	Train Signal (Std.), *24-32*	30	85	___	___	___
79	Flashing Signal, *28-40*	65	160	___	___	___
80	Automobile, *12-16*	720	1600	___	___	___
80/080/80N	Semaphore (Std.), *26-42*	50	130	___	___	___
81	Automobile, *12-16*	720	1600	___	___	___
81	Controlling Rheostat, *27-33*	2	5	___	___	___
82/082/82N	Semaphore, *27-42*	55	120	___	___	___
83	Flashing Traffic Signal, *27-42*	45	120	___	___	___
084	Semaphore, *28-32*	55	95	___	___	___
84	Semaphore, *27-32*	55	95	___	___	___
84	(2) Automobiles	1400	3200	___	___	___

		Good	Exc	Color	Cond	$
85	Telegraph Pole (Std.), *29-42*	12	25	___	___	___
85	(2) Automobiles	1400	3200	___	___	___
86	(6) Telegraph Poles, *29-42*	65	155	___	___	___
87	Flashing Crossing Signal, *27-42*	55	125	___	___	___
88	Battery Rheostat, *15-27*	2	5	___	___	___
88	Rheostat Controller, *33-42*	3	5	___	___	___
89	Flag Pole, *23-34*	20	55	___	___	___
90	Flag Pole, *27-42*	30	65	___	___	___
91	Circuit Breaker, *30-42*	20	45	___	___	___
092	Signal Tower, *23-27*	75	155	___	___	___
92	Floodlight Tower, *31-42**	105	220	___	___	___
93	Water Tower, *31-42*	25	65	___	___	___
94	High Tension Tower, *32-42**	95	220	___	___	___
95	Controlling Rheostat, *34-42*	2	5	___	___	___
96	Coal Elevator, manual, *38-40*	150	290	___	___	___
097	Telegraph Set (O)	50	85	___	___	___
97	Coal Elevator, *38-42*	110	265	___	___	___
98	Coal Bunker, *38-40*	195	470	___	___	___
99/099/99N	Train Control, *32-42*	45	110	___	___	___
100	Electric Loco (2-7/8"), *03-05**	3000	6000	___	___	___
100	Trolley (Std.), *10-16*	1300	3000	___	___	___
100	(2) Bridge Apprch. (Std.), *20-31*	15	35	___	___	___
100	Wooden Gondola (2-7/8"), *01*		NRS	___	___	___
101	Bridge Span (2) Approaches (Std.), *20-31*	25	70	___	___	___
101	Summer Trolley (Std.), *10-13*	1300	3000	___	___	___
102	(2) Bridge Spans (2) Approaches (Std.), *20-31*	35	110	___	___	___
103	Bridge (Std.), *13-16*	25	60	___	___	___
103	(3) Bridge Spans (2) Approaches (Std.), *20-31*	60	160	___	___	___
104	Bridge Span (Std.), *20-31*	20	45	___	___	___
104	Tunnel (Std.), *09-14*	50	130	___	___	___
105	Bridge (Std.), *11-14*	20	65	___	___	___
105	(2) Bridge Apprchs. (O), *20-31*	20	50	___	___	___
106	Bridge Span, (2) Approaches (O), *20-31*	30	70	___	___	___
107	DC Reducer, 110V, *23-32*		NRS	___	___	___
108	(2) Bridge Spans,					

		Good	Exc	Color	Cond	$
	(2) Approaches (O), 20-31	30	75	___	___	___
109	(3) Bridge Spans, (2) Approaches (O), 20-32	35	85	___	___	___
109	Tunnel (Std.), 13-14	30	65	___	___	___
110	Bridge Span (O), 20-31	12	25	___	___	___
111	Box of 50 Bulbs, 20-31	—	125	___	___	___
112	Gondola, Early (Std.), 10-12	150	300	___	___	___
112	Gondola, Later (Std.), 12-16	40	70	___	___	___
112	Gondola, Latest (Std.), 16-18	40	70	___	___	___
112	Gondola, Lionel Corp. (Std.), 18-26	35	60	___	___	___
112	Station, 31-35	120	255	___	___	___
113	Cattle Car, Later (Std.), 12-16	50	80	___	___	___
113	Cattle Car, Latest (Std.), 16-18	50	80	___	___	___
113	Cattle Car, Lionel Corp. (Std.), 18-26	40	60	___	___	___
113	Station, 31-34	135	280	___	___	___
114	Boxcar, Later (Std.), 12-16	35	60	___	___	___
114	Boxcar, Latest (Std.), 16-18	35	60	___	___	___
114	Boxcar, Lionel Corp. (Std.), 18-26	35	60	___	___	___
114	Station, 31-34	510	1300	___	___	___
115	Station, 35-42*	165	320	___	___	___
116	Station, 35-42*	600	1250	___	___	___
116	Ballast Car, Early and Later (Std.), 10-16	50	80	___	___	___
116	Ballast Car, Latest (Std.), 16-18	50	80	___	___	___
116	Ballast Car, Lionel Corp. (Std.), 18-26	50	80	___	___	___
117	Caboose, Early (Std.), 12	40	70	___	___	___
117	Caboose, Later (Std.), 12-16	40	70	___	___	___
117	Caboose, Latest (Std.), 16-18	40	70	___	___	___
117	Caboose, Lionel Corp. (Std.), 18-26	40	70	___	___	___
117	Station, 36-42	90	280	___	___	___
118	Tunnel, 8" long (O), 22-32	15	40	___	___	___
118L	Tunnel, 8" long, 27	15	40	___	___	___
119	Tunnel, 12" long, 20-42	12	40	___	___	___
119L	Tunnel, 12" long, 27-33	15	40	___	___	___
120	Tunnel, 17" long, 22-27	20	60	___	___	___
120L	Tunnel, 27-42	40	95	___	___	___
121	Station (Std.), 09-16	140	320	___	___	___
121	Station (Std.), 20-26	75	165	___	___	___
121X	Station (Std.), 17-19	110	285	___	___	___

PREWAR (1901-1942)	Good	Exc	Color	Cond	$
122 Station (Std.), *20-30*	65	150	___	___	___
123 Station (Std.), *20-23*	68	220	___	___	___
123 Tunnel, 18-1/2" long (O), *33-42*	65	190	___	___	___
124 Station, "Lionel Clty", *20-36**	65	165	___	___	___
125 Station, "Lionelville", *23-25*	65	170	___	___	___
125 Track Template, *38*	1	4	___	___	___
126 Station, "Lionelville", *23-36*	65	160	___	___	___
127 Station, "Lionel Town", *23-36*	65	130	___	___	___
128 124 Station & Terrace, *31-34*ᵃ	700	1700	___	___	___
128 115 Station & Terrace, *35-42**	700	1700	___	___	___
129 Terrace, *28-42**	600	1200	___	___	___
130 Tunnel, 26" long, *20-36*	130	400	___	___	___
130L Tunnel, 26" long, *27-33*	120	400	___	___	___
131 Corner Display, *24-28*	125	325	___	___	___
132 Corner Grass Plot, *24-28*	125	325	___	___	___
133 Heart Shaped Plot, *24-28*	125	325	___	___	___
134 Oval Shaped Plot, *24-28*	125	325	___	___	___
134 Station, "Lionel City", w/ stop, *37-42*	160	320	___	___	___
135 Circular Plot, *24-28*	125	325	___	___	___
136 Large Elevation, *24-28*		NRS	___	___	___
136 Station, "Lionelville", w/ stop, *37-42*	65	150	___	___	___
137 Station, w/ stop, *37-42*	55	135	___	___	___
140L Tunnel, 37" long, *27-32*	300	850	___	___	___
150 Electric 0-4-0, Early (O), *17*	80	165	___	___	___
150 Electric 0-4-0, Late (O), *18-25*	70	115	___	___	___
152 Electric 0-4-0 (O), *17-27*	80	130	___	___	___
152 Crossing Gate, *40-42*	18	45	___	___	___
153 Block Signal, *40-42*	20	55	___	___	___
153 Electric 0-4-0 (O), *24-25*	90	170	___	___	___
154 Electric 0-4-0 (O), *17-23*	90	170	___	___	___
154 Highway Signal, *40-42*	18	45	___	___	___
155 Freight Shed, *30-42**	135	330	___	___	___
156 Electric 4-4-4 (O), *17-23*	475	850	___	___	___
156 Electric 0-4-0 (O), *17-23*	380	750	___	___	___
156 Station Platform, *39-42*	70	145	___	___	___
156X Electric 0-4-0 (O), *23-24*	380	550	___	___	___
157 Hand Truck, *30-32*	20	45	___	___	___
158 Electric 0-4-0 (O), *19-23*	70	185	___	___	___

15

PREWAR (1901-1942)		Good	Exc	Color	Cond	$
158	(2) 156s and (1) 136, *40-42*	100	235			
159	Block Actuator, *40*	10	30			
161	Baggage Truck, *30-32**	30	75			
162	Dump Truck, *30-32**	30	75			
163	(2) 157 (1) 162 (1) 161, boxed, *30-42**	120	385			
164	Log Loader, *40-42*	100	245			
165	Magnetic Crane, *40-42*	150	300			
166	Whistle Controller, *40-42*	3	6			
167	Whistle Controller, *40-42*	4	10			
167X	Whistle Controller (OO), *40-42*	3	6			
169	Controller, *40-42*	2	6			
170	DC Reducer, 220V, *14-38*	2	5			
171	DC to AC Inverter, 110V, *36-42*	2	5			
172	DC to AC Inverter, 229V, *39-42*	2	5			
180	Pullman (Std.), *11-13*	100	175			
180	Pullman (Std.), *13-15*	80	175			
180	Pullman (Std.), *15-18*	80	175			
180	Pullman (Std.), *18-22*	80	100			
181	Combine (Std.), *11-13*	100	175			
181	Combine (Std.), *13-15*	80	175			
181	Combine (Std.), *15-18*	80	175			
181	Combine (Std.), *18-22*	80	100			
182	Observation (Std.), *11-13*	100	175			
182	Observation (Std.), *13-15*	80	175			
182	Observation (Std.), *15-18*	80	175			
182	Observation (Std.), *18-22*	80	100			
183	Pullman (Std.)		NM			
184	Bungalow, Illuminated, *23-32**	55	95			
184	Combine (Std.), *11*		NM			
185	Bungalow, *23-24*	45	95			
185	Observation (Std.), *11*		NM			
186	(5) 184 Bungalows, *23-32*	140	500			
186	Log Loader Outfit, *40-41*	130	300			
187	(5) 185 Bungalows, *23-24*	145	525			
188	Elevator and Car Set, *38-41*	110	350			
189	Villa, Illuminated, *23-32**	85	210			
190	Observation (Std.), *08*	800	1800			
190	Observation (Std.), *11-13*		NRS			

		Good	Exc	Color	Cond	$
190	Observation (Std.), *13-15*	200	300	___	___	___
190	Observation (Std.), *15-18*	200	300	___	___	___
190	Observation (Std.), *18-22*	80	150	___	___	___
190	Observation (Std.), *23-26*	275	600	___	___	___
191	Villa, Illuminated, *23-32**	120	240	___	___	___
192	Villa Set, Illuminated :					
	(1) 189; (1) 191; (2) 184, *27-32*		NRS	___	___	___
193	Accessory Set, boxed, *27-29*	145	360	___	___	___
194	Accessory Set, boxed, *27-29*	145	360	___	___	___
195	Terrace, *27-30*	320	820	___	___	___
196	Accessory Set, *27*	160	370	___	___	___
200	Electric Express (2-7/8"), *03*	4000	6000	___	___	___
200	Turntable, *28-33**	80	195	___	___	___
200	Wooden Gondola (2-7/8"), *01-02*		NRS	___	___	___
200	Trailer, matches #2 Trolley					
	(Std.), *11-16*	—	3600	___	___	___
200	Electric Express (2-7/8"), *03-05**	4000	7000	___	___	___
201	Steam 0-6-0 (O), *40-42*	350	785	___	___	___
202	Summer Trolley (Std.), *10-13*	1300	3000	___	___	___
203	Armored 0-4-0 (O), *17-21*	1000	1850	___	___	___
203	Steam 0-6-0 (O), *40-42*	280	500	___	___	___
204	Steam 2-4-2 (O), *40-42 u*	55	115	___	___	___
205	(3) Merch. Containers, *30-38**	125	300	___	___	___
206	Sack of Coal, *38-42*	5	18	___	___	___
208	Tool Set, boxed, *34-42**	40	120	___	___	___
0209	Barrels, *34-42*	5	15	___	___	___
209	Wooden Barrels, *34-42*	8	20	___	___	___
210	Switches, pair (Std.), *26, 34-42*	30	75	___	___	___
211	Flatcar (Std.), *26-40**	70	130	___	___	___
212	Gondola (Std.), *26-40**	75	150	___	___	___
213	Cattle Car (Std.), *26-40**	125	250	___	___	___
214	Boxcar (Std.), *26-40**	150	250	___	___	___
214R	Refrigerator Car (Std.), *29-40**	375	600	___	___	___
215	Tank Car (Std.), *26-40**	120	200	___	___	___
216	Hopper Car (Std.), *26-38**	175	300	___	___	___
217	Caboose (Std.), *26-40**	125	250	___	___	___
217	Lighting Set, *14-23*		NRS	___	___	___
218	Dump Car (Std.), *26-38**	175	325	___	___	___
219	Crane (Std.), *26-40**	120	175	___	___	___

PREWAR (1901-1942)		Good	Exc	Color	Cond	$
220	Floodlight Car (Std.), *31-40**	200	375	___	___	___
220	Switches, pair (Std.), *26**	20	55	___	___	___
222	Switches, pair (Std.), *26-32*	40	85	___	___	___
223	Switches, pair (Std.), *32-42*	35	95	___	___	___
224/224E	Steam 2-6-2 (O), *38-42*	95	205	___	___	___
225	222 Switches, 439 Panel, *29-32*	75	185	___	___	___
225/225E	Steam 2-6-2 (O), *38-42*	210	370	___	___	___
226/226E	Steam 2-6-4 (O), *38-41*	340	750	___	___	___
227	Steam 0-6-0 (O), *39-42*	550	1300	___	___	___
228	Steam 0-6-0 (O), *39-42*	550	1300	___	___	___
229	Steam 2-4-2 (O), *39-42*	55	120	___	___	___
230	Steam 0-6-0 (O), *39-42*	920	1880	___	___	___
231	Steam 0-6-0 (O), *39*	900	1800	___	___	___
232	Steam 0-6-0 (O), *40-42*	950	1900	___	___	___
233	Steam 0-6-0 (O), *40-42*	1000	2000	___	___	___
238	Steam 4-4-2 (O), *39-40, u*	200	400	___	___	___
238E	Steam 4-4-2 (O), *36-38*	100	200	___	___	___
248	Electric 0-4-0 (O), *27-32*	80	160	___	___	___
249/249E	Steam 2-4-2 (O), *36-39*	100	220	___	___	___
250	Electric 0-4-0, Early (O), *26*	100	220	___	___	___
250	Electric 0-4-0, Late (O), *34*	120	240	___	___	___
250E	Steam 0-4-0 Hiawatha (O), *35-42**	700	1500	___	___	___
251	Electric 0-4-0 (O), *25-32*	175	310	___	___	___
251E	Electric 0-4-0 (O), *27-32*	180	320	___	___	___
252	Electric 0-4-0 (O), *26-32*	65	130	___	___	___
252E	Electric 0-4-0 (O), *33-35*	85	170	___	___	___
253	Electric 0-4-0 (O), *24-32*	100	190	___	___	___
253E	Electric 0-4-0 (O), *31-36*	100	210	___	___	___
254	Electric 0-4-0 (O), *24-32*	120	240	___	___	___
254E	Electric 0-4-0 (O), *27-34*	140	265	___	___	___
255E	Steam 2-4-2 (O), *35-36*	400	800	___	___	___
256	Electric 0-4-4-0 (O), *24-30**	440	900	___	___	___
257	Steam 2-4-0 (O), *30-35 u*	140	320	___	___	___
258	Steam 2-4-0, Early (O), *30-35 u*	75	185	___	___	___
258	Steam 2-4-2, Late (O), *41 u*	30	85	___	___	___
259	Steam 2-4-2 (O), *32*	60	120	___	___	___
259E	Steam 2-4-2 (O), *33-42*	60	120	___	___	___
260E	Steam 2-4-2 (O), *30-35**	415	580	___	___	___
261	Steam 2-4-2 (O), *31*	150	245	___	___	___

PREWAR (1901-1942)		Good	Exc	Color	Cond	$
261E	Steam 2-4-2 (O), *35*	170	260	___	___	___
262	Steam 2-4-2 (O), *31-32*	120	215	___	___	___
262E	Steam 2-4-2 (O), *33-36*	135	235	___	___	___
263E	Steam 2-4-2 (O), *36-39**	300	620	___	___	___
264E	Steam 2-4-2 (O), *35-36*	140	280	___	___	___
265E	Steam 2-4-2 (O), *35-40*	150	310	___	___	___
267E/267W	Sets: 616,					
	(2) 617s, 618, *35-41*	240	425	___	___	___
270	Bridge, 10" long (O), *31-42*	15	50	___	___	___
270	Lighting Set, *15-23*		NRS	___	___	___
271	(2) 270 Spans (O), *31-33, 35-40*	35	100	___	___	___
271	Lighting Set, *15-23*		NRS	___	___	___
272	(3) 270 Spans (O), *31-33, 35-40*	38	110	___	___	___
280	Bridge, 14" long (Std.), *31-42*	35	80	___	___	___
281	(2) Bridge Spans (Std.),					
	31-33, 35-40	65	140	___	___	___
282	(3) Bridge Spans (Std.),					
	31-33, 35-40	85	175	___	___	___
289E	Steam 2-4-2 (O), *37u*	125	350	___	___	___
300	Electric Trolley Car					
	(2-7/8"), *01-05*	2000	4000	___	___	___
300	Hell Gate Bridge (Std.), *28-42**	580	1500	___	___	___
300	(See #3 Trolley)					
301	Batteries, set of 4 (2-7/8"), *03-05*		NRS	___	___	___
302	Plunge Battery (2-7/8"), *01-02*		NRS	___	___	___
303	Summer Trolley, *10-13*	1500	3500	___	___	___
303	Carbon Cylinders (2-7/8"), *02*		NRS	___	___	___
304	Composite Zincs (2-7/8"), *02*		NRS	___	___	___
306	Glass Jars (2-7/8"), *02*		NRS	___	___	___
308	(5) Signs (O), *40-42*	15	35	___	___	___
309	Electric Trolley Trailer					
	(2-7/8"), *01-05*	2500	4500	___	___	___
309	Pullman (Std.), *26-39*	100	175	___	___	___
310	Baggage (Std.), *26-39*	100	175	___	___	___
310	Rails and Ties, complete					
	section (2-7/8"), *01-02*	5	15	___	___	___
312	Observation (Std.), *24-39*	100	175	___	___	___
313	Bascule Bridge (O), *40-42*	220	495	___	___	___
314	Girder Bridge (O), *40-42*	10	27	___	___	___

PREWAR (1901-1942)		Good	Exc	Color	Cond	$
315	Trestle Bridge (O), 40-42	25	60	___	___	___
316	Trestle Bridge (O), 40-42	20	48	___	___	___
318	Electric 0-4-0 (Std.), 24-32	70	250	___	___	___
318E	Electric 0-4-0, 26-35	125	225	___	___	___
319	Pullman (Std.), 24-27	110	175	___	___	___
320	Baggage (Std.), 25-27	100	175	___	___	___
320	Switch and Signal (2-7/8"), 02-05		NRS	___	___	___
322	Observation (Std.), 24-27, 29-30 u	100	175	___	___	___
330	Crossing, 90° (2-7/8"), 02-05		NRS	___	___	___
332	Baggage (Std.), 26-33	50	80	___	___	___
337	Pullman (Std.), 25-32	100	200	___	___	___
338	Observation (Std.), 25-32	100	200	___	___	___
339	Pullman (Std.), 25-33	50	80	___	___	___
340	Suspension Bridge (2-7/8"), 02-05*		NRS	___	___	___
341	Observation (Std.), 25-33	50	80	___	___	___
350	Track Bumper (2-7/8"), 02-05		NRS	___	___	___
370	Jars and Plates (2-7/8"), 02-03		NRS	___	___	___
380	Electric 0-4-0 (Std.), 23-27	200	350	___	___	___
380	Elevated Pillars (2-7/8"), 04-05*	30	75	___	___	___
380E	Electric 0-4-0 (Std.), 26-29	300	350	___	___	___
381	Electric 4-4-4 (Std.), 28-29*	1800	3500	___	___	___
381E	Electric 4-4-4 (Std.), 28-36*	1500	3500	___	___	___
381U	Electric 4-4-4 Kit (Std.), 28-29	1600	4300	___	___	___
384	Steam 2-4-0 (Std.), 30-32*	400	500	___	___	___
384E	Steam 2-4-0 (Std.), 30-32*	400	500	___	___	___
385E	Steam 2-4-2 (Std.), 33-39*	450	750	___	___	___
390	Steam 2-4-2 (Std.), 29*	450	800	___	___	___
390E	Steam 2-4-2 (Std.), 29-31*	450	700	___	___	___
392E	Steam 4-4-2 (Std.), 32-39*	650	1100	___	___	___
400	Express Trail Car (2-7/8"), 03-05*	3500	6500	___	___	___
400E	Steam 4-4-4 (Std.), 31-39*	1200	2000	___	___	___
402	Electric 0-4-4-0 (Std.), 23-27	300	500	___	___	___
402E	Electric 0-4-4-0 (Std.), 26-29	300	450	___	___	___
404	Summer Trolley (Std.), 10		NRS	___	___	___
408E	Electric 0-4-4-0 (Std.), 27-36*	700	1500	___	___	___
412	Pullman, "California" (Std.), 29-35*	600	2000	___	___	___
413	Pullman, "Colorado" (Std.), 29-35*	600	2000	___	___	___
414	Pullman, "Illinois" (Std.), 29-35*	600	2000	___	___	___

No.	Description	Good	Exc	Color	Cond	$
416	Observation, "New York" (Std.), 29-35*	600	2000	___	___	___
418	Pullman (Std.), 23-32*	190	280	___	___	___
419	Combination (Std.), 23-32*	190	280	___	___	___
420	Pullman, "Faye" (Std.), 30-40*	525	1000	___	___	___
421	Pullman, "Westphal" (Std.), 30-40*	550	1000	___	___	___
422	Observation, "Tempel" (Std.), 30-40*	525	1000	___	___	___
424	Pullman, "Liberty Belle" (Std.), 31-40*	325	500	___	___	___
425	Pullman, "Stephen Girard" (Std.), 31-40*	325	500	___	___	___
426	Observation, "Coral Isle" (Std.), 31-40*	325	500	___	___	___
427	Diner (Std.), 30		NM	___	___	___
428	Pullman (Std.), 26-30*	250	325	___	___	___
429	Combine (Std.), 26-30*	250	325	___	___	___
430	Observation (Std.), 26-30*	250	325	___	___	___
431	Diner (Std.), 27-32*	350	600	___	___	___
435	Power Station, 26-38*	130	255	___	___	___
436	Power Station, 26-37*	120	235	___	___	___
437	Switch/Signal Tower, 26-37*	210	480	___	___	___
438	Signal Tower, 27-39*	215	465	___	___	___
439	Panel Board, 28-42*	50	130	___	___	___
440/0440/440N	Signal Bridge, 32-42*	190	460	___	___	___
440C	Panel Board, 32-42	45	100	___	___	___
441	Weighing Station (Std.), 32-36	450	1200	___	___	___
442	Landscape Diner, 38-42	90	200	___	___	___
444	Roundhouse (Std.), 32-35*	1100	3000	___	___	___
444-18	Roundhouse Clip, 33		NRS	___	___	___
450	Electric 0-4-0, Macy's (O), 30 u	300	695	___	___	___
450	Set: 450; matching 605; (2) 606s, 30 u	750	1400	___	___	___
455	Electric Range, 30, 32-33	320	980	___	___	___
490	Observation (Std.), 23-32*	190	280	___	___	___
500	Dealer Display, 27-28		NRS	___	___	___
500	Electric Derrick Car (2-7/8"), 03-04*	5000	7000	___	___	___
501	Dealer Display, 27-28		NRS	___	___	___

		Good	Exc	Color	Cond	$
502	Dealer Display, *27-28*		NRS	___	___	___
503	Dealer Display, *27-28*		NRS	___	___	___
504	Dealer Display, *24-28*		NRS	___	___	___
505	Dealer Display, *24-28*		NRS	___	___	___
506	Dealer Display, *24-28*		NRS	___	___	___
507	Dealer Display, *24-28*		NRS	___	___	___
508	Dealer Display, *24-28*		NRS	___	___	___
509	Dealer Display, *24-28*		NRS	___	___	___
510	Dealer Display, *27-28*		NRS	___	___	___
511	Flatcar (Std.), *27-40*	50	80	___	___	___
512	Gondola (Std.), *27-39*	40	60	___	___	___
513	Cattle Car (Std.), *27-38*	50	100	___	___	___
514	Boxcar (Std.), *29-40*	75	125	___	___	___
514	Refrigerator Car (Std.), *27-28*	225	400	___	___	___
514R	Refrigerator Car (Std.), *29-40*	120	175	___	___	___
515	Tank Car (Std.), *27-40*	90	150	___	___	___
516	Hopper Car (Std.), *28-40*	125	200	___	___	___
517	Caboose (Std.), *27-40*	40	75	___	___	___
520	Floodlight Car (Std.), *31-40*	75	150	___	___	___
529	Pullman (O), *26-32*	15	35	___	___	___
530	Observation (O), *26-32*	15	35	___	___	___
550	Miniature Figures, boxed (Std.), *32-36**	130	230	___	___	___
551	Engineer (Std.), *32*	20	38	___	___	___
552	Conductor (Std.), *32*	20	38	___	___	___
553	Porter (Std.), *32*	20	38	___	___	___
554	Male Passenger (Std.), *32*	20	38	___	___	___
555	Female Passenger (Std.), *32*	20	38	___	___	___
556	Red Cap Figure (Std.), *32*	20	38	___	___	___
600	Derrick Trailer (2-7/8"), *03-04**	4500	9500	___	___	___
600	Pullman, Early (O), *15-23*	40	80	___	___	___
600	Pullman, Late (O), *33-42*	45	85	___	___	___
601	Observation, Late (O), *33-42*	45	85	___	___	___
601	Pullman, Early (O), *15-23*	30	60	___	___	___
602	Baggage, Lionel Lines, Late (O), *33-42*	55	120	___	___	___
602	Baggage, NYC (O), *15-23*	20	45	___	___	___
602	Observation (O), *22 u*	15	35	___	___	___
603	Pullman, Early (O), *22 u*	25	70	___	___	___

		Good	Exc	Color	Cond	$
603	Pullman, Later (O), 20-25	18	50			
603	Pullman, Latest (O), 31-36	28	65			
604	Observation, Later (O), 20-25	28	65			
604	Observation, Latest (O), 31-36	28	65			
605	Pullman (O), 25-32	85	190			
606	Observation (O), 25-32	85	190			
607	Pullman (O), 26-27	35	75			
608	Observation (O), 26-37	35	75			
609	Pullman (O), 37	35	75			
610	Pullman, Early (O), 15-25	30	70			
610	Pullman, Late (O), 26-30	30	85			
611	Observation (O), 37	35	95			
612	Observation, Early (O), 15-25	25	65			
612	Observation, Late (O), 26-30	40	80			
613	Pullman (O), 31-40*	50	155			
614	Observation (O), 31-40*	50	155			
615	Baggage (O), 33-40*	85	195			
616E/616W	Diesel only (O), 35-41	50	115			
616E/616W	Set: 616, (2) 617s, 618	240	425			
617	Coach (O), 35-41	30	85			
618	Observation (O), 35-41	30	85			
619	Combine (O)	100	235			
620	Floodlight Car (O), 37-42	35	65			
629	Pullman (O), 24-32	15	35			
630	Observation, 24-32	15	35			
636W	Diesel only (O), 36-39	90	165			
636W	Set: 636W (2) 637s, 638, 36-39	220	480			
637	Coach (O), 36-39	70	115			
638	Observation (O), 36-39	50	115			
651	Flatcar (O), 35-40	15	45			
652	Gondola (O), 35-40	15	45			
653	Hopper Car (O), 34-40	30	65			
654	Tank Car (O), 34-42	20	45			
655	Boxcar (O), 34-42	20	45			
656	Cattle Car (O), 35-40	30	70			
657	Caboose (O), 34-42	17	42			
659	Dump Car (O), 35-42	40	70			
700	Electric 0-4-0 (O), 15-16	360	700			
700	Window Display (2-7/8"), 03-05		NRS			

		Good	Exc	Color	Cond	$
700E	Steam 4-6-4, Scale Hudson, 5344 (O), *37-42**	1900	4000	___	___	___
700K	Steam 4-6-4, unbuilt (O), *38-42*	3550	5400	___	___	___
701	Electric 0-4-0 (O), *15-16*	400	720	___	___	___
701	Steam 0-6-0 (see 708)					
702	Baggage (O), *17-21*	120	350	___	___	___
703	Electric 4-4-4 (O), *15-16*	1400	2600	___	___	___
706	Electric 0-4-0 (O), *15-16*	350	700	___	___	___
708	Steam 0-6-0, "8976" on boiler front (O), *39-42**	1500	3800	___	___	___
710	Pullman (O), *24-34*	140	240	___	___	___
711	R.C. Switches, pair (O72), *35-42*	75	170	___	___	___
712	Observation (O), *24-34*	140	280	___	___	___
714	Boxcar (O), *40-42**	300	600	___	___	___
714K	Boxcar, unbuilt (O), *40-42*	—	925	___	___	___
715	Tank Car (O), *40-42**	340	675	___	___	___
715K	Tank Car, unbuilt (O), *40-42*	—	745	___	___	___
716	Hopper Car (O), *40-42**	400	830	___	___	___
716K	Hopper, unbuilt (O), *40-42*	—	975	___	___	___
717	Caboose (O), *40-42**	390	625	___	___	___
717K	Caboose, unbuilt (O), *40-42*	—	745	___	___	___
720	90° Crossing (O72), *35-42*	20	42	___	___	___
721	Manual Switches, pair (O72), *35-42*	45	100	___	___	___
730	90° Crossing (O72), *35-42*	20	40	___	___	___
731	R.C. Switches, pair, T-rail (O72), *35-42*	90	175	___	___	___
751E/751W	Set: 752; (2) 753s; 754 (O), *34-41**	600	1000	___	___	___
752E	Diesel only(O), *34-41*	160	280	___	___	___
753	Coach (O), *36-41*	95	200	___	___	___
754	Observation (O), *36-41*	95	200	___	___	___
760	16-piece Curved Track (O72), *35-42*	35	80	___	___	___
761	Curved Track (O72), *34-42*	1	3	___	___	___
762	Straight Track (O72), *34-42*	1	3	___	___	___
762	Inside Straight Track (O72), *34-42*	2	5	___	___	___
763E	Steam 4-6-4 (O), *37-42*	1200	3000	___	___	___
771	Curved Track, T-rail (O72), *35-42*	3	8	___	___	___
772	Straight Track, T-rail (O72), *35-42*	4	12	___	___	___
773	Fishplate Outfit (O72), *36-42*	25	35	___	___	___

PREWAR (1901-1942)		Good	Exc	Color	Cond	$
782	Hiawatha Combine (O), *35-41* *	185	450	___	___	___
783	Hiawatha Coach (O), *35-41* *	185	450	___	___	___
784	Hiawatha Observation (O), *35-41* *	185	450	___	___	___
792	Rail Chief Combine (O), *37-41* *	300	925	___	___	___
793	Rail Chief Coach (O), *37-41* *	300	925	___	___	___
794	Rail Chief Observation (O), *37-41* *	300	925	___	___	___
800	Boxcar (O), *15-26*	25	50	___	___	___
800	Boxcar (2-7/8"), *04-05* *	2500	4500	___	___	___
801	Caboose (O), *15-26*	20	50	___	___	___
802	Stock Car (O), *15-26*	28	60	___	___	___
803	Hopper Car, Early (O), *23-28*	18	40	___	___	___
803	Hopper Car, Late (O), *29-34*	20	45	___	___	___
804	Tank Car (O), *23-28*	20	50	___	___	___
805	Boxcar (O), *27-34*	20	45	___	___	___
806	Stock Car (O), *27-34*	20	45	___	___	___
807	Caboose (O), *27-40*	10	20	___	___	___
809	Dump Car (O), *31-41*	30	70	___	___	___
810	Crane (O), *30-42*	95	175	___	___	___
811	Flatcar (O), *26-40*	40	80	___	___	___
812	Gondola (O), *26-42*	25	55	___	___	___
813	Stock Car (O), *26-42*	55	125	___	___	___
814	Boxcar (O), *26-42*	40	100	___	___	___
814R	Refrigerator Car (O), *29-42*	80	185	___	___	___
815	Tank Car (O), *26-42*	45	115	___	___	___
816	Hopper Car (O), *27-42*	60	130	___	___	___
817	Caboose (O), *26-42*	30	75	___	___	___
820	Boxcar (O), *15-26*	25	75	___	___	___
820	Floodlight Car (O), *31-42*	105	200	___	___	___
821	Stock Car (O), *15-16, 25-26*	45	95	___	___	___
822	Caboose (O), *15-26*	35	75	___	___	___
831	Flatcar (O), *27-34*	20	40	___	___	___
840	Industrial Power Station, *28-40* *	1200	3400	___	___	___
900	Ammunition Car (O), *17-21*	125	390	___	___	___
900	Box Trail Car (2-7/8"), *04-05* *	2000	4000	___	___	___
901	Gondola (O), *19-27*	20	40	___	___	___
902	Gondola (O), *27-34*	15	30	___	___	___
910	Grove of Trees, *32-42*	70	170	___	___	___
911	Country Estate	175	400	___	___	___
912	Suburban Home	175	400	___	___	___

PREWAR (1901-1942)		Good	Exc	Color	Cond	$
913	Landscaped Bungalow, *40-42*	140	315	___	___	___
914	Park Landscape, *32-35*	90	230	___	___	___
915	Tunnel, *32, 34-35*	160	485	___	___	___
916	Tunnel, 29-1/4" long, *35*	95	200	___	___	___
917	Scenic Hillside, *32-36*	90	230	___	___	___
918	Scenic Hillside, *32-36*	90	230	___	___	___
919	Park Grass, bag, *32-42*	7	17	___	___	___
920	Village, *32-33*	600	1750	___	___	___
921	Scenic Park, 3 pieces, *32-33*	980	2875	___	___	___
921C	Park Center, *32-33*	400	1160	___	___	___
922	Terrace, *32-36*	80	170	___	___	___
923	Tunnel, 40-1/4" long, *33-42*	90	250	___	___	___
924	Tunnel, 30" long (O72), *35-42*	50	150	___	___	___
925	Lubricant, *35-42*	1	3	___	___	___
927	Flag Plot, *37-42*	70	150	___	___	___
1000	Passenger Car (2-7/8"), *05**	4500	7500	___	___	___
1000	Trolley Trailer (Std.), *10-16*	1400	2500	___	___	___
1010	Electric 0-4-0, Winner (O), *31-32*	55	130	___	___	___
1010	Interurban Trailer (Std.), *10-16*	1000	2000	___	___	___
1011	Pullman, Winner (O), *31-32*	20	40	___	___	___
1011	Interurban (Std.), *10*		NM	___	___	___
1012	Station, *32*	35	65	___	___	___
1012	(See #1011 Interurban)					
1015	Steam 0-4-0 (O), *31-32*	75	155	___	___	___
1017	Winner Station, *33*	25	65	___	___	___
1019	Observation (O), *31-32*	25	55	___	___	___
1020	Baggage (O), *31-32*	50	115	___	___	___
1021	90° Crossover (O27), *32-42*	1	4	___	___	___
1022	Tunnel, 18-3/4" lg. (O), *35-42*	15	32	___	___	___
1023	Tunnel, 19" long, *34-42*	20	45	___	___	___
1024	Switches, pair (O27), *37-42*	4	16	___	___	___
1025	Bumper (O27), *40-42*	11	25	___	___	___
1027	Transformer, Tin Station, *34*	35	95	___	___	___
1028	Transformer, 40 watts, *39*	3	12	___	___	___
1030	Electric 0-4-0 (O), *32*	70	125	___	___	___
1035	Steam 0-4-0 (O), *32*	75	125	___	___	___
1045	Watchman, *38-42*	15	55	___	___	___
1050	Passenger Car Trailer (2-7/8"), *05**	5000	8000	___	___	___

PREWAR (1901-1942)	Good	Exc	Color	Cond	$
1100 Handcar, Mickey Mouse, *35-37**	400	685	____	____	____
1100 Summer Trolley Trailer (Std.),*10-13*		NRS	____	____	____
1103 Handcar, Peter Rabbit (O), *35-37**	400	1050	____	____	____
1105 Handcar, Santa Claus (O), *35-35**	575	1100	____	____	____
1107 Transformer, Tin Station, *33*	25	65	____	____	____
1107 Handcar, Donald Duck (O), *36-37**	450	1050	____	____	____
1121 Switches, pair (O27), *37-42*	15	35	____	____	____
1506L Steam 0-4-0 (O), *33-34*	95	140	____	____	____
1506M Steam 0-4-0 (O), *35*	250	475	____	____	____
1508 Steam 0-4-0, Commodore Vanderbilt w/ Mickey in 1509 Stoker Tender, *35*	320	525	____	____	____
1511 Steam 0-4-0 (O), *36-37*	110	180	____	____	____
1512 Gondola (O), *31-33, 36-37*	15	38	____	____	____
1514 Boxcar (O), *31-37*	15	38	____	____	____
1515 Tank Car (O), *33-37*	15	38	____	____	____
1517 Caboose (O), *31-37*	15	38	____	____	____
1518 Mickey Mouse Diner (O), *35*	75	190	____	____	____
1519 Mickey Mouse Band (O), *35*	75	190	____	____	____
1520 Mickey Mouse Animal (O), *35*	75	190	____	____	____
1536 Circus: 1508, 1509, 1518, 1519, 1520	700	1250	____	____	____
1550 Switches, pair, windup, *33-37*	2	6	____	____	____
1555 90° Crossover, windup, *33-37*	1	3	____	____	____
1560 Station, *33-37*	15	38	____	____	____
1569 Accessory Set, 8 pieces, *33-37*	20	55	____	____	____
1588 Steam 0-4-0 (O), *36-37*	150	275	____	____	____
1630 Pullman (O), *38-42*	25	55	____	____	____
1631 Observation (O), *38-42*	30	65	____	____	____
1651E Electric 0-4-0 (O), *33*	120	225	____	____	____
1661E Steam 2-4-0 (O), *33*	75	160	____	____	____
1662 Steam 0-4-0 (O27), *40-42*	155	260	____	____	____
1663 Steam 0-4-0 (O27), *40-42*	190	320	____	____	____
1664/1664E Steam 2-4-2 (O27), *38-42*	45	80	____	____	____
1666/1666E Steam 2-6-2 (O27), *38-42*	75	150	____	____	____
1668/1668E Steam 2-6-2 (O27), *37-41*	75	140	____	____	____
1673 Coach (O), *36-37*	30	75	____	____	____
1674 Pullman (O), *36-37*	30	75	____	____	____
1675 Observation (O), *36-37*	30	75	____	____	____

PREWAR (1901-1942)	Good	Exc	Color	Cond	$
1677 Gondola (O), *33-35, 39-42*	15	40	___	___	___
1679 Boxcar (O), *33-42*	10	30	___	___	___
1680 Tank Car (O), *33-42*	15	35	___	___	___
1681 Steam 2-4-0 (O), *34-35*	55	110	___	___	___
1681E Steam 2-4-0 (O), *34-35*	65	140	___	___	___
1682 Caboose (O), *33-42*	10	30	___	___	___
1684 Steam 2-4-2 (O27), *41-42*	35	80	___	___	___
1685 Coach (O), *u*	150	310	___	___	___
1686 Baggage (O), *u*	150	310	___	___	___
1687 Observation (O), *u*	150	310	___	___	___
1688/1688E Steam 2-4-2 (O27), *36-46*	40	85	___	___	___
1689E Steam 2-4-2 (O27), *36-37*	60	100	___	___	___
1690 Pullman (O), *33-40*	25	55	___	___	___
1691 Observation (O), *33-40*	22	55	___	___	___
1692 Pullman (O27), *39 u*	40	70	___	___	___
1693 Observation (O27), *39 u*	40	70	___	___	___
1700E Diesel, power unit only (O27), *35-37*	25	55	___	___	___
1700E Set: 1700 (2) 1701s, 1702 (O27), *35-37 u*	75	185	___	___	___
1701 Coach (O27), *35-37*	20	50	___	___	___
1702 Observation (O27), *35-37*	20	50	___	___	___
1703 Observation w/hooked coupler, *u*	35	85	___	___	___
1717 Gondola (O), *33-40 u*	15	35	___	___	___
1717X Gondola (O), *40 u*	20	42	___	___	___
1719 Boxcar (O), *33-40 u*	20	42	___	___	___
1719X Boxcar (O), *41-42 u*	20	42	___	___	___
1722 Caboose (O), *33-42 u*	20	42	___	___	___
1722X Caboose (O), *39-40 u*	15	35	___	___	___
1766 Pullman (Std.), *34-40**	300	600	___	___	___
1767 Baggage Car (Std.), *34-40**	300	800	___	___	___
1768 Observation (Std.), *34-40**	300	600	___	___	___
1811 Pullman (O), *33-37*	15	40	___	___	___
1812 Observation (O), *33-37*	30	65	___	___	___
1813 Baggage Car (O), *33-37*	60	120	___	___	___
1816/1816W Diesel (O), *35-37*	95	245	___	___	___
1817 Coach (O), *35-37*	20	50	___	___	___
1818 Observation (O), *35-37*	20	50	___	___	___
1835E Steam 2-4-2 (Std.), *34-39*	450	750	___	___	___

PREWAR (1901-1942)		Good	Exc	Color	Cond	$
1910	Electric 0-6-0, Early (Std.), *10-11*	800	1800	____	____	____
1910	Electric 0-6-0, Late (Std.), *12*	550	1100	____	____	____
1910	Pullman (Std.), *u*	1000	2000	____	____	____
1911	Electric 0-4-0, Early (Std.), *10-12*	1000	2000	____	____	____
1911	Electric 0-4-0, Late (Std.), *13*	700	1200	____	____	____
1911	Electric 0-4-4-0, Special (Std.), *11-12*	1000	2500	____	____	____
1912	Electric 0-4-4-0 (Std.), *10-12**	1500	2700	____	____	____
1912	Electric 0-4-4-0 Special (Std.), *11**	2500	5000	____	____	____
2200	Summer Trolley Trailer (Std.), *10-13*	1100	2500	____	____	____
2600	Pullman (O), *38-42*	55	135	____	____	____
2601	Observation (O), *38-42*	55	135	____	____	____
2602	Baggage Car (O), *38-42*	70	155	____	____	____
2613	Pullman (O), *38-42**	90	270	____	____	____
2614	Observation (O), *38-42**	90	270	____	____	____
2615	Baggage Car (O), *38-42**	115	285	____	____	____
2620	Floodlight Car (O), *38-42*	38	85	____	____	____
2623	Pullman (O), *41-42*	155	325	____	____	____
2624	Pullman (O), *41-42*	750	1890	____	____	____
2630	Pullman (O), *38-42*	25	60	____	____	____
2631	Observation (O), *38-42*	25	60	____	____	____
2640	Pullman Illuminated (O), *38-42*	25	65	____	____	____
2641	Observation Illuminated (O), *38-42*	25	65	____	____	____
2642	Pullman (O), *41-42*	20	60	____	____	____
2643	Observation (O), *41-42*	20	60	____	____	____
2651	Flatcar (O), *38-42*	20	45	____	____	____
2652	Gondola (O), *38-41*	20	45	____	____	____
2653	Hopper Car (O), *38-42*	25	60	____	____	____
2654	Tank Car (O), *38-42*	30	70	____	____	____
2655	Boxcar (O), *38-42*	25	70	____	____	____
2656	Stock Car (O), *38-41*	35	85	____	____	____
2657	Caboose (O), *40-41*	15	35	____	____	____
2657X	Caboose (O), *40-41*	12	25	____	____	____
2659	Dump Car (O), *38-41*	30	60	____	____	____
2660	Crane (O), *38-42*	42	85	____	____	____
2672	Caboose (O27), *41-42*	15	35	____	____	____
2677	Gondola (O27), *39-41*	12	30	____	____	____

PREWAR (1901-1942)		Good	Exc	Color	Cond	$
2679	Boxcar (027), 38-42	12	30			
2680	Tank Car (027), 38-42	12	30			
2682	Caboose (027), 38-42	15	30			
2682X	Caboose (027), 38-42	15	30			
2717	Gondola (O), 38-42u	15	40			
2719	Boxcar (O), 38-42u	15	40			
2722	Caboose (O), 38-42u	15	45			
2755	Tank Car (O), 41-42	35	80			
2757	Caboose (O), 41-42	20	35			
2757X	Caboose (O), 41-42	20	40			
2758	Automatic Boxcar (O), 41-42	35	50			
2810	Crane (O), 38-42	150	240			
2811	Flatcar (O), 38-42	65	130			
2812	Gondola (O), 38-42	38	95			
2813	Stock Car (O), 38-42	110	220			
2814	Boxcar (O), 38-42	90	205			
2814R	Refrigerator Car (O), 38-42	130	255			
2815	Tank Car (O), 38-42	65	165			
2816	Hopper Car (O), 35-42	110	230			
2817	Caboose (O), 36-42	85	155			
2820	Floodlight Car (O), 38-42	95	210			
2954	Boxcar (O), 40-42*	225	620			
2955	Sunoco Tank Car (O), 40-42*	225	620			
2956	Hopper Car (O), 40-42*	200	590			
2957	Caboose (O), 40-42*	200	550			
3300	Summer Trolley Trailer (Std.), 10-13	1400	2500			
3651	Operating Lumber Car (O), 39-42	15	40			
3652	Operating Gondola (O), 39-42	20	60			
3659	Operating Dump Car (O), 39-42	15	35			
3811	Operating Lumber Car (O), 39-42	35	70			
3814	Operating Merchandise Car (O), 39-42	110	240			
3859	Operating Dump Car (O), 38-42	40	85			
4351	(See 14, 17, 117)					
4400	(See #404 Summer Trolley)					
5344	(See 700E)					
5906	(See 14, 17)					
8118	(See 14)					

		Good	Exc	Color	Cond	$
8976	(See 227, 228, 229, 230, 706, 708)					
19050	(See 14)					
51906	(See 17)					
54078	(See 14, 114)					
62976	(See 114)					
65784	(See 12, 16, 112)					
76399	(See 16, 112)					
98237	(See 14, 114)					
342715	(See 17)					
A	Miniature Motor, *04*	50	105	___	___	___
A	Transformer, 40, 60 watts, *27-37*	8	26	___	___	___
B	New Departure Motor, *06-16*	50	112	___	___	___
B	Transformer, 50, 75 watts, *16-38*	6	25	___	___	___
C	New Departure Motor, *06-16*	50	110	___	___	___
D	New Departure Motor, *06-14*	50	110	___	___	___
E	New Departure Motor, *06-14*	50	110	___	___	___
F	New Departure Motor, *06-14*	50	110	___	___	___
G	Battery Fan Motor, *06-14*	50	110	___	___	___
K	Power Motor, *05*	50	110	___	___	___
K	Transformer, 150, 200 watts	30	80	___	___	___
L	Power Motor, *05*	50	110	___	___	___
L	Transformer, 50, 75 watts	7	24	___	___	___
M	Battery Motor, *15-20*	30	90	___	___	___
N	Transformer, 50 watts	7	25	___	___	___
Q	Transformer, 50, 75 watts	15	45	___	___	___
R	Battery Motor, *15-20*	30	85	___	___	___
R	Transformer, 100 watts, *38-42*	17	55	___	___	___
S	Transformer, 50, 80 watts	11	35	___	___	___
T	Transformer, 75, 100,150 watts	10	30	___	___	___
U	Transformer, Alladin	6	18	___	___	___
V	Transformer, 150 watts, *39-42*	65	125	___	___	___
W	Transformer, 75 watts	7	25	___	___	___
Y	Battery Motor, *15-20*	40	90	___	___	___
Z	Transformer, 250 watts, *39-42*	120	190	___	___	___

Other Transformers and Rheostats made by Lionel

		Good	Exc	Color	Cond	$
106	Rheostat, *11-14*	3	10	___	___	___
1029	25 watts, *36*	6	20	___	___	___
1030	40 watts, *35-38*	6	25	___	___	___

PREWAR (1901-1942)		Good	Exc	Color	Cond	$
1031	Rheosat, circa 1938	2	4	___	___	___
1036	Rheostat, circa 1941	2	5	___	___	___
1037	Tranformer, 40 watts, *40-42*	7	25	___	___	___
1038	Rheostat, circa 1940	2	4	___	___	___
1039	Transformer, 35 watts, *37-40*	7	20	___	___	___
1040	Transformer, 60 watts, *37-39*	12	30	___	___	___
1041	Transformer, 60 watts, *39-42*	12	30	___	___	___

Track, Lockons, and Contactors

	Good	Exc	Color	Cond	$
O Straight	.25	.75	___	___	___
O Curve	.25	.75	___	___	___
O72 Straight	1	2	___	___	___
O72 Curve	1	2	___	___	___
O27 Straight	.10	.50	___	___	___
O27 Curve	.10	.50	___	___	___
Standard Straight	.60	2	___	___	___
Standard Curve	.60	2	___	___	___
O Gauge Lockon	.10	.50	___	___	___
Standard Gauge Lockon	.25	1	___	___	___
UTC Lockon	.25	.75	___	___	___
145C Contactor	.50	2	___	___	___
153C Contactor	.50	3	___	___	___

	Good	Exc	Color	Cond	$
011-11 Fiber Pins (O), *46-50*	.10	.15			
011-43 Insulating Pins, dz. (O), *61*	1	1.50			
020 90° Crossover (O), *45-61*	5	7			
020X 45° Crossover (O), *46-59*	6	9			
022 R.C. Switches, pair (O), *45-69*	40	65			
022-500 Adapter Set (O), *57-61*	1	2			
022A R.C. Switches, pair (O), *47*	70	115			
025 Bumper (O), *46-47*	7	20			
026 Bumper, *48-50*	9	20			
027C-1 Track Clips, dz. (027), *47, 49*	.50	1			
30 Water Tower, *47-50*	70	140			
31 Curved Track (Super O), *57-66*	1	1.50			
31-7 Power Blade Con. (Super O), *57-61*	—	.50			
31-15 Ground Rail Pin (Super O), *57-66*	—	.90			
31-45 Power Blade Connection (Super O) *61-66*	—	.90			
32 Straight Track (Super O), *57-66*	.65	1.40			
32-10 Insulating Pin (Super O)	—	.50			
32-20 Power Blade Ins. (Super O)	—	.25			
32-25 Insulating Pin (Super O)	—	.25			
32-30 Ground Pin (Super O)	—	.25			
32-31 Power Pin (Super O)	—	.25			
32-32 Insulating Pin (Super O)	—	.25			
32-33 Ground Pin (Super O)	—	.25			
32-34 Power Pin (Super O)	—	.25			
32-45 Power Blade Insulators, dz. (Super O)	1	2			
32-55 Insulating Pins, dz. (Super O)	1	2			
33 Half Curved Track (Super O), *57-66*	.75	1			
34 Half Straight Track (Super O), *57-66*	.75	1			
35 Boulevard Lamp, *45-49*	10	30			
36 Remote Control Set (Super O), *57-66*	5	10			
37 Uncoupling Track Set (Super O), *57-66*	6	12			
38 Water Tower, *46-47*	75	230			
38 Accessory Adapter Track (Super O)	5	12			
39 Operating Set (Super O), *57*	4	9			
39-5 Operating Set (Super O), *57-58*	4	9			

		Good	Exc	Color	Cond	$
39-10	Operating Set (Super O), *58*	4	9	___	___	___
39-15	Operating Set, w/ blade (Super O), *57-58*	4	9	___	___	___
39-20	Operating Set (Super O), *57-58*	4	9	___	___	___
39-25	Operating Set (Super O), *61-66*	4	9	___	___	___
39-35	Operating Set (Super O), *59*	4	9	___	___	___
40	Hookup Wire, *50-51, 53-63*	1	3	___	___	___
40-25	Conductor Wire, *56-59*	2	4	___	___	___
40-50	Cable Reel, *60-61*	3	5	___	___	___
41	Contactor (Super O)	.50	1	___	___	___
41	U.S. Army Switcher, *55-57*	115	185	___	___	___
42	Picatinny Arsenal Switcher, *57*	150	300	___	___	___
042/42	Manual Switches, pr. (O), *46-59*	30	50	___	___	___
43	Power Track (Super O), *59-66*	3	6	___	___	___
44	U.S. Army Mobile Launcher, *59-62*	110	205	___	___	___
45	U.S. Marines Mobile Launcher, *60-62*	105	255	___	___	___
45	Automatic Gateman, *46-49*	30	60	___	___	___
45N	Automatic Gateman, *45*	30	60	___	___	___
48	Insl. Straight Track (Super O), *57-66*	4	9	___	___	___
49	Insl. Curved Track (Super O), *57-66*	4	9	___	___	___
50	Lionel Gang Car, *54-64*	35	65	___	___	___
51	Navy Yard Switcher, *56-57*	105	200	___	___	___
52	Fire Car, *58-61*	120	240	___	___	___
53	Rio Grande Snowplow, *57-60*					
	(A) Backwards "a" in Rio Grande	190	340	___	___	___
	(B) Correctly printed "a"	370	680	___	___	___
54	Ballast Tamper, *58-61, 66, 68-69*	120	245	___	___	___
54-6446	(See 6446 or 6446-25)					
55	Tie-jector, *57-61*	120	235	___	___	___
55-150	Ties, *57-60*	2	5	___	___	___
56	Lamp Post, *46-49*	20	50	___	___	___
56	M&St L Mine Transport, *58*	240	550	___	___	___
57	AEC Switcher, *59-60*	325	740	___	___	___
58	Lamp Post, *46-50*	20	48	___	___	___
58	GN Snowplow, *59-61*	315	600	___	___	___
59	Minuteman Switcher, *62-63*	280	595	___	___	___
60	Lionelville Rapid Transit Trolley, *55-58*	90	185	___	___	___
61	Ground Lockon (Super O), *57-66*	.25	.50	___	___	___

		Good	Exc	Color	Cond	$
62	Power Lockon (Super O), *57-66*	.25	.50	___	___	___
62-78	Wooden Barrels, *52-57*	5	10	___	___	___
64	Street Lamp, *45-49*	23	56	___	___	___
65	Lionel Lines Handcar, *62-66*	120	380	___	___	___
68	Executive Inspection Car, *58-61*	120	330	___	___	___
69	Lionel Maintenance Car, *60-62*	150	295	___	___	___
70	Yard Light, *49-50*	22	50	___	___	___
71	Lamp Post, *49-59*	12	22	___	___	___
75	Goose Neck Lamp, set of 2, *61-63*	11	25	___	___	___
76	Blvd. Street Lamp, *59-66, 68-69*	9	24	___	___	___
80	Controller		NRS	___	___	___
88	Controller, *46-60*	3	7	___	___	___
89	Flagpole, *56-58*	16	46	___	___	___
90	Controller	3	6	___	___	___
91	Circuit Breaker, *57-60*	6	18	___	___	___
92	Circuit Breaker, *59-66, 68-69*	4	9	___	___	___
93	Water Tower, *46-49*	15	35	___	___	___
96C	Controller	2	5	___	___	___
97	Coal Elevator, *46-50*	118	225	___	___	___
100	Multivolt-DC/AC, Trans., *58-66*		NRS	___	___	___
108	Trestle Set		NRS	___	___	___
109	Partial Trestle Set		NRS	___	___	___
110	Graduated Trestle Set, *55-69*	9	28	___	___	___
111	Elevated Trestle Set, *56-69*	8	??	___	___	___
111-100	Two Elevated Trestle Piers, *60-63*	5	18	___	___	___
112	R.C. Switches, pr. (Super O), *57-66*	45	95	___	___	___
114	Newsstand w/ horn, *57-59*	50	120	___	___	___
115	Passenger Station, *46-49*	155	310	___	___	___
118	Newsstand w/ whistle, *57-58*	35	90	___	___	___
119	Landscaped Tunnel, *57-58*		NRS	___	___	___
120	00° Crossing (Super O), *57-66*	4	10	___	___	___
121	Landscaped Tunnel, *59-66*		NRS	___	___	___
122	Lamp Assortment		NRS	___	___	___
123	Lamp Assortment, *55-59*		NRS	___	___	___
123-60	Lamp Assortment, *60-63*		NRS	___	___	___
125	Whistle Shack, *50-55*	17	42	___	___	___
128	Animated Newsstand, *57-60*	80	220	___	___	___
130	60° Crossing (Super O)	6	12	___	___	___
131	Curved Tunnel, *59-66*		NRS	___	___	___

	Good	Exc	Color	Cond	$
132 Passenger Station, *49-55*	45	105	___	___	___
133 Passenger Station, *57, 61-62, 66*	28	85	___	___	___
137 Passenger Station (See Prewar section), *46*		NM			
138 Water Tower, *53-57*	72	145	___	___	___
140 Automatic Banjo Signal, *54-66*	18	42	___	___	___
142 Man. Switches, pr. (Super O), *57-66*	28	52	___	___	___
145C Contactor, *50-60*	1	3	___	___	___
145 Automatic Gateman, *50-66*	26	49	___	___	___
147 Whistle Controller, *61-66*	1	4	___	___	___
148 Dwarf Trackside Signal, *57-60*	18	45	___	___	___
150 Telegraph Pole Set, *47-50*	14	45	___	___	___
151 Auto. Semaphore, *47-69*	22	46	___	___	___
152 Auto. Crossing Gate, *45-49*	16	38	___	___	___
153 Auto. Block Control, Signal, *45-59*	17	40	___	___	___
153C Contactor	1	5	___	___	___
154 Auto. Highway Signal, *45-69*	16	40	___	___	___
155 Blinking Light Signal w/bell, *55-57*	28	70	___	___	___
156 Station Platform, *46-49*	25	80	___	___	___
157 Station Platform, *52-59*	15	40	___	___	___
160 Unloading Bin, *52-57*	1	3	___	___	___
161 Mail Pickup Set, *61-63*	32	90	___	___	___
163 Single Target Block Signal, *61-69*	20	38	___	___	___
164 Log Loader, *46-50*	110	255	___	___	___
167 Whistle Controller, *45-46*	4	10	___	___	___
175 Rocket Launcher, *58-60*	105	300	___	___	___
175-50 Extra Rocket, *59-60*	5	20	___	___	___
182 Magnetic Crane, *46-49*	110	225	___	___	___
192 Oper. Control Tower, *59-60*	85	200	___	___	___
193 Industrial Water Tower, *53-55*	50	100	___	___	___
195 Floodlight Tower, *57-69*	28	60	___	___	___
195-75 Eight-Bulb Extension, *58-60*	7	18	___	___	___
196 Smoke Pellets, *46-47*	—	38	___	___	___
197 Rotating Radar Antenna, *57-59*	60	120	___	___	___
199 Microwave Relay Tower, *58-59*	32	85	___	___	___
202 UP Alco A unit, *57*	60	100	___	___	___
204 Santa Fe Alco AA units, *57*	75	160	___	___	___
205 Missouri Pacific Alco AA units, *57-58*	75	160	___	___	___
206 Artificial Coal, large bag, *46-68*	—	10	___	___	___

|---|---|---|---|---|---|
207 Artificial Coal, small bag	—	7			
208 Santa Fe Alco AA units, *58-59*	78	165			
209 New Haven Alco AA units, *58*	300	700			
209 Wooden Barrels, set of 4, *46-50*	5	10			
210 Texas Special Alco AA units, *58*	110	210			
211 Texas Special Alco AA units, *62-66*	80	190			
212 USMC Alco A unit, *58-59*	75	150			
212 Santa Fe Alco AA units, *64-66*	78	150			
212T USMC dummy A unit, *58-59 u*	285	575			
213 Railroad Lift Bridge, *50*		NM			
213 M&St L Alco AA units, *64*	75	190			
214 Plate Girder Bridge, *53-69*	8	20			
215 Santa Fe Alco units, *65 u*					
(A) AB units	80	180			
(B) Double A units (usually w/212T)	78	165			
216 Burlington Alco A unit, *58*	100	310			
216 M&St L Alco AA units,					
(usually w/213T), *64 u*	90	200			
217 B&M Alco AB units, *59*	74	180			
218 Santa Fe Alco units, *59-63*					
(A) Double A units	70	170			
(B) AB units	70	165			
219 Missouri Pacific Alco AA units, *59 u*	68	150			
220 Santa Fe Alco units, *60-61*					
(A) A unit only	75	135			
(B) AA units	100	230			
221 2-6-4, 221T/221W Tender, *46-47*	70	125			
221 Rio Grande Alco A unit, *63-64*	55	100			
221 USMC Alco A unit, *63-64 u*	100	255			
221 Santa Fe Alco A unit, *63-64 u*	175	420			
222 Rio Grande Alco A unit, *62 adv. cat.*	45	95			
223 218C Santa Fe Alco AB units, *63*	85	185			
224 Steam 2-6-2, 2466T/2466W					
Tender, *45-46*	80	110			
224 U.S. Navy Alco AB units, *60*	100	200			
225 C&O Alco A unit, *60*	65	120			
226 B&M Alco AB units, *60 u*	85	170			
227 CN Alco A unit, *60 u*	78	160			
228 CN Alco A unit, *61 u*	70	140			

229 M&St L Alco units, *61-62*					
(A) A unit only, 61	60	120	___	___	___
(B) AB units, *62*	95	180	___	___	___
230 C&O Alco A unit, *61*	55	105	___	___	___
231 Rock Island Alco A unit, *61-63*	50	115	___	___	___
232 New Haven Alco A unit, *62*	62	118	___	___	___
233 Steam 2-4-2, 233W Tender, *61-62*	50	105	___	___	___
235 Steam 2-4-2, 1130T/1060T Tender, *61 u*	18	45	___	___	___
236 Steam 2-4-2, 1130T/1050T Tender, *61-62*	18	45	___	___	___
237 Steam 2-4-2, *63-66*					
(A) w/ 1060T Tender	25	50	___	___	___
(B) w/ 234W Tender	48	105	___	___	___
238 Steam 2-4-2, 234W Tender, *63-64*	55	125	___	___	___
239 Steam 2-4-2, 234W Tender, *65-66*	55	100	___	___	___
240 Steam 2-4-2, 242T, *64 u*	130	255	___	___	___
241 Steam 2-4-2 w/ 234W Tender, *65 u*	75	165	___	___	___
242 Steam 2-4-2 w/ 1060T Tender or 1062T Tender, *62-66*	20	44	___	___	___
243 Steam 2-4-2, 243W Tender, *60*	70	140	___	___	___
244 Steam 2-4-2, 244T/1130T Tender, *60-61*	25	40	___	___	___
245 Steam 2-4-2, w/ 1060T Tender, *59-60 u*	35	70	___	___	___
246 Steam 2-4-2, 244T/1130T Tender, *59-61*	25	45	___	___	___
247 Steam 2-4-2, 247T Tender, *59*	28	65	___	___	___
248 Steam 2-4-2, 1130T Tender, *58*	28	65	___	___	___
249 Steam 2-4-2, 250T Tender, *58*	18	49	___	___	___
250 Steam 2-4-2, 250T Tender, *57*	20	49	___	___	___
251 Steam 2-4-2, 1062T Tender, *66 u*	140	280	___	___	___
252 Crossing Gate, *50-62*	13	28	___	___	___
253 Block Control Signal, *56-59*	18	42	___	___	___
256 Illuminated Freight Station, *50-53*	22	50	___	___	___
257 Freight Station w/ diesel horn, *56-57*	32	82	___	___	___
260 Bumper, *51-69*					
(A) Die-cast	10	20			
(B) Black plastic	20	46	___	___	___
262 Highway Crossing Gate, *62-69*	18	65	___	___	___
264 Operating Fork Lift Platform, includes 6264, *57-60*	120	210	___	___	___

POSTWAR (1945-1969)	Good	Exc	Color	Cond	$
270 Metal Bridge (O)	18	31			
282 Gantry Crane, *54-57*	85	175			
282R Gantry Crane, *56-57*	115	220			
299 Code Transmitter Beacon Set, *61-63*	65	145			
308 Railroad Sign Set, *45-49*	13	28			
309 Yard Sign Set, die-cast, *50-59*	11	28			
310 Billboard Set, *50-68*	7	15			
313 Bascule Bridge, *46-49*	240	550			
313-82 Fiber Pins, *46-60*	—	.05			
313-121 Fiber Pins, *61*	—	1.50			
314 Scale Model Girder Bridge, *45-50*	9	20			
315 Trestle Bridge, *46-48*	38	100			
316 Trestle Bridge, *49*	15	40			
317 Trestle Bridge, *50-56*	9	25			
321 Trestle Bridge, *58-64*	11	26			
332 Arch-Under Bridge, *59-66*	20	46			
334 Operating Dispatching Board, *57-60*	100	215			
342 Culvert Loader, *56-58*	115	285			
344-80 Missiles, *59-60*	5	10			
345 Culvert Unloader, *57-59*	165	365			
346 Manual Culvert Unloader, *65*	65	168			
347 Cannon Firing Range Set, *64 u*	120	460			
348 Manual Culvert Unloader, *66-69*	70	185			
350 Engine Transfer Table, *57-60*	155	350			
350-50 Transfer Table Extension, *57-60*	60	160			
352 Ice Depot, includes 6352, *55-57*	120	240			
353 Trackside Control Signal, *60-61*	14	40			
356 Operating Freight Station, *52-57*	38	105			
362 Barrel Loader, *52-57*	50	95			
364 Conveyor Lumber Loader, *48-57*	78	120			
364C On/Off Switch, *48-64*	3	7			
365 Dispatching Station, *58-59*	65	120			
375 Turntable, *62-64*	120	245			
390C Switch, d.p.d.t., *60-64*	3	9			
394 Rotary Beacon, *49-53*	25	50			
395 Floodlight Tower, *49-56*	22	46			
397 Diesel Operating Coal Loader, *48-57*	90	165			
400 B&O RDC Passenger, *56-58*	130	250			
404 B&O RDC Baggage-Mail, *57-58*	150	300			

		Good	Exc	Color	Cond	$
410	Billboard Blinker, *56-58*	22	44	____	____	____
413	Countdown Control Panel, *62*	38	72	____	____	____
415	Diesel Fueling Station, *55-57*	90	150	____	____	____
419	Heliport Control Tower, *62*	130	360	____	____	____
443	Missile Launch Platform, w/ 943 Ammo Dump, *60-62*	14	34	____	____	____
445	Switch Tower, lighted, *52-57*	38	62	____	____	____
448	Missile Firing Range Set, w/6448, *61-63*	70	140	____	____	____
450	Signal Bridge, two-track, *52-58*	26	58	____	____	____
450L	Signal Light Head	14	30	____	____	____
452	Signal Bridge, single-track, *61-63*	65	120	____	____	____
455	Operating Oil Derrick, *50-54*	115	180	____	____	____
456	Coal Ramp w/ 3456 Hopper, *50-55*	75	150	____	____	____
460	Piggyback Transportation, includes 3460, *55-57*	65	145	____	____	____
460P	Piggyback Platform, *55-57*	30	80	____	____	____
461	Platform w/ Truck and Trailer, *66*	65	145	____	____	____
462	Derrick Platform Set, *61-62*	135	290	____	____	____
464	Lumber Mill, *56-60*	80	165	____	____	____
465	Sound Dispatching Station, *56-57*	60	145	____	____	____
470	Missile Launching Platform w/ 6470, *59-62*	105	155	____	____	____
480-25	Conversion Coupler, *50-60*	1	3	____	____	____
480-32	Conv. Magnetic Coupler, *61-69*	1	3	____	____	____
494	Rotary Beacon, *54-66*	23	50	____	____	____
497	Coaling Station, *53-58*	80	150	____	____	____
520	Lionel Lines Box Cab Electric, *56-57*	70	140	____	____	____
600	MKT NW-2 Switcher, *55*					
	(A) Black frame and end rails	100	175	____	____	____
	(B) Gray frame and yellow end rails	215	400	____	____	____
601	Seaboard NW-2 Switcher, *56*	80	170	____	____	____
602	Seaboard NW-2 Switcher, *57-58*	85	195	____	____	____
610	Erie NW-2 Switcher, *55*					
	(A) Black frame	85	155	____	____	____
	(B) Yellow frame	280	590	____	____	____
611	Jersey Central NW-2 Switcher, *57-58*	120	200	____	____	____
613	UP NW-2 Switcher, *58*	125	415	____	____	____
614	Alaska NW-2 Switcher, *59-60*	120	200	____	____	____
616	Santa Fe NW-2 Switcher, *61-62*	85	175	____	____	____

		Good	Exc	Color	Cond	$
617	Santa Fe NW-2 Switcher, *63*	120	260			
621	Jersey Central NW-2 Switcher, *56-57*	60	130			
622	Santa Fe NW-2 Switcher, *49-50*	140	325			
623	Santa Fe NW-2 Switcher, *52-54*	75	185			
624	C&O NW-2 Switcher, *52-54*	100	245			
625	LV GE 44-ton Switcher, *57-58*	75	150			
626	B&O GE 44-ton Switcher, *59*	120	375			
627	LV GE 44-ton Switcher, *56-57*	80	145			
628	NP GE 44-ton Switcher, *56-57*	80	145			
629	Burlington GE 44-ton Switcher, *56*	110	340			
633	Santa Fe NW-2 Switcher, *62*	100	225			
634	Santa Fe NW-2 Switcher, *63, 65-66*					
	(A) w/ safety stripes	80	185			
	(B) w/o safety stripes	55	120			
635	UP NW-2 Switcher, *65 u*	60	120			
637	Steam 2-6-4, 2046W/736W Tender, *59-63*	80	160			
638-2361	Van Camp's Pork & Beans Boxcar, *62 u*	25	50			
645	Union Pacific NW-2 Switcher, *69*	60	125			
646	Steam 4-6-4, 2046W Tdr., *54-58*	100	230			
665	Steam 4-6-4, 2046W/6026W/ 736W Tender, *54-59, 66*	95	215			
670	Pennsylvania Turbine, 6-8-6, *52*		NM			
671	Steam 6-8-6, *46-49*					
	(A) 671W Tender	120	200			
	(B) 2671W Tender	115	185			
671R	Steam 0-8-6, 4424W/4671 Tender, *46-49*	130	315			
671RR	Steam 6-8-6, 2046W-50 Tender, *52*	130	215			
671S	Smoke Conversion Kit	—	42			
674	Steam 2-6-4, *52*		NM			
675	Steam 2-6-2, 2466W/2466WX/ 6466WX Tender, *47-49; 2-6-4, 52*	80	165			
681	Steam Turbine, 6-8-6, 2046W-50/ 2671W Tender, *50-51, 53*	120	255			
682	Steam 6-8-6, 2046W-50 Tender, *54-55*	210	385			
685	Steam 4-6-4, 6026W Tender, *53*	115	275			

	Good	Exc	Color	Cond	$
703 Steam 4-6-4, Hudson, *46*		NM			
703-10 Special Smoke Bulb, *46*	—	30	___	___	___
711 Remote Control Switches (O72)	100	195	___	___	___
721 Manual Switches (O72)	65	110	___	___	___
725 Steam 2-8-4, Berkshire, *52*		NM			
726 Steam 2-8-4 Berkshire					
(A) 2426W Tender, 46	275	475	___	___	___
(B) 2426W Tender, *47-49*	265	450	___	___	___
726RR Steam 2-8-4 Berkshire,					
2046W Tender, *52*	200	375	___	___	___
726S Smoke Conversion Kit		NRS	___	___	___
736 Steam 2-8-4, 2671WX/2046W/736W					
Tender, *50-66*	250	400	___	___	___
746 N&W Steam 4-8-4, *57-60*					
(A) Long stripe Tender	580	1300	___	___	___
(B) Short stripe Tender	500	1250	___	___	___
760 Curved Track, 16 sec. (O72), *54-57*	18	38	___	___	___
773 Steam 4-6-4 Hudson, 2426W					
Tender, *50*	700	1400	___	___	___
773 Steam 4-6-4 Hudson, *64-66*					
(A) w/ 773W Tender	500	1000	___	___	___
(B) w/ 736W Tender	455	800	___	___	___
902 Elevated Trestle Set, *60*		NRS	___	___	___
909 Smoke Fluid, *57-68*	—	10	___	___	___
919 Artificial Grass, *46-64*	—	8	___	___	___
920 Scenic Display Set, *57-58*	42	95	___	___	___
920-2 Tunnel Portals, pair, *58-59*	12	26	___	___	___
920-3 Green Grass, *57*		10	___	___	___
920-4 Yellow Grass, *57*		10	___	___	___
920-5 Artificial Rock, *58*	1	2	___	___	___
920-8 Lichen, *58*	1	2	___	___	___
925 Lionel Lubricant, lg. tube, *46-69*	1	5	___	___	___
926 Lionel Lubricant, sm. tube, *55*	.50	2	___	___	___
926-5 Instruction Booklet, *46-48*	1	5	___	___	___
927 Lubricating Kit, *50-59*	13	20	___	___	___
928 Maint. & Lubricating Kit, *60-63*	18	40	___	___	___
943 Ammo Dump, *59-61*	20	35	___	___	___
950 U.S. Railroad Map, *58-66*	18	48	___	___	___
951 Farm Set, *58*	14	38	___	___	___

	Good	Exc	Color	Cond	$
952 Miniature Figure Set, *58*	12	34			
953 Miniature Figure Set, *60-62*	14	35			
954 Swimming Pool/Playground Set, *59*	15	35			
955 Highway Set, *58*	12	30			
956 Stockyard Set, *59*	15	35			
957 Farm Building and Animal Set, *58*	16	40			
958 Vehicle Set, *58*	11	31			
959 Barn Set, *58*	13	33			
960 Barnyard Set, *59-61*	11	32			
961 School Set, *59*	12	32			
962 Turnpike Set, *58*	13	38			
963 Frontier Set, *59-60*	14	40			
963-100 Frontier Set w/ box for					
Halloween General Set	70	155			
964 Factory Set, *59*	13	35			
965 Farm Set, *59*	13	34			
966 Firehouse Set, *58*	13	35			
967 Post Office Set, *58*	13	35			
968 TV Transmitter Set, *58*	12	34			
969 Construction Set, *60*	12	34			
970 Ticket Booth, *58-60*	36	112			
971 Lichen Package, *60-64*	5	10			
972 Landscape Tree Assortment, *61-64*	5	10			
973 Complete Landscaping Set, *60-64*	10	25			
974 Scenery Set, *62-63*	5	10			
980 Ranch Set, *60*	14	36			
981 Freight Yard Set, *60*	12	34			
982 Suburban Split Level Set, *60*	12	34			
983 Farm Set, *60-61*	12	34			
984 Railroad Set, *61-62*	12	34			
985 Freight Area Set, *61*	11	32			
986 Farm Set, *62*	12	33			
987 Town Set, *62*	12	33			
988 Railroad Structure Set, *62*	12	33			
1001 Steam 2-4-2, 1001T Tender, *48*	22	45			
1002 Lionel Gondola, *48-52*					
(A) Black w/ white lettering	5	10			
(B) Blue w/ white lettering	6	12			
(C) Silver w/ black lettering	100	340			

POSTWAR (1945-1969)	Good	Exc	Color	Cond	$
(D) Yellow w/ black lettering	100	340	____	____	____
(E) Red w/ white lettering	110	350	____	____	____
(F) Light blue w/ black lettering		NRS	____	____	____
X1004 PRR Baby Ruth Boxcar, *48-52*	5	11	____	____	____
1005 Sunoco 1-D Tank Car, *48-50*	3	7	____	____	____
1007 LL SP-Type Caboose, *48-52*	3	8	____	____	____
1008 Camtrol Uncoupling Unit (O27), *57-62*	.50	1	____	____	____
1008-50 Camtrol w/ track (O27), *48*	.25	1	____	____	____
1010 Transformer, 35 watts, *61-66*	8	20	____	____	____
1011 Transformer, 25 watts, *48-49*	8	20	____	____	____
1012 Transformer, 35 watts, *50-54*	7	19	____	____	____
1013 Curved Track (O27), *45-69*	.10	.20	____	____	____
1013-17 Steel Pins (O27), *46-60*	—	.05	____	____	____
1013-42 Steel Pins (O27), *61-68*	—	.60	____	____	____
1014 Transformer, 40 watts, *55*	11	30	____	____	____
1015 Transformer, 45 watts, *56-60*	8	32	____	____	____
1016 Transformer, 35 watts, *59-60*	6	30	____	____	____
1018 Straight Track (O27), *45-69*	.15	.40	____	____	____
1018 1/2 Straight Track (O27), *55-69*	.15	.40	____	____	____
1019 R.C. Track Set (O27), *46-48*	2	8	____	____	____
1020 90° Crossing (O27), *55-69*	2	6	____	____	____
1021 90° Crossing (O27), *45-54*	2	6	____	____	____
1022 Man. Switches, pr. (O27), *53-69*	10	20	____	____	____
1122-34 R.C. Switches, pair, *52-53*	14	38	____	____	____
1023 45° Crossing (O27), *56-69*	2	5	____	____	____
1024 Man. Switches, pr. (O27), *46-52*	7	20	____	____	____
1025 Illuminated Bumper (O27), *46-47*	6	15	____	____	____
1025 Transformer, 45 watts, *61-69*	12	30	____	____	____
1026 Transformer, 25 watts, *61-64*	5	12	____	____	____
1032 Transformer, 75 watts, *48*	30	60	____	____	____
1033 Transformer, 90 watts, *48-56*	40	75	____	____	____
1034 Transformer, 75 watts, *48-54*	28	55	____	____	____
1035 Transformer, 60 watts, *47*	22	45	____	____	____
1037 Transformer, 40 watts, *46-47*	10	28	____	____	____
1041 Transformer, 60 watts, *45-46*	12	35	____	____	____
1042 Transformer, 75 watts, *47-48*	18	48	____	____	____
1043 Transformer					
(A) 50 watts, black, 53-57	12	35	____	____	____
(B) 60 watts, ivory, *57-58*	55	115	____	____	____

POSTWAR (1945-1969)	Good	Exc	Color	Cond	$
1044 Transformer, 90 watts, *57-69*	30	65	____	____	____
1045 Operating Watchman, *46-50*	14	35	____	____	____
1047 Operating Switchman, *59-61*	50	150	____	____	____
1050 Steam 0-4-0, 1050 Tender, *59 u*	50	100	____	____	____
1053 Transformer, 60 watts, *56-60*	18	40	____	____	____
1055 Texas Special Alco A unit, *59-60 adv. cat.*	30	75	____	____	____
1060 Steam 2-4-2, 1050T/1060T Tender, *60-62 adv. cat.*	12	30	____	____	____
1061 Steam 0-4-0, 1061T Tender, *64; 2-4-2, 69*	12	30	____	____	____
1062 Steam 2-4-2, 1062T Tender, *63-64*	12	30	____	____	____
1063 Transformer, 75 watts, *60-64*	18	55	____	____	____
1065 Union Pacific Alco A unit, *61 adv. cat.*	25	80	____	____	____
1066 Union Pacific Alco A unit, *64 u*	50	105	____	____	____
1073 Transformer, 60 watts, *61-66*	20	55	____	____	____
1101 Steam 2-4-2, 1001T Tender, *48*	20	40	____	____	____
1101 Transformer, 25 watts, *48*	8	15	____	____	____
1110 Steam 2-4-2, 1001T Tender, *49, 51-52*	10	38	____	____	____
1120 Steam 2-4-2, 1001T Tender, *50*	15	30	____	____	____
1121 R.C. Switches, pr. (O27), *46-51*	11	35	____	____	____
1122 R.C. Switches, pr. (O27), *52-53*	11	35	____	____	____
1122E R.C. Switches, pr. (O27), *53-69*	12	38	____	____	____
1122-500 Gauge Adapter (O27), *57-66*	.21	1	____	____	____
1130 Steam 2-4-2, 6066T/1130T Tender, *53-54*	16	32	____	____	____
1615 Steam 0-4-0, 1615T Tender, *55-57*	85	195	____	____	____
1625 Steam 0-4-0, 1625T Tender, *58*	75	190	____	____	____
1640-100 Presidential Kit, *60*	40	100	____	____	____
1654 Steam 2-4-2, 1654W Tender, *46-47*	35	70	____	____	____
1655 Steam 2-4-2, 6654W Tender, *48-49*	35	70	____	____	____
1656 Steam 0-4-0, 6403B Tender, *48-49*	145	280	____	____	____
1665 Steam 0-4-0, 2403B Tender, *46*	175	350	____	____	____
1666 Steam 2-6-2, 2466W/2466WX Tender, *46-47*	48	120	____	____	____
1862 General 4-4-0, 1862T Tender, *59-62*	100	225	____	____	____
1865 Western & Atlantic Coach, *59-62*	18	40	____	____	____
1866 Western & Atlantic Baggage, *59-62*	18	40	____	____	____

POSTWAR (1945-1969)	Good	Exc	Color	Cond	$
1872 General 4-4-0, 1872T Tender, *59-62*	100	300	____	____	____
1875 Western & Atlantic Coach, *59-62*	85	190			
1875W W&A Coach w/ whistle, *59-62*	65	150	____	____	____
1876 Western & Atlantic Baggage, *59-62*	28	75	____	____	____
1877 Flatcar w/ fence and horses, *59-62*	30	72	____	____	____
1882 General 4-4-0, 1882T Tender, *60 u*	200	420			
1885 Western & Atlantic Coach, *60 u*	95	275	____	____	____
1887 Flatcar w/ fences and horses, *60 u*	80	180	____	____	____
2001 Track Make-up kit (O27), *63*		NRS	____	____	____
2002 Track Make-up kit (O27), *63*		NRS	____	____	____
2003 Track Make-up kit (O27), *63*		NRS	____	____	____
2016 Steam 2-6-4, 6026W Tender, *55-56*	70	150	____	____	____
2018 Steam 2-6-4, *56-59, 61*					
(A) 6026T Tender	40	80			
(B) 6026W Tender	60	120			
(C) 1130T Tender	40	80	____	____	____
2020 Steam 6-8-6, 2020W/6020W Tender, *46-49*	95	195	____	____	____
2023 Union Pacific Alco AA, *50-51*					
(A) Yellow body	140	295	____	____	____
(B) Silver body	140	295	____	____	____
2024 C&O Alco A, *69*	30	80	____	____	____
2025 Steam 2-6-2, 2-6-4, with 2466W/ 6466W Tender, *47-49, 52*	70	140	____	____	____
2026 Steam 2-6-2, 2-6-4, *48-49, 51-53*					
(A) 6466W or 6466WX	60	110	____	____	____
(B) 6466T or 6066T	40	85	____	____	____
2028 Pennsylvania GP-7, *55*					
(A) Gold lettering	165	410	____	____	____
(B) Yellow lettering	140	375	____	____	____
(C) Tan frame	250	565	____	____	____
2029 Steam 2-6-4, 234W Tdr., *64-69*	70	125	____	____	____
2031 Rock Island Alco AA, *52-54*	150	380	____	____	____
2032 Erie Alco AA unit, *52-54*	125	250	____	____	____
2033 Union Pacific Alco AA, *52-54*	155	315	____	____	____
2034 Steam 2-4-2, 6066T Tender, *52*	22	45	____	____	____
2035 Steam 2-6-4, 6466W Tender, *50-51*	65	130	____	____	____
2036 Steam 2-6-4, 6466W Tender, *50*	65	150	____	____	____
2037 Steam 2-6-4, black engine, *54-55, 57-63*					

	Good	Exc	Color	Cond	$
(A) w/ 6026T, 1130T	40	90	___	___	___
(B) w/ 6026W, 233W, 234W	60	115	___	___	___
2037-500 Steam 2-6-4, pink engine, w/					
1130T-500 Tender, *57-58*	360	800	___	___	___
(no number), olive drab, *63-64 u*	90	200	___	___	___
2041 Rock Island Alco AA units, *69*	60	120			
2046 Steam 4-6-4, 2046W Tender,					
50-51, 53	135	235	___	___	___
2055 Steam 4-6-4, 2046W/6026W					
Tender, *53-55*	75	175	___	___	___
2056 Steam 4-6-4, 2046W Tender, *52*	105	230	___	___	___
2065 Steam 4-6-4, 2046W/6026W					
Tender, *54-56*	100	200	___	___	___
2240 Wabash F-3 AB unit, *56*	400	800	___	___	___
2242 New Haven F-3 AB unit, *58-59*	480	1200	___	___	___
2243 Santa Fe F-3 AB unit, *55-57*	300	495	___	___	___
2243C Santa Fe F-3 B unit, *55-57*	100	220	___	___	___
2245 Texas Special F-3 AB, *54-55*					
(A) B unit w/ portholes, 54	255	570	___	___	___
(B) B unit w/o portholes, *55*	430	835	___	___	___
2257 Lionel SP Type caboose, *47*					
(A) Red, no stack	5	10	___	___	___
(B) Tuscan, w/ stack	80	230	___	___	___
2321 Lackawanna Train Master, *54-56*					
(A) Gray roof	300	500	___	___	___
(B) Maroon roof	400	825	___	___	___
2322 Virginian Train Master, *65-66*					
(A) Unpainted blue stripe	300	625	___	___	___
(B) Painted blue stripe	400	825	___	___	___
2328 Burlington GP-7, *55-56*	200	450	___	___	___
2329 Virginian Rectifier, *58-59*	315	700	___	___	___
2330 Pennsylvania GG-1, green, *50*	625	1400	___	___	___
2331 Virginian TrainMaster, *55-58*					
(A) Black stripe/gold lettering, 55	720	1400	___	___	___
(B) Blue stripe/yellow lettering, 56-58	400	900	___	___	___
(C) Blue and yellow, gray mold	600	1200	___	___	___
2332 Pennsylvania GG-1, *47-49*					
(A) Black	900	2000	___	___	___
(B) Green	320	700	___	___	___

POSTWAR (1945-1969)	Good	Exc	Color	Cond	$
2333 Santa Fe F-3 AA unit, *48-49*	275	600	___	___	___
2333 NYC F-3 AA unit, *48-49*					
(A) Rubber-stamped lettering	425	900	___	___	___
(B) Heat-stamped lettering	295	700	___	___	___
2337 Wabash GP-7, *58*	110	315	___	___	___
2338 Milwaukee Road GP-7, *55-56*					
(A) Orange band around shell	800	1800	___	___	___
(B) Interrupted orange band	150	300	___	___	___
2339 Wabash GP-7, *57*	165	325	___	___	___
2340 Pennsylvania GG-1, *55*					
(A) Tuscan	700	1500	___	___	___
(B) Dark green	650	1350	___	___	___
2341 Jersey Central TrainMaster, *56*					
(A) High gloss orange	1100	2300	___	___	___
(B) Dull orange	950	2000	___	___	___
2343 Santa Fe F-3 AA units, *50-52*	250	600	___	___	___
2343C Santa Fe F-3 B unit, *50-55*	100	235	___	___	___
2344 NYC F-3 AA units, *50-52*	290	625	___	___	___
2344C NYC F-3 B unit, *50-55*	120	270	___	___	___
2345 WP F-3 AA units, *52*	1100	2100	___	___	___
2346 B&M GP-9, *65-66*	140	275	___	___	___
2347 C&O GP-7, *65 u*	1200	2600	___	___	___
2348 M&St L GP-9, *58-59*	175	425	___	___	___
2349 Northern Pacific GP-9, *59-60*	175	415	___	___	___
2350 New Haven EP-5, *56-58*					
(A) White "N", painted nose	370	750	___	___	___
(B) White "N", decal nose	220	500	___	___	___
(C) Orange "N", painted nose	1000	1600	___	___	___
(D) Orange "N", decal nose	500	1100	___	___	___
(E) White "N", orange paint through doors	380	800	___	___	___
2351 Milwaukee Road EP-5, *57-58*	200	550	___	___	___
2352 Pennsylvania EP-5, *58-59*					
(A) Tuscan body	200	495	___	___	___
(B) Chocolate brown body	225	550	___	___	___
2353 Santa Fe F-3 AA units, *53-55*	260	600	___	___	___
2354 NYC F-3 AA units, *53-55*	265	650	___	___	___
2355 Western Pacific F-3 AA units, *53*	800	1700	___	___	___
2356 Southern F-3 AA units, *54-56*	500	1000	___	___	___

	Good	Exc	Color	Cond	$
2356C Southern F-3 B unit, *54-56*	160	375	___	___	___
2357 Lionel SP-Type Caboose, *47-48*					
(A) Red w/ red stack	100	275	___	___	___
(B) Tuscan w/ Tuscan stack	15	30	___	___	___
2358 Great Northern EP-5, *59-60*	350	1000	___	___	___
2359 Boston & Maine GP-9, *61-62*	185	280	___	___	___
2360 Penn GG-1, *56-58, 61-63*					
(A) Tuscan, 5 gold stripes	580	1500	___	___	___
(B) Dark green, 5 gold stripes	525	1300	___	___	___
(C) Tuscan, single gold stripe, heat-stamped lettering	425	1000	___	___	___
(D) Tuscan, single gold stripe, decal lettering	400	885	___	___	___
2363 Illinois Central F-3 AB units, *55-56*	400	1100	___	___	___
2365 C&O GP-7, *62-63*	135	320	___	___	___
2367 Wabash F-3 AB unit, *55*	400	1000	___	___	___
2368 B&O F-3 AB unit, *56*	650	1700	___	___	___
2373 CP F-3 AA unit, *57*	950	2100	___	___	___
2378 Milwaukee Road F-3 AB unit, *56*					
(A) w/ roof line stripes	1050	1800	___	___	___
(B) w/o roof line stripes	1000	1700	___	___	___
2379 Rio Grande F-3 AB units, *57-58*	580	1200	___	___	___
2383 Santa Fe F-3 AA unit, *58-66*	225	475	___	___	___
2400 Maplewood Pullman, green, *48-49*	60	175	___	___	___
2401 Hillside Obc., green, *48-49*	60	175	___	___	___
2402 Chatham Pullman, green, *48-49*	60	155	___	___	___
2404 Santa Fe Vista Dome, *64-65*	30	70	___	___	___
2405 Santa Fe Pullman, *64-65*	30	70	___	___	___
2406 Santa Fe Observation, *64-65*	30	70	___	___	___
2408 Santa Fe Vista Dome, *66*	35	78	___	___	___
2409 Santa Fe Pullman, *66*	35	78	___	___	___
2410 Santa Fe Observation, *66*	35	75	___	___	___
2411 Lionel Lines Flatcar, *46-48*					
(A) w/ pipes, 46	65	100	___	___	___
(B) w/ logs, *47-48*	12	35	___	___	___
2412 Santa Fe Vista Dome, *59-63*	25	95	___	___	___
2414 Santa Fe Pullman, *59-63*	25	95	___	___	___
2416 Santa Fe Observation, *59-63*	22	65	___	___	___
2419 DL&W Work Caboose, *46-47*	22	40	___	___	___

POSTWAR (1945-1969)	Good	Exc	Color	Cond	$
2420 DL&W Work Caboose, w/ light, *46-48*	40	95	___	___	___
2421 Maplewood Pullman, *50-53*					
(A) Gray roof	40	85	___	___	___
(B) Silver roof	40	70	___	___	___
2422 Chatham Pullman, *50-53*					
(A) Gray roof	40	85	___	___	___
(B) Silver roof	35	70	___	___	___
2423 Hillside Observation, *50-53*					
(A) Gray roof	40	80	___	___	___
(B) Silver roof	35	65	___	___	___
2429 Livingston Pullman, *52-53*	50	120	___	___	___
2430 Blue Pullman, *46-47*	24	65	___	___	___
2431 Blue Observation, *46-47*	25	65	___	___	___
2432 Clifton Vista Dome, *54-58*	20	45	___	___	___
2434 Newark Pullman, *54-58*	20	45	___	___	___
2435 Elizabeth Pullman, *54-58*	30	75	___	___	___
2436 Mooseheart Observation, *57-58*	20	60	___	___	___
2436 Summit Observation, *54-56*	25	60	___	___	___
2440 Green Pullman, *46-47*	20	55	___	___	___
2441 Green Observation, *46-47*	20	50	___	___	___
2442 Clifton Vista Dome, *56*	45	115	___	___	___
2442 Brown Pullman, *46-48*	20	70	___	___	___
2443 Brown Observation, 46-48	20	70	___	___	___
2444 Newark Pullman, 56	25	80	___	___	___
2445 Elizabeth Pullman, 56	45	190	___	___	___
2446 Summit Observation, *56*	40	95	___	___	___
2452 Pennsylvania Gondola, *45-47*	8	13	___	___	___
2452X Pennsylvania Gondola, *46-47*	5	12	___	___	___
X2454 Pennsylvania Boxcar, *46*	70	180	___	___	___
X2454 Baby Ruth Boxcar, "PRR" logo, *46-47*	7	22	___	___	___
2456 Lehigh Valley Hopper, *48*	7	23	___	___	___
2457 PRR Caboose, metal, N5, *45-47*	10	30	___	___	___
X2458 Pennsylvania Boxcar, *46-47*	15	45	___	___	___
2460 Bucyrus Erie Crane, 12-wheel, *46-50*					
(A) Gray Cab	65	165	___	___	___
(B) Black Cab	35	85	___	___	___
2461 Transformer Car, die-cast, *47-48*					

	Good	Exc	Color	Cond	$
(A) Red transformer	40	110			
(B) Black transformer	30	85			
2465 Sunoco 2-D Tank Car, *46-48*	5	17			
2472 PRR Caboose, metal, N5, *46-47*	10	25			
2481 Plainfield Pullman, yellow, *50*	105	275			
2482 Westfield Pullman, yellow, *50*	105	275			
2483 Livingston Observation, yellow, *50*	85	230			
2521 President McKinley Obs., *62-66*	60	170			
2522 President Harrison V. D., *62-66*	80	180			
2523 President Garfield Pullman, *62-66*	80	180			
2530 REA Baggage, *54-60*					
(A) Large doors	250	500			
(B) Small doors	75	155			
2531 Silver Dawn Observation, *52-60*	50	95			
2532 Silver Range Vista Dome, *52-60*	50	95			
2533 Silver Cloud Pullman, *52-59*	50	95			
2534 Silver Bluff Pullman, *52-59*	50	95			
2541 Alexander Hamilton Obs., *55-56**	75	200			
2542 Betsy Ross Vista Dome, *55-56**	75	200			
2543 William Penn Pullman, *55-56**	75	200			
2544 Molly Pitcher Pullman, *55-56**	75	200			
2550 B&O RDC Baggage Mail, *57-58*	200	500			
2551 Banff Park Observation, *57**	100	225			
2552 Skyline 500 Vista Dome, *57**	100	225			
2553 Blair Manor Pullman, *57**	150	350			
2554 Craig Manor Pullman, *57**	150	350			
2555 Sunoco 1-D Tank Car, *46-48*	12	35			
2559 B&O RDC Passenger, *57-58*	150	305			
2560 Lionel Lines Crane, 8-wheel, *46-47*	20	58			
2561 Vista Valley Observation, *59-61**	100	245			
2562 Regal Pass Vista Dome, *59-61**	125	310			
2563 Indian Falls Pullman, *59-61**	125	310			
2625 Madison Pullman, *46-47**	95	235			
2625 Manhattan Pullman, *46-47**	100	240			
2625 Irvington Pullman, *46-50**					
(A) No silhouettes	80	220			
(B) w/ silhouettes	105	265			
2627 Madison Pullman, *48-50**					
(A) No silhouettes	80	225			

	Good	Exc	Color	Cond	$
(B) w/ silhouettes	80	255	___	___	___
2628 Manhattan Pullman, *48-50**			___	___	___
(A) No silhouettes	80	220	___	___	___
(B) w/ silhouettes	95	260	___	___	___
2671 TCA Tender, *68*	—	75			
2755 SUNX 1-D Tank Car, *45*	35	125			
2855 SUNX 1-D Tank Car, *46-47*					
(A) Black	65	200	___	___	___
(B) Gray	50	175	___	___	___
2856 B&O Scale Hopper Car, *46-47*		NM	___	___	___
2857 NYC Scale Caboose, *46*		NM	___	___	___
X2954 Pennsylvania Scale Boxcar, *41-42*	125	250			
2955 SUNX 1-D Scale Tankcar, *40-42, 46*	100	250			
2956 B&O Scale Hopper Car, *40-42*	150	310			
2957 NYC Scale Caboose, *46*	60	225	___	___	___
(3309) Turbo Missile Launch Car, *63-64*					
(A) Red body	25	65	___	___	___
(B) Olive body	70	280	___	___	___
3330 Flatcar w/ Submarine Kit, *60-62*	60	150	___	___	___
3330-100 Oper. Submarine Kit, *60-61*	50	100	___	___	___
(3349) Turbo Missile Launch Car, *62-65*	25	65	___	___	___
3356 Operating Horse Car only, *56-60, 64-66*	40	85	___	___	___
3356 Operating Horse Car and Corral set, *56-60, 64-66*	85	185			
3356-100 (9) Black Horses, *56-59*	6	18			
3356-150 Horse Car Corral	30	80	___	___	___
3357 Hydraulic Maintenance Car, *62-64*	20	65	___	___	___
3359 Lionel Lines Two-bin Dump, *55-58*	18	50	___	___	___
3360 Operating Burro Crane, *56-57*	130	280	___	___	___
3361 Operating Log Dump Car, *55-58*	20	48	___	___	___
3362 Flatcar w/ helium tanks or logs, *61-63*	10	40	___	___	___
3362/3364 Log Dump Car, *65-69*	10	35	___	___	___
3366 Circus Car Corral Set, *59-62*	115	220	___	___	___
3366 Circus Car only, *59-62*	50	100	___	___	___
3366-100 (9) White Horses, *59-60*	16	40	___	___	___
3370 W&A Outlaw Car, *61-64*	18	65	___	___	___
3376 Bronx Zoo Car, *60-66, 69*					

	Good	Exc	Color	Cond	$
(A) Blue w/ white lettering	20	50	___	___	___
(B) Green w/ yellow lettering	35	110	___	___	___
(C) Blue w/ yellow lettering	110	310	___	___	___
3386 Bronx Zoo Car, *60 adv. cat.*	25	65	___	___	___
3409 Helicopter Car, *61 adv. cat.*	45	120	___	___	___
3410 Helicopter Car, *61-63*	40	100	___	___	___
(3413) Mercury Capsule Car, *62-64*	65	145	___	___	___
3419 Helicopter Car, *59-65*	40	115	___	___	___
3424 Wabash Operating Boxcar, *56 58*	30	80	___	___	___
3424-100 Low Bridge Signal Set	10	30	___	___	___
3428 U.S. Mail Oper. Boxcar, *59-60*	30	105	___	___	___
3429 USMC Helicopter Car, *60*	200	465	___	___	___
3434 Poultry Dispatch car, *59-60, 64-66*	25	95	___	___	___
3435 Traveling Aquarium Car, *59-62*					
(A) Gold circle	400	1000	___	___	___
(B) Tank 1, Tank 2	280	800	___	___	___
(C) Gold letter	150	300	___	___	___
(D) Yellow rubber stamp	100	250	___	___	___
3444 Erie Operating Gondola, *57-59*	30	70	___	___	___
3451 Operating Log Dump Car, *46-48*	10	30	___	___	___
3454 PRR Operating Merchandise Car, *46-47*					
(A) Red lettering		NRS	___	___	___
(B) Blue lettering	40	130	___	___	___
3456 N&W Operating Hopper Car, *50-55*	15	40	___	___	___
3459 LL Operating Dump Car, *46-48*					
(A) Aluminum bin	85	240	___	___	___
(B) Black bin	12	45	___	___	___
(C) Green bin	20	65	___	___	___
3460 Flatcar w/ trailers, *55-57*	22	65	___	___	___
3461 Lionel Operating Log Car, *49-55*	9	35	___	___	___
3462 Automatic Milk Car, *47-48*	15	48	___	___	___
3462P Milk Car Platform	3	14	___	___	___
X3464 ATSF Operating Boxcar, *49-52*	10	25	___	___	___
X3464 NYC Operating Boxcar, *49-52*	10	25	___	___	___
3469 LL Operating Dump Car, *49-55*	12	42	___	___	___
3470 Target Launcher, *62-64*	30	72	___	___	___
3472 Automatic Milk Car, *49-53*	20	55	___	___	___
3474 Western Pacific Boxcar, *52-53*	14	50	___	___	___
3482 Automatic Milk Car, *54-55*	18	55	___	___	___

	Good	Exc	Color	Cond	$
3484 Pennsylvania Opeating Boxcar, *53*	15	48	___	___	___
3484-25 ATSF Operating. Boxcar, *54*	30	90	___	___	___
3494-1 NYC Pacemaker Boxcar, *55*	40	105	___	___	___
3494-150 MP Operating Boxcar, *56*	55	135	___	___	___
3494-275 State of Maine Operating Boxcar, *56-58*	55	130	___	___	___
3494-550 Monon Operating Boxcar, *57-58*	100	350	___	___	___
3494-625 Soo Operating Boxcar, *57-58*	115	350	___	___	___
3509 Satellite Car, *61*	22	60	___	___	___
(3510) Satellite Car, *62 adv. cat.*	40	155	___	___	___
3512 Fireman and Ladder Car, *59-61*					
(A) Black rooftop ladder	30	95	___	___	___
(B) Silver rooftop ladder	40	125	___	___	___
3519 Satellite Car, *61-64*	20	55	___	___	___
3520 Searchlight Car, *52-53*	30	58	___	___	___
3530 GM Generator Car, *56-58*	60	120	___	___	___
3530-50 Searchlight w/ pole and base	24	75	___	___	___
3535 A E C Security Car, *60-61*	28	105	___	___	___
3540 Operating Radar Car, *59-60*	35	135	___	___	___
3545 Lionel TV Car, *61-62*	50	170	___	___	___
3559 Operating Coal Dump Car, *46-48*	15	40	___	___	___
3562-1 ATSF Operating Barrel Car, black, *54*	65	175	___	___	___
3562-25 ATSF Operating Barrel Car, gray, *54*					
(A) Red lettering	125	325	___	___	___
(B) Blue lettering	20	55	___	___	___
3562-50 ATSF Oper. Barrel Car, yellow, *55-56*					
(A) Painted	35	85	___	___	___
(B) Unpainted	20	55	___	___	___
3562-75 ATSF Operating Barrel Car, orange, *57-58*	35	65	___	___	___
3619 Helicopter Boxcar, *62-64*					
(A) Light yellow	30	90	___	___	___
(B) Dark yellow	40	150	___	___	___
3620 Searchlight Car, *54-56*	25	50	___	___	___
3650 Extension Searchlight Car, *56-59*					
(A) Light gray	30	65	___	___	___
(B) Dark gray	65	135	___	___	___
3656 Armour Operating Cattle Car, *49-55*					

	Good	Exc	Color	Cond	$
(A) Black letters, Armour sticker	70	180			
(B) White letters, Armour sticker	32	80			
(C) White lettering	22	75			
3656 Stockyard w/ cattle	20	55			
3662 Automatic Milk Car, *55-60, 64-66*	30	70			
3665 Minuteman Operating Car, *61-64*					
(A) Medium blue roof	75	170			
(B) Dark blue roof	50	130			
3666 Minuteman Boxcar w/ missile, *64 u*	170	500			
3672 Bosco Operating Boxcar, *59-60*					
(A) Unpainted	80	220			
(B) Painted	95	260			
3820 Flatcar w/ submarine, *60-62*	60	200			
3830 Flatcar w/ submarine, *60-63*	50	115			
3854 Operating Merchandise Car, *46-47*	180	420			
3927 Lionel Lines Track Cleaner, *56-60*	50	125			
3927-50 Track Cleaning Fluid, *57-69*	2	5			
3927-75 Track Cleaning Pads, *57-69*	3	10			
4357 PRR SP-Type Caboose, elec., *48-49*	55	165			
4452 PRR Gondola, electronic, *40-49*	40	100			
4454 Baby Ruth PRR Boxcar, elec., *46-49*	60	170			
4457 PRR N5 Caboose, electronic, *46-47*	45	160			
4681 Steam 6-8-6, electronic, *50*		NM			
4776-18 (See 2457, 2472)					
5159 Maintenance Kit, *63-65*	2	5			
5159-50 Maintenance and Lube Kit, *66-69*	2	5			
5180 Viewing Stand	50	145			
5459 LL Dump Car, electronic, *46-49*	40	115			
6002 NYC Gondola, *50*	4	12			
X6004 Baby Ruth PRR Boxcar, *50*	4	8			
6007 Lionel Lines SP-Type Caboose, *50*	3	6			
6009 R.C. Uncoupling Track, *53-54*	1	5			
6012 Lionel Gondola, *51-56*	2	6			
6014 Airex Boxcar, *60, u*	25	70			
6014 Bosco PRR Boxcar, *58*					
(A) White body	35	65			
(B) Red body	5	10			
(C) Orange body	5	10			
6014 Chun King Boxcar, *57 u*	60	130			

	Good	Exc	Color	Cond	$
6014 Frisco Boxcar, *57, 63-69*					
(A) White body	4	8	___	___	___
(B) Red body	4	8	___	___	___
(C) White w/ coin slot	20	45	___	___	___
(D) Orange body	20	40	___	___	___
X6014 Baby Ruth PRR Boxcar	5	10	___	___	___
6014-150 Wix Boxcar, *59 u*	85	185	___	___	___
6015 Sunoco 1-D Tank Car, *54-55*					
(A) Painted tank	35	90	___	___	___
(B) Unpainted tank	4	8	___	___	___
6017 Lionel Lines SP-Type Caboose, *51-62*	2	5	___	___	___
6017 Lionel SP-Type Caboose, *56 only*	15	40	___	___	___
6017-50 USMC SP-Type Caboose, *58*	20	55	___	___	___
6017-85 LL SP-Type Caboose, gray, *58*	25	58	___	___	___
6017-100 B&M SP-Type Caboose, *59, 62, 65-66*					
(A) Purplish blue	250	520	___	___	___
(B) Medium or light blue	10	35	___	___	___
6017-185 ATSF SP-Type Caboose, *59-60*	10	35	___	___	___
6017-200 U.S. Navy SP-Type Caboose, *60*	35	85	___	___	___
6017-225 ATSF SP-Type Caboose, *c. 63 u*	15	45	___	___	___
6017-235 ATSF SP-Type Caboose, *62*	25	55	___	___	___
6019 RCS Track Set (O27), *48-66*	2	7	___	___	___
6024 Nabisco Shredded Wheat Boxcar, *57*	10	24	___	___	___
6024 RCA Whirlpool Boxcar, *57 u*	28	68	___	___	___
6025 Gulf 1-D Tank Car, *56-58*	5	15	___	___	___
6027 Alaska SP-Type Caboose, *59*	25	70	___	___	___
6029 Remote Control Uncoupling Track, *55-63*	1	4	___	___	___
6032 Lionel Gondola, black (O27), *52-54*	2	6	___	___	___
X6034 Baby Ruth PRR Boxcar, *53-54*	5	14	___	___	___
6035 Sunoco 1-D Tank Car, *52-53*	3	6	___	___	___
6037 Lionel Lines Caboose SP-Type, *52-54*	2	5	___	___	___
6042 Lionel Gondola, *59-61, 62-64 u*	2	6	___	___	___
6044 Airex Boxcar, orange lettering, *59-60 u*					
(A) Medium blue	5	15	___	___	___
(B) Teal blue	40	85	___	___	___
(C) Dark blue/purple	80	260	___	___	___
6044-1X Nestles/McCall's Boxcar					

POSTWAR (1945-1969)	Good	Exc	Color	Cond	$
(no lettering), *62-63 u*	450	900			
6045 LL 2-D Tank Car, *59-64 adv. cat.*					
(A) Gray	15	25			
(B) Orange	15	40			
6045 Cities Service 2-D Tank, *60 u*	12	35			
6047 Lionel Lines SP-Type Caboose, *62*	2	4			
6050 Lionel Savings Bank Boxcar, *61*	12	30			
6050 Swift Refrigerator Car, *62-63*	9	18			
6050 Libby's Boxcar, *63 u*	18	45			
6057 LL SP-Type Caboose, *59-62*	3	9			
6057-50 LL SP-Type Caboose, orange, *62*	12	25			
6058 C&O SP-Type Caboose, *61*	15	45			
6059 M&St L SP-Type Caboose, *61-69*					
(A) Painted, red	6	15			
(B) Unpainted, red	3	7			
(C) Unpainted, maroon	5	10			
6062 NYC Gondola, w/ cable reels, *59-62*	7	18			
6062-50 NYC Gondola, w/ 2 canisters, *69*	5	20			
(6067) Caboose (no lett.), SP-Type, *62*	3	7			
6076 ATSF Hopper, *63 u*	10	22			
6076 LV Hopper, red, black, or gray body	7	15			
(6076) Hopper, no lettering, gray or yellow body	10	20			
6110 Steam 2-4-2, 6001T Tender, *50-51*	15	35			
(6111) Flatcar w/ logs, *55-57*	5	15			
6112 Lionel Gondola, *56 58*					
(A) Black body	4	10			
(B) Blue body	4	10			
(C) White body	8	23			
6119 DL&W Work Caboose, red, *55-56*	10	25			
6119-25 DL&W Work Caboose, orange, *56-59*	10	30			
6119-50 DL&W Caboose, brown, *56*	15	60			
6119-75 DL&W Caboose, gray, *57*	12	30			
6119-100 DL&W Work Caboose, red/gray, *57-66, 69*	9	22			
(6119-125) Rescue Unit Work Caboose (no number), olive drab, *63-64 u.*	60	140			

	Good	Exc	Color	Cond	$
(6120) Work Caboose (no lettering), yellow, *61-62 adv. cat.*	7	20	___	___	___
(6121) Flatcar (various colors) w/ pipes, *56-57*	5	15	___	___	___
6130 ATSF Work Caboose, *61, 65-69*	10	30	___	___	___
6139 R.C. Uncoupling Track (O27), *63*	1	4	___	___	___
6142 Lionel Gondola; green, blue, or black, *63-66, 69*	2	8	___	___	___
6149 Remote Control Uncoupling Track (O27), *64-69*	1	5	___	___	___
(6151) Flatcar (various colors) w/ patrol truck, *58*	40	122	___	___	___
6162 NYC Gondola, *59-68*					
(A) Blue body	5	12	___	___	___
(B) Red body	40	105	___	___	___
6162-60 Alaska Gondola, *59*	25	58	___	___	___
6167 LL SP Type Caboose, red, *63*	3	8	___	___	___
(6167) Unstamped SP Type Caboose w/o end rails					
(A) Red body	3	8	___	___	___
(B) Yellow body	10	25	___	___	___
(C) Brown body	15	40	___	___	___
6167-85 UP SP Type Caboose, *69*	10	28	___	___	___
6175 Flatcar w/ rocket, red or black body, *58-61*	25	65	___	___	___
6176 LV Hopper, yellow, gray, or black body, *64-66, 69*	3	9	___	___	___
(6176) Hopper (no lettering)					
(A) Yellow	5	15	___	___	___
(B) Gray	5	15	___	___	___
(C) Olive	30	70	___	___	___
6219 C&O Work Caboose, *60*	25	70	___	___	___
6220 Santa Fe NW-2 Switcher, *49-50*	125	275	___	___	___
6250 Seaboard NW-2 Switcher, *54-55*					
(A) Decals	115	295	___	___	___
(B) Rubber stamped	105	275	___	___	___
6257 Lionel SP Type Caboose, *48-56, 63-64*	3	10	___	___	___
6257-100 Lionel Lines SP-Type Caboose	9	20	___	___	___
6257-25 Lionel SP-Type Caboose	3	6	___	___	___

	Good	Exc	Color	Cond	$
6257-50 Lionel SP-Type Caboose	3	6			
6257X Lionel SP-Type Caboose	12	28			
6262 Flatcar w/ wheels, *56-57*					
(A) Black, 56-57	30	70			
(B) Red, *56*	160	450			
6264 Flatcar w/ lumber for Fork Lift set, *57-60*	20	55			
6311 Flatcar w/ three pipes, *55*	15	35			
6315 Gulf 1-D Chemical Tank Car, *56-59, 68-69*					
(A) Early, painted	20	48			
(B) Late, unpainted	30	65			
(C) Late, unpainted w/ built date	40	80			
6315 Lionel Lines 1-D Tank Car, *63-66*	13	32			
6342 NYC Gondola, *56-58, 64-66*	9	25			
6343 Barrel Ramp Car, *61-62*	15	40			
6346 Alcoa Quad Hopper, *56*	20	45			
6352 PFE Reefer from 352 Ice Depot, *55-57*	45	105			
6356 NYC Stock Car, 2 level, *54-55*	10	35			
6357 Lionel SP-Type Caboose, *48-61*	6	18			
6357-50 ATSF SP-Type Caboose	320	900			
6361 Flatcar w/ timber, *60-61, 64-69*	25	65			
6362 Truck Car w/ three trucks, *55-56*					
(A) Shiny orange	20	60			
(B) Dull orange	75	150			
6376 I L Circus Stock Car, *56-57*	30	65			
(6401) Flatcar, no load, gray	2	6			
(6402) Flatcar w/ reels or boat, *62, 64-66, 69*					
(A) w/ reels	6	14			
(B) w/ boat	25	60			
6404 Black Flatcar w/ brown auto, *60*	—	270			
6405 Maroon Flatcar w/ trailer, *61*	12	40			
(6406) Flatcar w/ yellow auto, *61*	35	85			
(6407) Flatcar w/ rocket, *63*	125	450			
(6408) Flatcar w/ pipes, *63*	10	20			
(6409) Flatcar w/ pipes, *63*	10	20			
6411 Flatcar w/ logs, *48-50*	11	25			
6413 Mercury Project Car, *62-63*	60	140			
6414 Evans Auto Loader w/ four cars, *55-66*					
(A) Early premium cars w/windows,					

	Good	Exc	Color	Cond	$
chrome bumpers, and rubber tires;					
red, yellow, blue, and white	40	100	___	___	___
(B) Four cheap cars, w/o trim,					
two red, two yellow	300	600	___	___	___
(C) Four red cars w/ gray bumpers	50	175	___	___	___
(D) Four yellow cars w/ gray bumpers	150	400	___	___	___
(E) Four brown cars w/ gray bumpers	300	750	___	___	___
(F) Four green cars w/ gray bumpers	400	950	___	___	___
6415 Sunoco 3-D Tank Car, *53-55, 64-66, 69*	7	22	___	___	___
6416 Boat Loader Car, *61-63*	80	200	___	___	___
6417 PRR Porthole Caboose, *53-57*					
(A) w/ "NEW YORK ZONE"	10	25	___	___	___
(B) w/o "NEW YORK ZONE"	100	230	___	___	___
6417-3 (See 6417-25)					
6417-25 Lionel Lines N5C Caboose, *54*	15	40	___	___	___
6417-50 LV N5C Caboose, *54*					
(A) Tuscan	350	1000	___	___	___
(B) Gray	50	140	___	___	___
6417-51 (See 6417-50)					
6417-53 (See 6417-25)					
6418 (See 214)					
6418 Flatcar w/ steel girders, *55-57*	45	100	___	___	___
6419 DL&W Work Caboose, early frame, *48-50, 52-57*	13	25	___	___	___
6419-25 DL&W Work Caboose, *54-55*	13	25	___	___	___
6419-50 DL&W Work Caboose, late frame, *56-57*	15	40	___	___	___
6419-57 (See 6419-100)					
6419-75 DL&W Work Caboose, late frame, *56-57*	15	40	___	___	___
6419-100 N&W Work Caboose, *57-58*	45	135	___	___	___
6420 DL&W Work Caboose, w/ light, *48-50*	35	100	___	___	___
6424 Flatcar w/ two autos, *56-59*	16	40	___	___	___
6425 Gulf 3-D Tank Car, *56-58*	15	35	___	___	___
6427 Lionel Lines N5C Caboose, *54-60*	12	25	___	___	___
6427-60 Virginian N5C Caboose, *58*	90	285	___	___	___
6427-500 PRR N5C Girls' Caboose,					

POSTWAR (1945-1969)	Good	Exc	Color	Cond	$
57-58*	125	350	___	___	___
6428 U.S. Mail Boxcar, 60-61, 65-66	10	28	___	___	___
6429 DL&W Work Caboose, AAR trucks, 63	100	310	___	___	___
6430 Flat. w/ Cooper-Jarrett vans, 56-58	20	50	___	___	___
6431 Flatcar w/ vans, 66	80	250	___	___	___
6434 Poultry Dispatch, 58-59	35	78	___	___	___
6436-1 LV Quad Hopper, black, 55	15	32	___	___	___
6436-25 LV Quad Hoppper, maroon, 55-57	15	28	___	___	___
6436-57 (See 6436-500)					
6436-110 LV Quad Hopper, red, 63-68					
(A) w/o cover	15	30	___	___	___
(B) w/ cover and "NEW 3-55"	80	155	___	___	___
6436-500 LV Girls' Hopper, lilac, "643657," 57-58*	75	225	___	___	___
6436-1969 TCA Quad Hopper, 69	50	110	___	___	___
6437 Pennsylvania N5C Caboose, 61-68	12	30	___	___	___
6440 Flatcar with vans, 61-63	25	80	___	___	___
6440 Green Pullman, 48-49	20	45	___	___	___
6441 Green Observation, 48-49	20	45	___	___	___
6442 Brown Pullman, 49	30	70	___	___	___
6443 Brown Observation, 49	30	70	___	___	___
6445 Fort Knox Gold Reserve, 61-63	50	140	___	___	___
(6446) N&W Quad Hopper "546446", black or gray, 54-55	18	40	___	___	___
6446-25 N&W Quad Hopper "644625", black or gray, 55 57	18	40	___	___	___
6446-60 See 6436-110(B)					
6447 Pennsylvania N5C Caboose, 63	125	350	___	___	___
6448 Target Car, 61-64	10	20	___	___	___
6452 Pennsylvania Gondola, black, 48-49	5	13	___	___	___
X6454(A) Baby Ruth PRR Boxcar, 48	60	200	___	___	___
X6454(B) NYC Boxcar, orange, 48	45	155	___	___	___
X6454(C) NYC Boxcar, brown, 48	15	40	___	___	___
X6454(D) NYC Boxcar, tan, 48	8	30	___	___	___
X6454(E) ATSF Boxcar, 48	12	40	___	___	___
X6454(F) SP Boxcar, 49-52	12	40	___	___	___
X6454(G) Erie Boxcar, 49-52	20	50	___	___	___
X6454(H) PRR Boxcar, 49-52	20	50	___	___	___

POSTWAR (1945-1969)	Good	Exc	Color	Cond	$
6456 Lehigh Valley Short Hopper, *48-55*					
(A) Black	5	10			
(B) Maroon	5	10			
(C) Gray	15	35			
(D) Enamel red, yellow lettering	50	100			
(E) Enamel red, white lettering	200	500			
6457 Lionel SP-Type, *49-52*	12	25			
6460 Bucyrus Erie black cab Crane, 8-wheel, *52-54*	20	55			
6460-25 Bucyrus Erie red cab Crane, 8-wheel, w/ box, *54*	40	95			
6461 Transformer Car, *49-50*	25	75			
6462 NYC Gondola, *49-57*					
(A) Black,	5	11			
(B) Green,	7	18			
(C) Red,	4	10			
6462-500 NYC Girls' Gondola, pink, *57-58**	65	170			
6463 Rocket Fuel 2-D Tank, *62-63*	10	35			
6464-1 WP Boxcar, *53-54*					
(A) Blue lettering	35	90			
(B) Red lettering	450	1200			
6464-25 GN Boxcar, *53-54*	35	95			
6464-50 M&St L Boxcar, *53-56*	38	85			
6464-75 RI Boxcar, *53-54, 69*	40	85			
6464-100 WP Boxcar, *54-55*					
(A) Silver body, yellow feather	60	140			
(B) Orange body, blue feather	350	830			
6464-125 NYC Boxcar, *54-56*	40	120			
6464-150 MP Boxcar, *54-55, 57*	32	115			
6464-175 Rock Island Boxcar, *54-55*					
(A) Blue lettering	50	125			
(B) Black lettering	450	1050			
6464-200 Pennsylvania Boxcar, *54-55, 69*	60	140			
6464-225 SP Boxcar, *54-56*	50	120			
6464-250 WP Boxcar, *66*	90	195			
6464-275 State of Maine Boxcar, *55, 57-59*					
(A) Striped doors	40	95			
(B) Solid doors	55	130			
6464-300 Rutland Boxcar, *55-56*					

	Good	Exc	Color	Cond	$
(A) Rubber-stamped	40	95			
(B) Split door	310	760			
(C) Solid shield	850	2500			
(D) Heat-stamped	50	150			
6464-325 B&O Sentinel Boxcar, *56*	280	585			
6464-350 MKT Katy Boxcar, *56*	115	255			
6464-375 Central of Georgia Boxcar, *56-57, 66*					
(A) Unpainted, maroon body	45	110			
(B) Painted, red body	800	1700			
6464-400 B&O Timesaver Boxcar, *56-57, 69*	40	110			
6464-425 New Haven Boxcar, *56-58*	30	75			
6464-450 Great Northern Boxcar, *56-57, 66*	60	135			
6464-475 B&M Boxcar, *57-60, 65-66, 68*	25	60			
6464-500 Timken Boxcar, yellow and white charcoal lettering (Also see 6464-500 in Modern Era.) *57-58, 69*	60	130			
6464-510 NYC Pacemaker Boxcar, *57-58*	300	620			
6464-515 MKT Boxcar, *57-58*	260	590			
6464-525 M&St L Boxcar, *57-58, 64-66*	30	70			
6464-650 D&RGW Box., *57-58, 66*					
(A) Unpainted yellow body	50	130			
(B) Painted yellow body & roof	500	1050			
6464-700 Santa Fe Boxcar, *61, 66*	45	120			
6464-725 New Haven Boxcar, *62-66, 68*					
(A) Orange body	30	70			
(B) Black body	65	195			
6464-825 Alaska Boxcar, *59-60*	105	230			
6464-900 NYC Boxcar, *60-66*	40	115			
6464-1965 TCA Pittsburgh Boxcar, *65*	—	270			
6464-1970 (See Modern Era)					
6464-1971 (See Modern Era)					
6465 Sunoco 2-D Tank Car, *48-56*	4	11			
6465 Cities Service 2-D Tank, *60-62*	12	30			
6465 Gulf 2-D Tank Car, *58*					
(A) Black tank	25	75			
(B) Gray tank	10	25			
6465 LL 2-D Tank Car, *59, 63-64*					
(A) Black tank	10	30			
(B) Orange tank	5	10			

		Good	Exc	Color	Cond	$
6467	Bulkhead Flatcar, *56*	18	50	___	___	___
6468	B&O Auto Boxcar, *53-55*					
	(A) Tuscan	140	320	___	___	___
	(B) Blue	20	60	___	___	___
6468-25	NH Auto Boxcar, *56-58*	20	50	___	___	___
(6469)	Lionel Liquified Gases Car, *63*	55	165	___	___	___
6470	Explosives Boxcar, *59-60*	12	40	___	___	___
6472	Refrigerator Car, *50-53*	18	35	___	___	___
6473	Horse Transport Car, *62-69*	10	28	___	___	___
6475	Heinz 57 Vat Car, post-factory					
	alteration	50	100	___	___	___
6475	Libby's Crushed Pineapple					
	Vat Car, *63, u*	18	50	___	___	___
6475	Pickles Vat Car, *60-62*	15	45	___	___	___
6476	LV Hopper, red, black, and					
	gray body, *57-69*	5	12	___	___	___
6476-1	LV Hopper, gray, TTOS, *69*	25	75	___	___	___
6476-135	LV Hopper, yellow, *64-66, 68*	5	10	___	___	___
6476-160	LV Hopper, black, *69*	5	10	___	___	___
6476-185	LV Hopper, yellow, *69*	5	10	___	___	___
6477	Bulkhead Car w/ pipes, *57-58*	15	65	___	___	___
6480	Explosives Boxcar, red, *61, adv. cat.*	18	45	___	___	___
6482	Refrigerator Car, *57*	30	60	___	___	___
(6500)	Flatcar w/ Bonanza plane, *62, 65*	280	540	___	___	___
(6501)	Flatcar w/ jet boat, *62-63*	55	125	___	___	___
(6502)	Flatcar w/ bridge girder, *62*	20	48	___	___	___
6511	Flatcar w/ pipes, *53-56*	11	38	___	___	___
(6512)	Cherry Picker Car, *62-63*	35	95	___	___	___
6517	LL Bay Window Caboose, *55-59*					
	(A) Underscored	30	75	___	___	___
	(B) Not underscored	20	55	___	___	___
6517-75	Erie B/W Caboose, *66*	180	465	___	___	___
6517-1966	TCA B/W Caboose, *66*	90	200	___	___	___
6518	Transformer Car, *56-58*	45	115	___	___	___
6519	Allis-Chalmers Flatcar, *58-61*					
	(A) Dark/medium orange base	35	80	___	___	___
	(B) Dull light orange base	40	110	___	___	___
6520	Searchlight Car, *49-51*					
	(A) Tan diesel generator	200	500	___	___	___

POSTWAR (1945-1969)	Good	Exc	Color	Cond	$
(B) Green diesel generator	100	285	___	___	___
(C) Maroon or orange diesel gen.	25	65	___	___	___
6530 Fire Fighting Car, red, *60-61*	30	70	___	___	___
6536 M&St L Quad Hopper, *58-59, 63*	20	50	___	___	___
6544 Missile Firing Car, *60-64*					
(A) White-lettered console	45	110	___	___	___
(B) Black-lettered console	175	400	___	___	___
6555 Sunoco 1-D Tank Car, *49-50*	15	40	___	___	___
6556 MKT Stock Car, *58*	60	225	___	___	___
6557 Lionel SP-Type Caboose, smoke, *58-59*	85	230	___	___	___
6560 Bucyrus Erie Crane w/ stack, 8-wheel, *55-58, 68-69*					
(A) Reddish-orange or black cab, early construction	65	175	___	___	___
(B) Gray cab	40	90	___	___	___
(C) Red cab	20	50	___	___	___
(D) Dark blue (Hagerstown)	40	95	___	___	___
6560-25 Bucyrus Erie Crane, 8-whl., *56*	45	110	___	___	___
6561 Reel Car, *53-56*					
(A) Orange reels	20	65	___	___	___
(B) Gray reels	25	75	___	___	___
6562 NYC Gondola w/ canisters, black, red, or gray, *56-58*	12	35	___	___	___
6572 REA Refrig. Car, *58-59, 63*	45	100	___	___	___
6630 IRBM Rocket Launcher, *61, adv. cat.*	30	95	___	___	___
6636 Alaska Quad Hopper, *50 60*	15	40	___	___	___
6640 USMC Rocket Launcher, *60*	85	225	___	___	___
6646 Lionel Lines Stock Car, *57*	12	40	___	___	___
6650 IRBM Rocket Launcher, *59-63*	25	60	___	___	___
6650-80 Missile, *60*	3	8	___	___	___
6651 USMC Cannon Car, *64 u*	60	150	___	___	___
6656 Lionel Lines Stock Car, *49-55*	5	20	___	___	___
6657 Rio Grande SP-Type Caboose, *57-58*	50	135	___	___	___
6660 Flatcar w/ crane, *58*	30	80	___	___	___
6670 Flatcar w/ crane, *59-60*	20	70	___	___	___
6672 Santa Fe Refrigerator Car, *54-56*					
(A) Blue lettering, two lines	22	60	___	___	___
(B) Black lettering, two lines	25	65	___	___	___

	Good	Exc	Color	Cond	$
(C) Blue lettering, three lines	60	200			
6736 Detroit & Mack. Quad Hopper, *60-62*	15	45			
6800 Flatcar w/ airplane, *57-60*	75	170			
6801 Flatcar w/ boat, *57-60*	45	110			
6802 Flatcar w/ bridge, *58-59*	12	30			
6803 Flatcar w/ tank and truck, *58-59*	70	185			
6804 Flatcar w/ USMC trucks, *58-59*	70	185			
6805 Atomic Disposal Flatcar, *58-59*	35	100			
6806 Flatcar w/ USMC trucks, *58-59*	70	165			
6807 Lionel Flatcar w/ boat, *58-59*	60	130			
6808 Flatcar w/ USMC trucks, *58-59*	100	240			
6809 Flatcar w/ USMC trucks, *58-59*	85	195			
6810 Flatcar w/ trailer, *58*	18	45			
6812 Track Maintenance Car, *59*	18	90			
6814 Lionel Rescue Caboose, *59-61*	30	105			
6816 Flatcar w/ bulldozer, *59-60*					
(A) Red car	200	420			
(B) Black car	260	650			
6816-100 Allis-Chalmers Tractor, *59-60*	50	170			
6817 Flatcar w/ scraper, *59-60*					
(A) Black car	340	680			
(B) Red car	200	400			
6817-100 Allis-Chalmers Scraper, *59-60*	75	200			
6818 Transformer Car, *58*	20	55			
6819 Flatcar w/ helicopter, *59-60*	22	65			
6820 Flatcar w/ missile transport helicopter, *60-61*					
(A) Light blue-painted flatcar	80	225			
(B) Darker blue flatcar	50	150			
6821 Flatcar w/ crates, *59-60*	15	25			
6822 Searchlight Car, *61-69*	20	50			
6823 Flatcar w/ RBM missiles, *59-60*	20	55			
6824 USMC Work Caboose, *60*	60	165			
6825 Flatcar w/ bridge, *59-62*	20	45			
6826 Flatcar w/ trees, *59-60*	65	145			
6827 Flatcar w/ steam shovel, *60-63*	65	140			
6827-100 Harnischfeger Shovel, *60*	40	95			
6828 Flatcar w/ crane, *60-63, 66*	80	180			
6828-100 Harnischfeger Crane, *60*	40	100			

POSTWAR (1945-1969)

		Good	Exc	Color	Cond	$
6830	Flatcar w/ submarine, *60-61*	50	120	___	___	___
6844	Flatcar w/ missiles, *59-60*					
	(A) Black plastic flatcar	20	60	___	___	___
	(B) Red plastic flatcar	300	650	___	___	___
63132	(See 3464)					
64173	(See 6427 LL)					
65400	(See 2454 or 6454)					
81000	(See 6417 PRR)					
96743	(See 6454)					
159000	(See 3464)					
336155	(See 3361)					
477618	(See 2457 or 2472)					
536417	(See 6417 PRR)					
546446	(See 6446)					
576419	(See 6419-100)					
576427	(See 6427-500)					
641751	(See 6417-50)					
A	Transformer, 90 watts, *47-48*	25	75	___	___	___
CTC	Lockon (O and O27), *47-69*	—	1	___	___	___
ECU-1	Electronic Control Unit, *46*	18	60	___	___	___
KW	Transformer, 190 watts, *50-65*	100	195	___	___	___
LTC	Lockon (O and O27), *50-69*	—	5	___	___	___
LW	Transformer, 125 watts, *55-56*	90	140	___	___	___
OC	Curved Track (O), *45-61*	—	1.50	___	___	___
OC1/2	Half Sec. Curve Track (O), *45-66*	—	1.50	___	___	___
OCS	Curved Insulated Track (O), *46-50*	NRS		___	___	___
OS	Straight Track (O), *45-61*	—	1.50	___	___	___
OSS	Straight Insulated Track, *46-50*	NRS		___	___	___
OTC	Lockon Track (O and O27)	—	5	___	___	___
Q	Transformer, 75 watts, *46*	20	65	___	___	___
R	Transformer, 110 watts, *46-47*	30	80	___	___	___
RW	Transformer, 110 watts, *48-54*	40	85	___	___	___
RCS	Remote Control Track (O), *45-48*	5	9	___	___	___
SP	Smoke Pellets, bottle, *48-69*	5	12	___	___	___
SW	Transformer, 130 watts, *61-66*	60	120	___	___	___
TW	Transformer, 175 watts, *53-60*	70	145	___	___	___
TOC	Curved Track (O), *62-66, 68-69*	—	2	___	___	___
TOC1/2	Half Sec. Str. Trk. (O), *62-66*	—	2	___	___	___
TOS	Straight Track (O), *62-69*	—	2	___	___	___

		Good	Exc	Color	Cond	$
UCS	Remote Control Track (O), *45-69*	—	12	____	____	____
UTC	Lockon (O, O27, Standard), *45*	—	1.50	____	____	____
V	Transformer, 150 watts, *46-47*	75	145	____	____	____
VW	Transformer, 150 watts, *48-49*	70	155	____	____	____
Z	Transformer, 250 watts, *45-47*	100	225	____	____	____
ZW	Transformer, 250 watts, *48-49*	120	275	____	____	____
ZW	Transformer, 275 watts, *50-66*	150	295	____	____	____

No Number SP-Type Caboose,
(see 6067, 6167)

No Number Work Caboose,
(see 6119-125, 6120)

No Number Flatcar (see 6401, 6402, 6406)

No Number Gondola (see 6142)

No Number Hopper (see 6176)

No Number Turbo Missile Car (see 3309, 3349)

No Number Rolling Stock
(see 3413, 3510, 6111, 6121, 6151, 6407,
6408, 6409, 6469, 6500, 6501, 6502, 6512)

		Exc	New	Cond/$
[00002]	Midwest TCA Stock Car, *75 u*		NRS	_____
[00005]	Midwest TCA Covered Quad Hopper, *78 u*		NRS	_____
3	(See 8104, 8630, 8701)			
[4]	Midwest TCA C&NW F-3 A Unit, shell only, *77 u*		NRS	_____
[10]	METCA Jersey Central F-3 A Unit, shell only, *71 u*		NRS	_____
[303]	LOTS Stauffer Chemical 1-D Tank Car, *85 u*	60	75	_____
484	(See 8587)			
491	(See 7203)			
(0511)	TCA St. Louis Baggage Car "1981", *81 u*	60	75	_____
0512	Toy Fair Reefer, *81 u*	100	125	_____
550	(See 8378)			
(550C)	Curved Track 31" (O), *70*	.75	1.25	_____
(550S)	Straight Track (O), *70*	.75	1.25	_____
577	(See 9562)			
578	(See 9563)			
579	(See 9564)			
580	(See 9565)			
581	(See 9566)			
582	(See 0567)			
611	(See 8100)			
634	Santa Fe NW-2, *70 u*	55	100	_____
659	(See 8101)			
665E	Johnny Cash "Blue Train" 4-6-4, *71 u*		NRS	_____
672	(See 8610)			
779	(See 8215)			
0780	LRRC Boxcar, *82 u*	75	100	_____
0781	LRRC Flatcar w/ trailers, *83 u*	100	125	_____
0782	LRRC 1-D Tank Car, *85 u*	60	75	_____
783	(See 8406)			
0784	LRRC Covered Quad Hopper, *84 u*	75	100	_____
784	(See 8606)			
[1018-1979]	TCA Mortgage Burning Hi-cube Boxcar, *79 u*	40	50	_____

		Exc	New	Cond/$
(1050)	New Englander set, *80-81*	160	180	_____
(1051)	T&P Diesel set, *80*		NM	
(1052)	Chesapeake Flyer set, *80*	140	160	_____
(1053)	The James Gang set, *80-82*	225	250	_____
(1070)	The Royal Limited set, *80*	400	450	_____
(1071)	Mid Atlantic Limited set, *80*	375	425	_____
(1072)	Cross Country Express set, *80-81*	300	350	_____
(1076)	Lionel Clock, *76-77 u*	200	250	_____
(1081)	Wabash Cannonball set, *70-72*	110	125	_____
(1082)	Yard Boss set, *70*	125	150	_____
(1083)	Pacemaker set, *70*	110	125	_____
(1084)	Grand Trunk & Western set, *70*	125	150	_____
(1085)	Santa Fe Express Diesel Freight set, *70*	175	200	_____
(1085)	Santa Fe Twin Diesel set, *71*	175	200	_____
(1086)	The Mountaineer set, *70*		NM	
(1087)	Midnight Express set, *70*		NM	
(1091)	Sears Special set, *70 u*		NRS	_____
(1092)	79N97081C Sears set, *70 u*		NRS	_____
(1092)	79C97105C Sears 6-unit set, *71 u*		NRS	_____
(1100)	Happy Huff n' Puff, *74-75 u*	50	60	_____
(1150)	L.A.S.E.R. Train set, *81-82*	175	200	_____
(1151)	Union Pacific Thunder Freight set, *81-82*	160	185	_____
(1153)	JCPenney Thunderball Freight set, *81 u*	170	190	_____
(1154)	Reading Yard King set, *81-82*	225	250	_____
(1155)	Cannonball Freight set, *82*	75	90	_____
(1157)	Lionel Leisure Wabash Cannonball set, *81 u*		NRS	_____
(1158)	Maple Leaf Limited set, *81*	500	550	_____
(1159)	Toys 'R Us Midnight Flyer set, *81 u*	135	150	_____
(1160)	Great Lakes Limited set, *81*	400	450	_____
(T-1171)	Canadian National Steam Loco set, *71 u*	195	225	_____
(T-1172)	Yardmaster set, *71 u*		NRS	_____
(T-1173)	Grand Trunk & Western set, *71-73 u*	185	210	_____
(T-1174)	Canadian National set, *71-73 u*	300	350	_____
(1182)	The Yardmaster set, *71-72*	85	110	_____
(1183)	The Silver Star set, *71-72*	75	100	_____
(1184)	The Allegheny set, *71*	125	160	_____
(1186)	Cross Country Express set, *71-72*	200	250	_____
(1187)	Illinois Central set, *71 (SSS)*	450	550	_____
(1190)	Sears Special #1 set, *71 u*		NRS	_____

		Exc	New	Cond/$
(1195)	JCPenney Special set, *71 u*		NRS	_____
(1198)	Unnamed set, *71 u*		NRS	_____
(1199)	Ford Autolite Allegheny set, *71 u*	185	210	_____
(1200)	Gravel Gus, *75 u*		NRS	_____
[1203]	NETCA B&M NW-2, shell only, *72 u*	—	70	_____
[1223]	LOTS Seattle & North Coast Hi-cube Boxcar, *86 u*	125	150	_____
(1250)	New York Central set, *72 (SSS)*	400	475	_____
(1252)	Heavy Iron set, *82-83*	100	145	_____
(1253)	Quicksilver Express set, *82-83*	300	350	_____
(1254)	Black Cave Flyer set, *82*	80	110	_____
(1260)	Continental Limited set, *82*	450	550	_____
(1261)	49N95211 Sears Black Cave Flyer set, *82 u*		NRS	_____
(1262)	Toys 'R Us Heavy Iron set, *82 u*		NRS	_____
(1263)	XU671-0701A JCPenney Overland Freight set, *82 u*		NRS	_____
(1264)	Nibco Express set, *82 u*	175	225	_____
(1265)	Tappan Special set, *82 u*	135	165	_____
(T-1272)	Yardmaster set, *72-73 u*		NRS	_____
(T-1273)	Silver Star set, *72-73 u*		NRS	_____
(1280)	Kickapoo Valley & Northern set, *72*	60	75	_____
(1284)	Allegheny set, *72*	150	175	_____
(1285)	Santa Fe Twin Diesel set, *72*	100	150	_____
(1287)	Pioneer Dockside Switcher set, *72*	—	100	_____
[1287]	Midwest TCA C&NW Reefer, *84 u*		NRS	_____
(1290)	Sears set, *72 u*		NRS	_____
(1291)	Sears set, *72 u*		NRS	_____
(1350)	Canadian Pacific set, *73 (SSS)*	800	1000	_____
(1351)	Baltimore & Ohio set, *83-84*	200	225	_____
(1352)	Rocky Mountain Freight set, *83-84*	75	100	_____
(1353)	Southern Streak set, *83-85*	75	100	_____
(1354)	Northern Freight Flyer set, *83-85*	275	325	_____
(1355)	Commando Assault Train set, *83-84*	150	200	_____
(1359)	Train Display Case for set 1355, *83 u*	75	100	_____
(1361)	Gold Coast Limited set, *83*	750	900	_____
(1362)	Lionel Leisure Express set, *83 u*		NRS	_____
(1380)	US Steel Industrial Switcher set, *73-75*	60	75	_____
(1381)	Cannonball set, *73-75*	60	75	_____
(1382)	Yardmaster set, *73-74*	100	125	_____

MPC MODERN ERA (1970-1986)		Exc	New	Cond/$
(1383)	Santa Fe Freight set, *73-75*	100	130	_____
(1384)	Southern Express set, *73-76*	100	125	_____
(1385)	Blue Streak Freight set, *73-74*	100	125	_____
(1386)	Rock Island Express set, *73-74*	125	150	_____
(1387)	Milwaukee Road Special set, *73*	200	250	_____
(1388)	Golden State Arrow set, *73-75*	200	225	_____
(1390)	Sears 7-unit set, *73 u*		NRS	_____
(1392)	79C95224C Sears 8-unit set, *73 u*		NRS	_____
(1393)	79C95223C Sears 6-unit set, *73 u*		NRS	_____
(1395)	JCPenney set, *73 u*		NRS	_____
(1400)	Happy Huff n' Puff Junior, *75 u*		NRS	_____
(1402)	Chessie System set, *84-85*	125	150	_____
(1403)	Redwood Valley Express set, *84-85*	190	225	_____
(1450)	D&RGW set, *74 (SSS)*	400	450	_____
(1451)	Erie-Lackawanna Limited set, *84*	600	700	_____
(1460)	Grand National set, *74*	275	300	_____
(1461)	Black Diamond set, *74 u, 75*	100	125	_____
(1463)	Coca-Cola Special set, *74 u, 75*	225	275	_____
(1487)	Broadway Limited set, *74-75*	225	275	_____
(1489)	Santa Fe Double Diesel set, *74-76*	150	175	_____
(1492)	79N96185C Sears 7-unit set, *74 u*		NRS	_____
(1493)	79N96185C Sears 7-unit set, *74 u*		NRS	_____
(1499)	JCPenney Great Express set, *74 u*		NRS	_____
(1501)	Midland Freight set, *85-86*	75	100	_____
(1502)	Yard Chief set, *85-86*	200	225	_____
(1506)	Sears Chessie System set, *85 u*		NRS	_____
(1512)	JCPenney Midland Freight set, *85 u*		NRS	_____
(1549)	Toys 'R Us Heavy Iron set, *85-89 u*	200	250	_____
(1552)	Burlington Northern Limited set, *85*	500	600	_____
(1560)	North American Express set, *75*	225	275	_____
(1562)	Fast Freight Flyer set, *85 u*	125	150	_____
(1577)	Liberty Special set, *75 u*	200	250	_____
(1579)	Milwaukee Road set, *75 (SSS)*	400	475	_____
(1581)	Thunderball Freight set, *75-76*	75	100	_____
(1582)	Yard Chief set, *75-76*	120	165	_____
(1584)	Norfolk & Western "Spirit of America" set, *75*	250	275	_____
(1585)	75th Anniversary Special set, *75-77*	225	275	_____
(1586)	Chesapeake Flyer set, *75-77*	150	175	_____
(1587)	Capitol Limited set, *75*	250	275	_____

		Exc	New	Cond/$
(1594)	Sears set, *75 u*		NRS	_____
(1595)	79C9716C Sears 6-unit set, *75 u*		NRS	_____
(1602)	Nickel Plate Special set, *86-91*	150	175	_____
(1606)	Sears Nickel Plate Special set, *86 u*		NRS	_____
(1608)	American Express General set, *86 u*	250	300	_____
(1615)	Cannonball Express set, *86-90*	85	95	_____
(1632)	Santa Fe Work Train set, *86 (SSS)*	275	325	_____
(1652)	B&O Freight set, *86*	225	275	_____
(1658)	Town House set, *86 u*	80	100	_____
(1660)	Yard Boss set, *76*	100	120	_____
(1661)	Rock Island Line set, *76-77*	95	125	_____
(1662)	Black River Freight set, *76-78*	100	125	_____
(1663)	Amtrak Lake Shore Limited set, *76 77*	200	275	_____
(1664)	Illinois Central Freight set, *76-77*	300	350	_____
(1665)	NYC Empire State Express set, *76*	450	550	_____
(1672)	Northern Pacific set, *76 (SSS)*	350	400	_____
(1685)	True Value Freight Flyer set, *86-87 u*		NRS	_____
(1686)	Kay Bee Toys Freight Flyer set, *86 u*		NRS	_____
(1693)	Toys 'R Us Rock Island Line set, *76 u*		NRS	_____
(1694)	Toys 'R Us Black River Freight set, *76 u*		NRS	_____
(1696)	Sears set, *76 u*		NRS	_____
(1698)	True Value Rock Island Line set, *76 u*		NRS	_____
(1760)	Trains n' Truckin' Steel Hauler set, *77-78*	90	100	_____
(1761)	Trains n' Truckin' Cargo King set, *77-78*	100	125	_____
(1762)	Wabash Cannonball set, *77*	125	175	_____
(1764)	Heartland Express set, *77*	225	275	_____
(1765)	Rocky Mountain Special set, *77*	250	300	_____
(1766)	B&O Budd Car set, *77 (SSS)*	400	450	_____
1776	(See 8559, 8665, 9170)			
1776	Seaboard U36B, *74-76*	100	125	_____
(1790)	Lionel Leisure Steel Hauler set, *77 u*		NRS	_____
(1791)	Toys 'R Us Steel Hauler set, *77 u*		NRS	_____
(1792)	True Value Rock Island Line set, *77 u*		NRS	_____
(1793)	Toys 'R Us Black River Freight set, *77 u*		NRS	_____
(1796)	JCPenney Cargo Master set, *77 u*		NRS	_____
(1860)	Workin' On The Railroad Timberline set, *78*	60	75	_____
(1862)	Workin' On The Railroad Logging Empire set, *78*	75	100	_____
(1864)	Santa Fe Double Diesel set, *78-79*	150	175	_____

		Exc	New	Cond/$
(1865)	Chesapeake Flyer set, *78-79*	150	175	_____
(1866)	Great Plains Express set, *78-79*	275	300	_____
(1867)	Milwaukee Road Limited set, *78*	300	350	_____
(1868)	M&St L set, *78 (SSS)*	225	275	_____
(1892)	JCPenney Logging Empire set, *78 u*		NRS	_____
(1893)	Toys 'R Us Logging Empire set, *78 u*		NRS	_____
(1960)	Midnight Flyer set, *79-81*	60	80	_____
(1962)	Wabash Cannonball set, *79*	90	110	_____
(1963)	Black River Freight set, *79-81*	75	90	_____
(1964)	Radio Control Express set, *79 u*		NM	_____
(1965)	Smokey Mountain Line set, *79*		NRS	_____
1970	(See 8615)			
(1970)	Southern Pacific Limited set, *79 u*	550	650	_____
(1971)	Quaker City Limited set, *79*	450	500	_____
[1971-1976]	Rocky Mountain TCA Reefer, *76 u*		NRS	_____
1973	TCA Bicentennial Observation Car (O27), *76 u*	40	60	_____
1974	TCA Bicentennial Passenger Car (O27), *76 u*	40	60	_____
1975	TCA Bicentennial Passenger Car (O27), *76 u*	40	60	_____
1976	TCA Seaboard U36B, *76 u*	150	200	_____
[1976]	Southern TCA Florida East Coast F-3 ABA,			
	shells only, *76 u*		NRS	_____
[1979]	IETCA Boxcar, *79 u*	—	15	_____
[1980]	IETCA SP Caboose, *80 u*	—	15	_____
[1980]	Atlantic TCA Flatcar w/ trailers, *80 u*	25	30	_____
1980	(See 8068, 9544)			
[1981]	IETCA Quad Hopper, *81 u*	—	15	_____
[1981]	LCOL Boxcar, *81 u*	—	25	_____
1981	(See 0511)			
[1982]	IETCA 3-D Tank Car, *82 u*	—	15	_____
1982	(See 7205)			
[1983]	IETCA Reefer, *83 u*	—	15	_____
[1983]	TTOS Phoenix 3-D Tank Car, *83 u*		NRS	_____
[1983]	Great Lakes TCA Churchill Downs Boxcar, *83 u*		NRS	_____
[1983]	Great Lakes TCA Churchill Downs Reefer, *83 u*		NRS	_____
1983	(See 7206)			
[1984]	TTOS Sacramento Northern Boxcar, *84 u*	80	100	_____
[1984]	Ft. Pitt TCA Iron City Boxcar, *84 u*	—	170	_____
[1984]	Ft. Pitt TCA Iron City Reefer, *84 u*	—	170	_____
[1984]	Ft. Pitt TCA Heinz Pickles Boxcar, *84 u*		NRS	_____

		Exc	New	Cond/$
1984	(See 7212)			
[1984-30x]	Ft. Pitt TCA Heinz Ketchup Boxcar, *84 u*	—	200	_____
[1985]	TTOS Snowbird Covered Quad Hopper, *85 u*	40	50	_____
[1986]	IETCA Bunk Car, *86 u*	—	15	_____
[1986]	Southern TCA Bunk Car, *86 u*	—	30	_____
[1986]	LCOL Work Caboose, shell only, *86 u*	—	18	_____
(1990)	Mystery Glow Midnight Flyer set, *79 u*		NRS	_____
(1991)	JCPenney Wabash Cannonball Deluxe Express set, *79 u*		NRS	_____
(1993)	Toys 'R Us Midnight Flyer set, *79 u*		NRS	_____
2110	Graduated Trestle set (22), *70-88*	10	15	_____
2111	Elevated Trestle set (10), *70-88*	10	15	_____
(2113)	Tunnel Portals (2), *84-87*	10	15	_____
(2115)	Dwarf Signal, *84-87*	13	15	_____
(2117)	Block Target Signal, *84-87*	20	25	_____
(2122)	Extension Bridge w/ rock piers, *76-87*	30	40	_____
2125	Whistling Freight Shed, *71*	40	50	_____
2126	Whistling Freight Shed, *76-87*	25	30	_____
2127	Diesel Horn Shed, *76-87*	25	30	_____
(2128)	Operating Switchman, *83-86*	30	35	_____
2129	Illuminated Freight Station, *83-86*	30	35	_____
(2133)	Lighted Freight Station, *72-78, 80-84*	30	40	_____
2140	Automatic Banjo Signal, *70-84*	20	25	_____
(2145)	Automatic Gateman, *72-84*	35	45	_____
(2151)	Operating Semaphore, *78-82*	20	25	_____
(2152)	Automatic Crossing Gate, *70-84*	25	30	_____
2154	Automatic Highway Flasher, *70-87*	20	25	_____
2156	Illuminated Station Platform, *70-71*	30	40	_____
2162	Automatic Crossing Gate and Signal, *70-87, 94*		CP	_____
(2163)	Block Target Signal, *70-78*	20	25	_____
(2170)	Street Lamps (3), *70-87*	15	20	_____
(2171)	Gooseneck Street Lamps (2), *80-81, 83-84*	20	25	_____
(2175)	Sandy Andy Gravel Loader kit, *76-79*	40	60	_____
(2180)	Road Signs (16), *77-94*		CP	_____
(2181)	Telephone Poles (10), *77-94*		CP	_____
(2195)	Floodlight Tower, *70-71*	45	60	_____
(2199)	Microwave Tower, *72-75*	30	40	_____
(2214)	Girder Bridge, *70-71, 72 u, 73-87*	5	10	_____
2256	Station Platform, *73-81*	15	20	_____

		Exc	New	Cond/$
[2256]	TCA Station Platform, *75 u*	25	35	_____
(2260)	Illuminated Bumper, *70-71, 72 u, 73*	25	40	_____
(2280)	Non-Illuminated Bumpers (3), *73-84*	3	5	_____
2282	Die-cast Bumpers (2), *83 u*	20	25	_____
2283	Die-cast Bumpers (2), *84-94*		CP	_____
(2290)	Illuminated Bumpers (2), *75 u, 76-86*	10	12	_____
2292	Station Platform, *85-87*	6	10	_____
(2300)	Operating Oil Drum Loader, *83-87*	100	150	_____
(2301)	Operating Sawmill, *80-84*	90	125	_____
2302	Union Pacific Manual Gantry Crane, *80-82*	20	25	_____
2303	Santa Fe Manual Gantry Crane, *80-81*	20	25	_____
2305	Operating Oil Derrick, *81-84*	150	175	_____
(2306)	Operating Ice Station w/ 6700 PFE			
	Ice Car, *82-83*	175	225	_____
(2307)	Billboard Light, *82-86*	20	25	_____
2308	Animated Newsstand, *82-83*	150	175	_____
(2309)	Mechanical Crossing Gate, *82-92*	4	8	_____
(2310)	Mechanical Crossing Gate, *73-77*	3	5	_____
(2311)	Mechanical Semaphore, *82-92*	4	8	_____
(2312)	Mechanical Semaphore, *73-77*	3	5	_____
(2313)	Floodlight Tower, *75-86*	20	25	_____
(2314)	Searchlight Tower, *75-84*	20	25	_____
(2315)	Operating Coaling Station, *83-84*	125	175	_____
2316	N&W Operating Gantry Crane, *83-84*	150	175	_____
2317	Operating Drawbridge, *75 u, 76-81*	100	125	_____
(2318)	Operating Control Tower, *83-86*	75	100	_____
2319	Illuminated Watchtower, *75-78, 80*	30	35	_____
2320	Flagpole kit, *83-87*	20	25	_____
2321	Operating Sawmill, *84, 86-87*	100	150	_____
2323	Operating Freight Station, *84-87*	100	125	_____
2324	Operating Switch Tower, *84-87*	75	100	_____
(2390)	Lionel Mirror, *82 u*	65	100	_____
2494	Rotary Beacon, *72-74*	40	50	_____
(2709)	Rico Station kit, *81-94*		CP	_____
2710	Billboards (5), *70-84*	3	5	_____
(2714)	Tunnel, *75 u, 76-77*	40	50	_____
(2717)	Short Extension Bridge, *77-87*	3	5	_____
(2718)	Barrel Platform kit, *77-84*	3	5	_____
(2719)	Watchman's Shanty kit, *77-87*	3	5	_____

MPC MODERN ERA (1970-1986)

		Exc	New	Cond/$
(2720)	Lumber Shed kit, *77-84, 87*	3	5	_____
(2721)	Operating Log Mill kit, *78*	3	5	_____
(2722)	Barrel Loader kit, *78*	3	5	_____
(2729)	Water Tower kit, *85*		NM	
(2783)	Freight Station kit, *84*	7	10	_____
(2784)	Freight Platform kit, *81-90*	6	9	_____
(2785)	Engine House kit, *73-77*	40	50	_____
(2786)	Freight Platform kit, *73-77*	4	7	_____
(2787)	Freight Station kit, *73-77, 83*	7	10	_____
(2788)	Coal Station kit, *75 u, 76-77*	20	40	_____
(2789)	Water Tower kit, *75-77, 80*	20	25	_____
(2791)	Cross Country set, *70-71*	25	35	_____
(2792)	Whistle Stop set, *70-71*	25	35	_____
(2792)	Layout Starter Pak, *80-84*	10	25	_____
(2793)	Alamo Junction set, *70-71*	25	35	_____
(2796)	Grain Elevator kit, *76 u, 77*	60	75	_____
(2797)	Rico Station kit, *76-77*	30	45	_____
(2900)	Lockon, *70-94*		CP	_____
(2901)	Track Clips (12) (O27), *71-94*		CP	_____
(2905)	Lockon and Wire, *74-94*		CP	_____
2909	Smoke Fluid, *70-94*		CP	_____
2910	OTC Contactor, *84-86, 88*	4	8	_____
(2911)	Smoke Pellets, *70-73*	10	15	_____
2925	Lubricant, *70-71, 72 u, 73-75*	—	2	_____
(2927)	Maintenance kit, *70, 78-94*	5	7	_____
2928	Oil, *71*	—	2	_____
2951	Track Layout Book, *70-86*	1	2	_____
2952	Train and Accessory Manual, *70-74*	1	2	_____
2953	Train and Accessory Manual, *75-86*	1	2	_____
(2960)	Lionel 75th Anniversary Book, *75 u, 76*	10	20	_____
(2980)	Magnetic Conversion Coupler, *70, 71*	1	2	_____
(2985)	The Lionel Train Book, *86-94*	10	12	_____
3100	Great Northern 4-8-4 (FARR #3), *81*	500	600	_____
[3764]	LOTS Kahn Boxcar, *81 u*	60	75	_____
4044	Transformer 45-watt, *70-71*	3	5	_____
4045	Safety Transformer, *70-71*	3	4	_____
4050	Safety Transformer, *72-79*	3	4	_____
4060	AC/DC Power Master Transformer, *80-93*	15	25	_____
4065	DC Hobby Transformer, *81-83*	3	4	_____

		Exc	New	Cond/$
4090	Power Master Transformer, *70-84*	40	55	_____
4125	Transformer 25-watt, *72*	3	4	_____
4150	Trainmaster Transformer, *72-73, 75-77*	6	12	_____
4250	Trainmaster Transformer, *74*	6	12	_____
4449	(See 8307)			
4501	(See 8309)			
4651	Trainmaster Transformer, *78-79*	2	3	_____
4690	MW Transformer, *86-89*	75	95	_____
4851	DC Transformer, *85-91, 94*	3	4	_____
4870	DC Hobby Transformer and Throttle Controller, *77-78*	3	4	_____
4935	(See 8150)			
(5012)	Curved Track 27", card of 4 (O27), *70-94*		CP	_____
(5013)	Curved Track 27" (O27), *70-78*	.50	.55	_____
(5014)	Half-Curved Track 27" (O27), *70-94*		CP	_____
(5017)	Straight Track, card of 4 (O27), *70-94*		CP	_____
(5018)	Straight Track (O27), *70-78*	.50	.75	_____
(5019)	Half-Straight Track (O27), *70-94*		CP	_____
5020	90° Crossover (O27), *70-94*		CP	_____
(5021)	Left Manual Switch 27" (O27), *70-94*		CP	_____
(5022)	Right Manual Switch 27" (O27), *70-94*		CP	_____
5023	45° Crossover (O27), *70-94*		CP	_____
(5025)	Manumatic Uncoupler, *71-72*	1	2	_____
(5027)	Pair Manual Switches 27" (O27), *74-84*	15	25	_____
(5030)	Track Expander set (O27), *71-84*	20	30	_____
(5033)	Curved Track 27" (O27), *79-94*		CP	_____
(5038)	Straight Track (O27), *79-94*		CP	_____
(5041)	Insulator Pins (12) (O27), *70-94*		CP	_____
(5042)	Steel Pins (12) (O27), *70-94*		CP	_____
(5090)	Three Pair Manual Switches 27" (O27), *78-84*	60	80	_____
(5113)	Curved Track 54" (O27), *79-94*		CP	_____
5121	Left Remote Switch 27" (O27), *70-94*		CP	_____
5122	Right Remote Switch 27" (O27), *70-94*		CP	_____
(5125)	Pair Remote Switches 27" (O27), *71-83*	25	35	_____
5132	Right Remote Switch 31" (O), *80-94*		CP	_____
5133	Left Remote Switch 31" (O), *80-94*		CP	_____
(5149)	Remote Uncoupling Section (O27), *70-94*		CP	_____
(5193)	Three Pair Remote Switches 27" (O27), *78-83*	90	110	_____
5484	TCA 4-6-4, *85 u*	400	500	_____

MPC MODERN ERA (1970-1986)

		Exc	New	Cond/$
(5500)	Straight Track (O), *71-94*		CP	_____
(5501)	Curved Track 31" (O), *71-94*		CP	_____
(5502)	Remote Uncoupling Section (O), *71-72*	8	10	_____
(5504)	Half-Curved Track 31" (O), *83-94*		CP	_____
(5505)	Half-Straight Track (O), *83-94*		CP	_____
5520	90° Crossover (O), *71-72*	7	10	_____
5530	Remote Uncoupling Section (O), *81-94*		CP	_____
5540	90° Crossover (O), *81-94*		CP	_____
(5543)	Insulator Pins (12) (O), *70-94*		CP	_____
5545	45° Crossover (O), *83-94*		CP	_____
(5551)	Steel Pins (12) (O), *70-94*		CP	_____
(5572)	Curved Track 72" (O), *79-94*		CP	_____
5600	Curved Track, *73-74 (TT)*	1	2	_____
5601	Curved Track, card of 4, *73-74 (TT)*	6	10	_____
5602	Curved Track Ballast, card of 4, *73-74 (TT)*	6	10	_____
5605	Straight Track, *73-74 (TT)*	1	2	_____
5606	Straight Track, card of 4, *73-74 (TT)*	6	10	_____
5607	Straight Track Ballast, card of 4, *73-74 (TT)*	6	10	_____
5620	Left Manual Switch, *73-74 (TT)*	5	15	_____
5625	Left Remote Switch, *73-74 (TT)*	10	20	_____
5630	Right Manual Switch, *73-74 (TT)*	5	15	_____
5635	Right Remote Switch, *73-74 (TT)*	10	20	_____
5640	Left Switch Ballast, card of 2, *73-74 (TT)*	6	10	_____
5650	Right Switch Ballast, card of 2, *73-74 (TT)*	6	10	_____
5655	Lockon, *73-74 (TT)*	1	2	_____
5660	Terminal Track w/ lockon, *74 (TT)*	2	4	_____
5700	Oppenheimer Reefer, *81*	40	50	_____
[5700]	Ozark TCA Oppenheimer Reefer, *81 u*	50	100	_____
5701	Dairymen's League Reefer, *81*	30	40	_____
5702	National Dairy Despatch Reefer, *81*	30	40	_____
5703	North American Despatch Reefer, *81*	30	40	_____
5704	Budweiser Reefer, *81-82*	50	80	_____
5705	Ball Glass Jars Reefer, *81-82*	40	50	_____
5706	Lindsay Brothers Reefer, *81-82*	30	40	_____
5707	American Refrigerator Reefer, *81-82*	30	40	_____
5708	Armour Reefer, *82-83*	20	25	_____
5709	REA Reefer, *82-83*	35	45	_____
5710	Canadian Pacific Reefer, *82-83*	25	30	_____
[5710]	NETCA CP Reefer, *82 u*	25	30	_____

		Exc	New	Cond/$
[5710]	LCAC CP Reefer, *83 u*		NRS	_____
5711	Commercial Express Reefer, *82-83*	25	30	_____
5712	Lionel Lines Reefer, *82 u*	225	275	_____
5713	Cotton Belt Reefer, *83-84*	20	30	_____
5714	Michigan Central Reefer, *83-84*	20	30	_____
[5714]	LCAC Michigan Central Reefer, *85 u*		NRS	_____
5715	Santa Fe Reefer, *83-84*	25	45	_____
5716	Vermont Central Reefer, *83-84*	25	30	_____
[5716]	NETCA Vermont Central Reefer, *83 u*	25	30	_____
5717	Santa Fe Bunk Car, *83*	30	40	_____
5718	(See 9849)			
5719	Canadian National Reefer, *84*	25	30	_____
5720	Great Northern Reefer, *84*	150	175	_____
5721	Soo Line Reefer, *84*	25	30	_____
5722	NKP Reefer, *84*	25	30	_____
5724	PRR Bunk Car, *84*	25	40	_____
[5724]	LCOL PRR Bunk Car, *84 u*	30	40	_____
5726	Southern Bunk Car, *84 u*	35	45	_____
5727	US Marines Bunk Car, *84-85*	25	35	_____
5728	Canadian Pacific Bunk Car, *86*	20	25	_____
5730	Strasburg RR Reefer, *85-86*	20	30	_____
5731	L&N Reefer, *85-86*	20	25	_____
[5731]	TCA Museum L&N Reefer, *90 u*	100	150	_____
5732	Jersey Central Reefer, *85-86*	20	25	_____
5733	Lionel Lines Bunk Car, *86 u*	40	50	_____
5734-85	TCA REA Reefer, *85 u*	150	175	_____
5735	NYC Bunk Car, *85-86*	50	60	_____
5739	B&O Tool Car, *86*	50	65	_____
5745	Santa Fe Bunk Car, *86 (SSS)*	50	75	_____
5760	Santa Fe Tool Car, *86 (SSS)*	50	75	_____
5900	AC/DC Converter, *79-83*	4	6	_____
[6014-900]	LCCA Frisco Boxcar (O27), *75-76 u*	25	40	_____
6076	TTOS Santa Fe Hopper (O27), *70 u*		NRS	_____
6076	LV Hopper (O27), *70 u*	20	25	_____
6100	Ontario Northland Covered Quad Hopper, *81-82*	30	40	_____
[6100]	LCAC Ontario Northland Covered Quad Hopper, *82 u*		NRS	_____
6101	Burlington Northern Covered Quad Hopper, *81-82*	20	35	_____

MPC MODERN ERA (1970-1986)	Exc	New	Cond/$
[6101] Atlantic TCA Burlington Northern Covered Quad Hopper, *82 u*	20	25	_____
6102 GN Covered Quad Hopper (FARR #3), *81*	50	65	_____
6103 Canadian National Covered Quad Hopper, *81*	40	50	_____
6104 Southern Quad Hopper w/ coal load (FARR #4), *83*	75	95	_____
6105 Reading Operating Hopper, *82*	60	75	_____
6106 N&W Covered Quad Hopper, *82*	40	50	_____
6107 Shell Covered Quad Hopper, *82*	25	30	_____
6109 C&O Operating Hopper, *83*	40	60	_____
6110 Missouri Pacific Covered Quad Hopper, *83-84*	15	25	_____
6111 L&N Covered Quad Hopper, *83-84*	20	30	_____
[6111] LOTS L&N Covered Quad Hopper, *83 u*	40	60	_____
[6111] Southern TCA L&N Covered Quad Hopper, *83 u*	25	30	_____
6112 LCCA Commonwealth Edison Quad Hopper w/ coal load, *83 u*	75	95	_____
6113 Illinois Central Hopper (O27), *83-85*	10	15	_____
6114 C&NW Covered Quad Hopper, *83*	150	175	_____
6115 Southern Hopper (O27), *83-86*	15	20	_____
6116 Soo Line Ore Car, *84*	30	40	_____
6117 Erie Operating Hopper, *84*	40	50	_____
6118 Erie Covered Quad Hopper, *84*	50	65	_____
6122 Penn Central Ore Car, *84*	30	40	_____
6123 PRR Covered Quad Hopper (FARR #5), *84-85*	60	75	_____
6124 D&H Covered Quad Hopper, *84*	20	30	_____
[6124] NETCA D&H Covered Quad Hopper, *84 u*	25	30	_____
6126 Canadian National Ore Car, *86*	30	35	_____
6127 Northern Pacific Ore Car, *86*	30	35	_____
6127 (See 5735)			
6131 Illinois Terminal Covered Quad Hopper, *85-86*	20	25	_____
6134 Burlington Northern 2-bay ACF Hopper (Std. O), *86 u*	150	200	_____
6135 C&NW 2-bay ACF Hopper (Std. O), *86 u*	150	200	_____
6137 Nickel Plate Road Hopper (O27), *86-91*	15	20	_____
6138 B&O Quad Hopper w/ coal load, *86*	30	40	_____
6150 Santa Fe Hopper (O27), *85-86, 92 u*	15	20	_____
6177 Reading Hopper (O27), *86-90*	20	25	_____
6200 FEC Gondola w/ canisters, *81-82*	15	25	_____
6200 (See 8404)			

		Exc	New	Cond/$
6201	Union Pacific Animated Gondola, *82-83*	25	35	_____
6202	WM Gondola w/ coal load, *82*	40	45	_____
(6203)	Black Cave Gondola (O27), *82*	3	5	_____
6205	CP Gondola w/ canisters, *83*	30	35	_____
6206	C&IM Gondola w/ canisters, *83-85*	20	30	_____
6207	Southern Gondola w/ canisters (O27), *83-85*	6	8	_____
6208	Chessie System Gondola w/ canisters, *83 u*	35	40	_____
6209	NYC Gondola w/ coal load (Std. O), *84-85*	60	75	_____
6210	Erie-Lackawanna Gondola w/ canisters, *84*	30	40	_____
6211	C&O Gondola w/ canisters, *84-85*	—	12	_____
[6211]	LOTS C&O Gondola w/ canisters, *86 u*	50	75	_____
6214	Lionel Lines Gondola w/ canisters, *84 u*	40	50	_____
6230	Erie-Lackawanna Reefer (Std. O), *86 u*	125	150	_____
6231	Railgon Gondola w/ coal load (Std. O), *86 u*	150	175	_____
6232	Illinois Central Boxcar (Std. O), *86 u*	125	150	_____
6233	Canadian Pacific Flatcar w/ stakes (Std. O), *86 u*	125	150	_____
6234	Burlington Northern Boxcar (Std. O), *85*	45	60	_____
6235	Burlington Northern Boxcar (Std. O), *85*	45	60	_____
6236	Burlington Northern Boxcar (Std. O), *85*	45	60	_____
6237	Burlington Northern Boxcar (Std. O), *85*	45	60	_____
6238	Burlington Northern Boxcar (Std. O), *85*	45	60	_____
6239	Burlington Northern Boxcar (Std. O), *86 u*	60	75	_____
6251	NYC Coal Dump Car, *85*	15	20	_____
6254	NKP Gondola w/ canisters, *86-91*	10	12	_____
6258	Santa Fe Gondola w/ canisters (O27), *85-86, 92 u*	—	6	_____
X6260	NYC Gondola w/ canisters, *85-86*	15	18	_____
6272	Santa Fe Gondola w/ cable reels, *86 (SSS)*	20	25	_____
6300	Corn Products 3-D Tank Car, *81-82*	25	35	_____
6301	Gulf 1-D Tank Car, *81*	20	25	_____
6302	Quaker State 3-D Tank Car, *81*	40	50	_____
6304	GN 1-D Tank Car (FARR #3), *81*	60	75	_____
6305	British Columbia 1-D Tank Car, *81*	50	65	_____
6306	Southern 1-D Tank Car (FARR #4), *83*	60	75	_____
6307	PRR 1-D Tank Car (FARR #5), *84-85*	75	100	_____
6308	Alaska 1-D Tank Car (O27), *82-83*	25	30	_____
6310	Shell 2-D Tank Car (O27), *83-84*	20	25	_____
6312	C&O 2-D Tank Car (O27), *84-85*	20	30	_____
6313	Lionel Lines 1-D Tank Car, *84 u*	50	65	_____
6314	B&O 3-D Tank Car, *86*	50	60	_____

		Exc	New	Cond/$
6315	TCA Pittsburgh 1-D Tank Car, *72 u*	65	75	_____
6317	Gulf 2-D Tank Car (O27), *84-85*	20	25	_____
6323	LCCA Virginia Chemicals 1-D Tank Car, *86 u*	50	65	_____
6325	(See 6579)			
6357	Frisco 1-D Tank Car, *83*	65	95	_____
6401	Virginian B/W Caboose, *81*	45	65	_____
[6401]	Sacramento-Sierra TCA Virginian B/W Caboose, *84 u*	—	45	_____
6403	Amtrak Vista Dome Car (O27), *76-77*	50	60	_____
6404	Amtrak Passenger Car (O27), *76-77*	50	60	_____
6405	Amtrak Passenger Car (O27), *76-77*	50	60	_____
6406	Amtrak Observation Car (O27), *76-77*	50	60	_____
6410	Amtrak Passenger Car (O27), *77*	40	60	_____
6411	Amtrak Passenger Car (O27), *77*	30	50	_____
6412	Amtrak Vista Dome Car (O27), *77*	30	50	_____
6420	Reading Transfer Caboose, *81-82*	15	20	_____
6421	Joshua L. Cowen B/W Caboose, *82*	50	60	_____
6422	DM&IR B/W Caboose, *81*	30	40	_____
6425	Erie-Lackawanna B/W Caboose, *83-84*	35	40	_____
6426	Reading Transfer Caboose, *82-83*	10	15	_____
6427	Burlington Northern Transfer Caboose, *83-84*	10	20	_____
6428	C&NW Transfer Caboose, *83-85*	20	25	_____
6430	Santa Fe SP Caboose, *83-89*	6	8	_____
6431	Southern B/W Caboose (FARR #4), *83*	50	60	_____
6432	Union Pacific SP Caboose, *81-82*	10	12	_____
6433	Canadian Pacific B/W Caboose, *81*	60	75	_____
6434	Southern SP Caboose, *83-85*	6	8	_____
6435	US Transfer Caboose, *83-84*	10	20	_____
6438	GN B/W Caboose (FARR #3), *81*	50	60	_____
6439	Reading B/W Caboose, *84-85*	20	30	_____
6441	Alaska B/W Caboose, *82-83*	40	50	_____
6446-25	N&W Covered Quad Hopper, *70 u*	175	200	_____
6449	Wendy's N5C Caboose, *81-82*	50	65	_____
6464-500	Timken Boxcar, *70 u*	150	200	_____
6464-1970	TCA Chicago Boxcar, *70 u*	125	160	_____
6464-1971	TCA Disneyland Boxcar, *71 u*	200	225	_____
(6476-135)	Lehigh Valley Hopper "25000" (O27), *70-71 u*		NRS	_____
(6478)	Black Cave SP Caboose, *82*	5	10	_____
6482	Nibco Express SP Caboose, *82 u*	30	40	_____

		Exc	New	Cond/$
6483	LCCA Jersey Central SP Caboose, *82 u*	30	40	_____
6485	Chessie System SP Caboose, *84-85*	5	10	_____
6491	Erie-Lackawanna Transfer Caboose, *85-86*	8	15	_____
6493	L&C B/W Caboose, *86-87*	25	45	_____
6494	Santa Fe Bobber Caboose, *85-86*	8	10	_____
6496	Santa Fe Work Caboose, *86 (SSS)*	25	35	_____
(6504)	L.A.S.E.R. Flatcar w/ helicopter (O27), *81-82*	20	30	_____
(6505)	L.A.S.E.R. Radar Car, *81-82*	20	30	_____
(6506)	L.A.S.E.R. Security Car, *81-82*	20	30	_____
(6507)	L.A.S.E.R. Flatcar w/ cruise missile, *81-82*	20	30	_____
6508	Canadian Pacific Crane Car, *81*	60	80	_____
[6508]	LCOL Canadian Pacific Crane Car, *83 u*	—	45	_____
(6509)	Depressed Flatcar w/ girders, *81*	75	100	_____
6510	Union Pacific Crane Car, *82*	75	85	_____
6515	Union Pacific Flatcar (O27), *83-84, 86*	5	10	_____
6521	NYC Flatcar w/ stakes (Std. O), *84-85*	60	75	_____
6522	C&NW Searchlight Car, *83-85*	30	35	_____
6524	Erie Crane Car, *84*	75	85	_____
6526	US Marines Searchlight Car, *84-85*	30	35	_____
6529	NYC Searchlight Car, *85-86*	20	25	_____
6531	Express Mail Flatcar w/ trailers, *85-86*	30	45	_____
6560	Bucyrus Erie Crane Car, *71*	150	175	_____
(6561)	Flatcar w/ cruise missile (O27), *83-84*	15	30	_____
(6562)	Flatcar w/ fences (O27), *83-84*	15	25	_____
(6564)	Flatcar w/ two USMC tanks (O27), *83-84*	15	25	_____
(6567)	LCCA ICG Crane Car "100408", *85 u*	60	85	_____
(6573)	Redwood Valley Express Dump Car (O27), *84-85*	8	15	_____
(6574)	Redwood Valley Express Crane Car (O27), *84-85*	8	15	_____
(6575)	Redwood Valley Express Flatcar w/ fences (O27), *84-85*	8	15	_____
6576	Santa Fe Crane Car (O27), *85-86*	8	12	_____
6576	Santa Fe Flatcar w/ fences (O27), *92 u*	8	12	_____
6579	NYC Crane Car, *85-86*	40	50	_____
6582	TTOS Portland Flatcar w/ wood load, *86 u*	75	100	_____
6585	PRR Flatcar w/ fences (O27), *86-90*	5	10	_____
6587	W&ARR Flatcar w/horses, *86 u*	20	30	_____
6593	Santa Fe Crane Car, *86 (SSS)*	50	60	_____
6670	(See 9378)			
6700	PFE Ice Car (See 2306)			

MPC MODERN ERA (1970-1986)

		Exc	New	Cond/$
6900	N&W E/V Caboose, *82*	90	125	_____
6901	Ontario Northland E/V Caboose, *82 u*	60	80	_____
6903	Santa Fe E/V Caboose, *83*	150	200	_____
6904	Union Pacific E/V Caboose, *83*	150	175	_____
6905	NKP E/V Caboose, *83 u*	75	95	_____
6906	Erie-Lackawanna E/V Caboose, *84*	100	125	_____
6907	NYC Woodside Caboose (Std. O), *86 u*	150	175	_____
6908	PRR N5C Caboose (FARR #5), *84-85*	100	125	_____
6910	NYC E/V Caboose, *84 u*	100	125	_____
(6912)	Redwood Valley Express SP Caboose, *84-85*	10	20	_____
6913	Burlington Northern E/V Caboose, *85*	100	125	_____
6916	NYC Work Caboose, *85-86*	15	20	_____
6917	Jersey Central E/V Caboose, *86*	60	75	_____
6918	B&O SP Caboose, *86*	10	15	_____
6919	NKP SP Caboose, *86-91*	5	10	_____
6920	B&A Woodside Caboose (Std. O), *86 u*	125	150	_____
6921	PRR SP Caboose, *86-90*	5	10	_____
6926	TCA New Orleans E/V Caboose, *86 u*	45	60	_____
7200	Quicksilver Passenger Car (O27), *82-83*	50	60	_____
7201	Quicksilver Passenger Car (O27), *82-83*	50	60	_____
7202	Quicksilver Observation Car (O27), *82-83*	50	60	_____
(7203)	N&W Dining Car "491", *82 u*	350	450	_____
(7204)	Southern Pacific Dining Car, *82 u*	350	450	_____
(7205)	TCA Denver Combination Car "1982", *82 u*	50	80	_____
(7206)	TCA Louisville Passenger Car "1983", *83 u*	50	80	_____
7207	NYC Dining Car, *83 u*	175	250	_____
(7208)	PRR Dining Car, *83 u*	175	225	_____
7210	Union Pacific Dining Car, *84*	100	125	_____
(7211)	Southern Pacific Vista Dome Car, *83 u*	300	400	_____
(7212)	TCA Pittsburgh Passenger Car "1984", *84 u*	60	80	_____
7215	B&O Passenger Car, *83-84*	50	60	_____
7216	B&O Passenger Car, *83-84*	50	60	_____
7217	B&O Baggage Car, *83-84*	50	60	_____
7220	Illinois Central Baggage Car, *85, 87*	100	125	_____
7221	Illinois Central Combination Car, *85, 87*	100	125	_____
7222	Illinois Central Passenger Car, *85, 87*	100	125	_____
7223	Illinois Central Passenger Car, *85, 87*	100	125	_____
7224	Illinois Central Dining Car, *85, 87*	100	125	_____
7225	Illinois Central Observation Car, *85, 87*	100	125	_____

		Exc	New	Cond/$
7227	Wabash Dining Car (FF #1), *86-87*	100	125	_____
7228	Wabash Baggage Car (FF #1), *86-87*	100	125	_____
7229	Wabash Combination Car (FF #1), *86-87*	100	125	_____
7230	Wabash Passenger Car (FF #1), *86-87*	100	125	_____
7231	Wabash Passenger Car (FF #1), *86-87*	100	125	_____
7232	Wabash Observation Car (FF #1), *86-87*	100	125	_____
7241	W&ARR Passenger Car, *86 u*	50	60	_____
7242	W&ARR Baggage Car, *86 u*	50	60	_____
7301	Norfolk & Western Stock Car, *82*	40	50	_____
7302	Texas & Pacific Stock Car (O27), *83-84*	15	20	_____
7303	Erie Stock Car, *84*	50	65	_____
7304	Southern Stock Car (FARR #4), *83 u*	60	75	_____
7309	Southern Stock Car (O27), *85-86*	15	20	_____
7312	W&ARR Stock Car (O27), *86 u*	25	30	_____
7401	Chessie System Stock Car (O27), *84-85*	15	20	_____
7403	LCCA LNAC Boxcar, *84 u*	35	50	_____
7404	Jersey Central Boxcar, *86*	60	75	_____
7500	Lionel 75th Anniversary U36B, *75-77*	125	150	_____
7501	Lionel 75th Anniversary Boxcar, *75-77*	25	35	_____
7502	Lionel 75th Anniversary Reefer, *75-77*	25	35	_____
7503	Lionel 75th Anniversary Reefer, *75-77*	25	35	_____
7504	Lionel 75th Anniversary Covered Quad Hopper, *75-77*	30	40	_____
7505	Lionel 75th Anniversary Boxcar, *75-77*	25	35	_____
7506	Lionel 75th Anniversary Boxcar, *75-77*	25	35	_____
7507	Lionel 75th Anniversary Reefer, *75-77*	25	35	_____
7508	Lionel 75th Anniversary N5C Caboose, *75-77*	30	40	_____
7509	Kentucky Fried Chicken Reefer, *81-82*	25	30	_____
7510	Red Lobster Reefer, *81-82*	25	30	_____
7511	Pizza Hut Reefer, *81-82*	25	30	_____
7512	Arthur Treacher's Reefer, *82*	25	30	_____
7513	Bonanza Reefer, *82*	25	30	_____
7514	Taco Bell Reefer, *82*	25	30	_____
7515	Denver Mint Car, *81*	65	85	_____
7517	Philadelphia Mint Car, *82*	60	75	_____
7518	Carson City Mint Car, *83*	40	50	_____
[7518]	IETCA Carson City Mint Car, *84 u*	—	40	_____
7519	Toy Fair Reefer, *82 u*	75	100	_____
7520	Nibco Express Boxcar, *82 u*	350	500	_____

		Exc	New	Cond/$
7521	Toy Fair Reefer, *83 u*	75	100	_____
7522	New Orleans Mint Car, *84 u*	40	50	_____
[7522]	Lone Star TCA New Orleans Mint Car			
	w/ coin, *86 u*	—	275	_____
7523	Toy Fair Reefer, *84 u*	100	125	_____
7524	Toy Fair Reefer, *85 u*	100	125	_____
7525	Toy Fair Boxcar, *86 u*	100	125	_____
7530	Dahlonega Mint Car, *86 u*	75	85	_____
7600	Frisco "Spirit of '76" N5C Caboose, *74-76*	40	50	_____
[7600]	Midwest TCA Frisco "Spirit of '76" N5C			
	Caboose "00003", *76 u*	—	50	_____
7601	Delaware Boxcar, *74-76*	20	25	_____
7602	Pennsylvania Boxcar, *74-76*	25	30	_____
7603	New Jersey Boxcar, *74-76*	25	30	_____
7604	Georgia Boxcar, *74 u, 75-76*	25	30	_____
7605	Connecticut Boxcar, *74u, 75-76*	25	30	_____
7606	Massachusetts Boxcar, *74u, 75-76*	25	30	_____
7607	Maryland Boxcar, *74 u, 75-76*	25	30	_____
7608	South Carolina Boxcar, *75 u, 76*	30	40	_____
7609	New Hampshire Boxcar, *75 u, 76*	50	60	_____
7610	Virginia Boxcar, *75 u, 76*	175	225	_____
7611	New York Boxcar, *75 u, 76*	75	100	_____
7612	North Carolina Boxcar, *75 u, 76*	25	50	_____
7613	Rhode Island Boxcar, *75 u, 76*	25	50	_____
[7679]	VTC Boxcar, *79 u*	—	20	_____
[7681]	VTC N5C Caboose, *81 u*	—	25	_____
[7682]	VTC Covered Quad Hopper, *82 u*	—	25	_____
[7683]	VTC Virginia Fruit Express Reefer, *83 u*	—	28	_____
[7684]	VTC Vitraco Oil 3-D Tank Car, *84 u*	—	25	_____
[7685]	VTC Boxcar, *85 u*	—	30	_____
[7686]	VTC GP-7, *86 u*	—	125	_____
7700	Uncle Sam Boxcar, *75 u*	60	75	_____
7701	Camel Boxcar, *76-77*	15	25	_____
7702	Prince Albert Boxcar, *76-77*	15	25	_____
7703	Beechnut Boxcar, *76-77*	15	25	_____
7704	Toy Fair Boxcar, *76 u*	125	150	_____
7705	Canadian Toy Fair Boxcar, *76 u*	175	225	_____
7706	Sir Walter Raleigh Boxcar, *77-78*	20	30	_____
7707	White Owl Boxcar, *77-78*	20	30	_____

No.	Description	Exc	New	Cond/$
7708	Winston Boxcar, *77-78*	20	30	_____
7709	Salem Boxcar, *78*	20	30	_____
7710	Mail Pouch Boxcar, *78*	20	30	_____
7711	El Producto Boxcar, *78*	20	30	_____
7712	Santa Fe Boxcar (FARR #1), *79*	40	50	_____
[7780]	TCA Museum Boxcar, *80 u*	—	30	_____
[7781]	TCA Hafner Boxcar, *81 u*	—	30	_____
[7782]	TCA Carlisle & Finch Boxcar, *82 u*	—	30	_____
[7783]	TCA Ives Boxcar, *83 u*	—	30	_____
[7784]	TCA Voltamp Boxcar, *84 u*	—	30	_____
[7785]	TCA Hoge Boxcar, *85 u*	—	30	_____
7800	Pepsi Boxcar, *76 u, 77*	50	60	_____
7801	A&W Boxcar, *76 u, 77*	25	35	_____
7802	Canada Dry Boxcar, *76 u, 77*	25	35	_____
7803	Trains n' Truckin' Boxcar, *77 u*	25	35	_____
7806	Season's Greetings Boxcar, *76 u*	100	125	_____
7807	Toy Fair Boxcar, *77 u*	100	125	_____
7808	Northern Pacific Stock Car, *77*	50	65	_____
7809	Vernors Boxcar, *77 u, 78*	20	30	_____
7810	Orange Crush Boxcar, *77 u, 78*	20	30	_____
7811	Dr. Pepper Boxcar, *77 u, 78*	20	30	_____
7812	TCA Houston Stock Car, *77 u*	20	30	_____
7813	Season's Greetings Boxcar, *77 u*	100	125	_____
7814	Season's Greetings Boxcar, *78 u*	100	125	_____
7815	Toy Fair Boxcar, *78 u*	100	125	_____
7816	Toy Fair Boxcar, *79 u*	100	125	_____
7817	Toy Fair Boxcar, *80 u*	125	175	_____
7900	D&RGW Operating Cowboy Car, *82-83*	25	30	_____
7901	Lionel Lines Cop & Hobo Car, *82-83*	40	45	_____
7902	Santa Fe Boxcar (O27), *82-85*	6	8	_____
7903	Rock Island Boxcar (O27), *83*	6	8	_____
7904	San Diego Zoo Giraffe Car, *83-84*	40	50	_____
(7905)	Black Cave Boxcar (O27), *82*	7	10	_____
7908	Tappan Boxcar (O27), *82 u*	50	65	_____
7909	L&N Boxcar (O27), *83-84*	40	50	_____
7910	Chessie System Boxcar (O27), *84-85*	20	25	_____
7912	Toys 'R Us Giraffe Car, *82-84 u*	75	100	_____
7913	Turtleback Zoo Giraffe Car, *85-86*	35	40	_____
7914	Toys 'R Us Giraffe Car, *85-89 u*	75	100	_____

		Exc	New	Cond/$
7920	Sears Centennial Boxcar (O27), *85-86 u*	40	60	_____
7925	Erie-Lackawanna Boxcar (O27), *86-90*	8	12	_____
7926	NKP Boxcar (O27), *86-91*	8	11	_____
7930	True Value Boxcar (O27), *86-87 u*	40	60	_____
7931	Town House TV & Appliances Boxcar (O27), *86 u*	40	50	_____
7932	Kay Bee Toys Boxcar (O27), *86-87 u*	40	50	_____
8001	NKP 2-6-4, *80 u*	60	75	_____
8002	Union Pacific 2-8-4 (FARR #2), *80*	500	600	_____
8003	Chessie System 2-8-4, *80*	550	600	_____
8004	Rock Island 4-4-0, *80-82*	150	170	_____
8005	Santa Fe 4-4-0, *80-82*	60	75	_____
8006	ACL 4-6-4, *80 u*	650	800	_____
8007	NYNH&H 2-6-4, *80-81*	60	75	_____
8008	Chessie System 4-4-2, *80*	75	85	_____
8010	Santa Fe NW-2, *70, 71 u*	60	75	_____
8020	Santa Fe Alco A Unit, *70-72, 74-76*	75	100	_____
8020	Santa Fe Alco A Unit Dummy, *70*	50	70	_____
8021	Santa Fe Alco B Unit, *71-72, 74-76*	60	75	_____
8022	Santa Fe Alco A Unit, *71 u*	100	125	_____
8025	CN Alco A Unit, *71-73 u*	100	125	_____
8025	CN Alco A Unit Dummy, *71-73 u*	50	75	_____
8030	Illinois Central GP-9, *70-72*	85	125	_____
8031	Canadian National GP-7, *71-73 u*	70	125	_____
8031	Illinois Central GP-9 Dummy, *70*		NM	
8040	NKP 2-4-2, *70-72*	30	40	_____
8040	Canadian National 2-4-2, *71 u*	50	100	_____
8041	NYC 2-4-2, *70*	60	75	_____
8041	PRR 2-4-2, *71 u*	60	75	_____
8042	GTW 2-4-2, *70, 71-73 u*	30	40	_____
8043	NKP 2-4-2, *70 u*	50	75	_____
8050	D&H U36C, *80*	125	175	_____
8051	D&H U36C Dummy, *80*	100	125	_____
[8051]	NETCA Hood's Milk Boxcar, *86 u*	45	55	_____
8054/8055	Burlington F-3 AA set, *80*	400	500	_____
8056	C&NW Trainmaster, *80*	350	425	_____
8057	Burlington NW-2, *80*	125	175	_____
8059	Pennsylvania F-3 B Unit, *80 u*	375	500	_____
8060	Pennsylvania F-3 B Unit, *80 u*	400	550	_____

		Exc	New	Cond/$
8061	Chessie System U36C, *80*	160	190	_____
8062	Burlington F-3 B Unit, *80 u*	200	275	_____
8062	Great Northern 4-6-4, *70*		NM	
8063	Seaboard SD-9, *80*	125	175	_____
8064	Florida East Coast GP-9, *80*	115	150	_____
8065	Florida East Coast GP-9 Dummy, *80*	80	100	_____
8066	TP&W GP-20, *80-81*	100	125	_____
8067	Texas & Pacific Alco A Unit, *80*		NM	
(8068)	LCCA Rock Island GP-20 "1980", *80 u*	100	150	_____
8071	Virginian SD-18, *80 u*	140	175	_____
8072	Virginian SD-18 Dummy, *80 u*	95	125	_____
(8100)	Norfolk & Western 4-8-4 "611", *81*	700	900	_____
(8101)	Chicago & Alton 4-6-4 "659", *81*	450	550	_____
8102	Union Pacific 4-4-2, *81-82*	60	75	_____
[8103]	LCAC Toronto, Hamilton & Buffalo Boxcar, *81 u*		NRS	_____
(8104)	Union Pacific 4-4-0 "3", *81 u*	275	325	_____
8111	DT&I NW-2, *71-74*	50	75	_____
8140	Southern 2-4-0, *71 u*	25	35	_____
8141	PRR 2-4-2, *71-72*	40	60	_____
8142	C&O 4-4-2, *71-72*	55	65	_____
(8150)	PRR GG-1 "4935", *81*	575	800	_____
8151	Burlington SD-28, *81*	150	195	_____
8152	Canadian Pacific SD-24, *81*	195	225	_____
8153	Reading NW-2, *81-82*	125	150	_____
8154	Alaska NW-2, *81-82*	125	175	_____
8155	Monon U36B, *81-82*	100	125	_____
8156	Monon U36B Dummy, *81-82*	60	75	_____
8157	Santa Fe Trainmaster, *81*	400	500	_____
8158	DM&IR GP-35, *81-82*	75	125	_____
8159	DM&IR GP-35 Dummy, *81-82*	60	75	_____
8160	Burger King GP-20, *81-82*	100	125	_____
8161	L.A.S.E.R. Diesel Switcher, *81-82*	30	75	_____
8162	Ontario Northland SD-18, *81 u*	125	150	_____
8163	Ontario Northland SD-18 Dummy, *81 u*	100	125	_____
8164	Pennsylvania F-3 B Unit, *81 u*	450	600	_____
8182	Nibco Express NW-2, *82 u*	100	150	_____
(8190)	Diesel Horn kit, *81 u*	—	45	_____
8200	"Kickapoo" Dockside 0-4-0, *72*	30	40	_____
8203	PRR 2-4-2, *72, 74 u, 75*	30	40	_____

		Exc	New	Cond/$
8204	C&O 4-4-2, *72*	60	70	_____
[8204]	LCAC Algoma Central Boxcar, *82 u*		NRS	_____
8206	NYC 4-6-4, *72-75*	175	225	_____
8209	"Pioneer" Dockside 0-4-0 w/ tender, *72*	50	75	_____
8209	"Pioneer" Dockside 0-4-0 w/o tender, *73-76*	45	60	_____
8210	Joshua L. Cowen 4-6-4, *82*	350	400	_____
8212	Black Cave 0-4-0, *82*	30	50	_____
8213	D&RGW 2-4-2, *82-83, 84-91 u*	60	70	_____
8214	Pennsylvania 2-4-2, *82-83*	60	75	_____
(8215)	Nickel Plate Road 2-8-4 "779", *82 u*	600	650	_____
8250	Santa Fe GP-9, *72, 74-75*	90	120	_____
(8251-50)	Horn/Whistle Controller, *72-74*	2	3	_____
8252	D&H Alco A Unit, *72*	75	100	_____
8253	D&H Alco B Unit, *72*	50	75	_____
8254	Illinois Central GP-9 Dummy, *72*	60	75	_____
8255	Santa Fe GP-9 Dummy, *72,*	75	90	_____
8258	Canadian National GP-7 Dummy, *72-73 u*	65	80	_____
8260/8262	Southern Pacific F-3 AA set, *82*	675	725	_____
8261	Southern Pacific F-3 B Unit, *82 u*	700	900	_____
8263	Santa Fe GP-7, *82*	75	100	_____
8264	CP Vulcan Switcher w/ snowplow, *82*	150	175	_____
8265	Santa Fe SD-40, *82*	375	425	_____
8266	Norfolk & Western SD-24, *82*	150	200	_____
8268	Texas & Pacific Alco A Unit, *82-83*	100	125	_____
8269	Texas & Pacific Alco A Unit Dummy, *82-83*	60	75	_____
8272	Pennsylvania EP-5, *82 u*	275	325	_____
8300	Santa Fe 2-4-0, *73-74*	20	25	_____
8302	Southern 2-4-0, *73-76*	25	30	_____
8303	Jersey Central 2-4-2, *73-74*	40	50	_____
8304	Rock Island 4-4-2, *73-75*	100	125	_____
8304	Pennsylvania 4-4-2, *74-75*	90	125	_____
8304	B&O 4-4-2, *75*	90	125	_____
8304	C&O 4-4-2, *75-77*	90	125	_____
8305	Milwaukee Road 4-4-2, *73*	90	125	_____
(8307)	Southern Pacific 4-8-4 "4449", *83*	1000	1300	_____
8308	Jersey Central 2-4-2, *73-74 u*	40	50	_____
(8309)	Southern 2-8-2 "4501" (FARR #4), *83*	450	550	_____
8310	Santa Fe 2-4-0, *74-75 u*	30	40	_____
8310	Jersey Central 2-4-0, *74-75 u*	30	60	_____

		Exc	New	Cond/$
8310	Nickel Plate Road 2-4-0, *73 u*	30	60	_____
8311	Southern 0-4-0, *73 u*	30	40	_____
8313	Santa Fe 0-4-0, *83-84*	15	20	_____
8314	Southern 2-4-0, *83-85*	20	25	_____
8315	B&O 4-4-0, *83-84*	85	120	_____
8350	US Steel Diesel Switcher, *73-75*	20	30	_____
8351	Santa Fe Alco A Unit, *73-75*	60	75	_____
8352	Santa Fe GP-20, *73-75*	60	100	_____
8353	Grand Trunk GP-7, *73-75*	60	100	_____
8354	Erie NW-2, *73, 75*	90	120	_____
8355	Santa Fe GP-20 Dummy, *73-74*	80	125	_____
8356	Grand Trunk GP-7 Dummy, *73-75*	60	75	_____
8357	PRR GP-9, *73-75*	125	150	_____
8358	PRR GP-9 Dummy, *73-75*	60	100	_____
(8359)	Chessie System GP-7 "GM50", *73*	100	150	_____
8360	Long Island GP-20, *73-74*	75	100	_____
8361	Western Pacific Alco A Unit, *73-75*	75	100	_____
8362	Western Pacific Alco B Unit, *73-75*	50	75	_____
8363	B&O F-3 A Unit, *73-75*	250	300	_____
8364	B&O F-3 A Unit Dummy, *73-75*	150	200	_____
8365/8366	CP F-3 AA set, *73 (SSS)*	450	600	_____
8367	Long Island GP-20 Dummy, *73-75*	100	125	_____
8368	Alaska Vulcan Switcher, *83*	125	175	_____
8369	Erie-Lackawanna GP-20, *83-85*	125	150	_____
8370/8372	NYC F-3 AA set, *83*	400	550	_____
8371	NYC F-3 B Unit, *83*	150	225	_____
8374	Burlington Northern NW-2, *83-85*	125	150	_____
8375	C&NW GP-7, *83-85*	125	150	_____
8376	Union Pacific SD-40, *83*	400	450	_____
8377	US Switcher, *83-84*	60	75	_____
(8378)	Wabash Trainmaster "550", *83 u*	1100	1300	_____
8379	PRR Fire Car, *83 u*	155	200	_____
8380	Lionel Lines SD-28, *83 u*	175	225	_____
8402	Reading 4-4-2, *84-85*	60	75	_____
8403	Chessie System 4-4-2, *84-85*	60	75	_____
(8404)	PRR 6-8-6 "6200" (FARR #5), *84-85*	450	600	_____
(8406)	NYC 4-6-4 "783", *84*	900	1000	_____
8410	Redwood Valley Express 4-4-0, *84-85*	40	60	_____
8452	Erie Alco A Unit, *74-75*	80	100	_____

		Exc	New	Cond/$
8453	Erie Alco B Unit, *74-75*	50	75	_____
8454	D&RGW GP-7, *74-75*	100	125	_____
8455	D&RGW GP-7 Dummy, *74-75*	50	80	_____
8458	Erie-Lackawanna SD-40, *84*	350	400	_____
8459	D&RGW Vulcan Rotary Snowplow, *84*	155	200	_____
8460	MKT NW-2, *74-75*	50	75	_____
8463	Chessie System GP-20, *74 u*	135	150	_____
8464/8465 D&RGW F-3 AA set, *74 (SSS)*		300	425	_____
8466	Amtrak F-3 A Unit, *74-76*	200	300	_____
8467	Amtrak F-3 A Unit Dummy, *74-76*	100	150	_____
8468	B&O F-3 B Unit, *74-75 (SSS)*	125	150	_____
8469	CP F-3 B Unit, *74 (SSS)*	150	200	_____
8470	Chessie System U36B, *74*	100	150	_____
8471	Pennsylvania NW-2, *74-76*	200	250	_____
8473	Coca-Cola NW-2, *74 u, 75*	125	150	_____
8474	D&RGW F-3 B Unit, *74 (SSS)*	125	150	_____
8475	Amtrak F-3 B Unit, *74 (SSS)*	125	150	_____
8477	NYC GP-9, *84 u*	325	375	_____
8480/8482 Union Pacific F-3 AA set, *84*		350	450	_____
8481	Union Pacific F-3 B Unit, *84*	200	225	_____
8485	US Marines NW-2, *84-85*	100	150	_____
8490	(See 8690)			
8500	Pennsylvania 2-4-0, *75-76*	20	25	_____
8502	Santa Fe 2-4-0, *75*	20	25	_____
8506	PRR 0-4-0, *75-77*	100	150	_____
8507	Santa Fe 2-4-0, *75 u*	25	30	_____
[8507]	LCAC CN F-3 A Unit, shell only, *85 u*		NRS	_____
[8508]	LCAC CN F-3 A Unit, shell only, *85 u*		NRS	_____
8512	Santa Fe 0-4-0, *85-86*	25	35	_____
8516	NYC 0-4-0, *85-86*	125	150	_____
8550	Jersey Central GP-9, *75-76*	100	125	_____
8551	Pennsylvania EP-5, *75-76*	200	250	_____
8552/8553/8554 Southern Pacific Alco ABA set, *75-76*		200	250	_____
8555/8557 Milwaukee Road F-3 AA set, *75 (SSS)*		300	400	_____
8556	Chessie System NW-2, *75-76*	200	250	_____
8558	Milwaukee Road EP-5, *76-77*	175	200	_____
(8559)	N&W GP-9 "1776", *75*	100	130	_____
8560	Chessie System U36B Dummy, *75*	75	100	_____
8561	Jersey Central GP-9 Dummy, *75-76*	60	80	_____

		Exc	New	Cond/$
8562	Missouri Pacific GP-20, *75-76*	100	125	_____
8563	Rock Island Alco A Unit, *75-76 u*	75	100	_____
8564	Union Pacific U36B, *75*	125	175	_____
8565	Missouri Pacific GP-20 Dummy, *75-76*	60	75	_____
8566	Southern F-3 A Unit, *75-77*	250	350	_____
8567	Southern F-3 A Unit Dummy, *75-77*	125	175	_____
8568	Preamble Express F-3 A Unit, *75 u*	125	175	_____
8569	Soo Line NW-2, *75-77*	60	75	_____
8570	Liberty Special Alco A Unit, *75 u*	100	125	_____
8571	Frisco U36B, *75-76*	75	100	_____
8572	Frisco U36B Dummy, *75-76*	60	75	_____
8573	Union Pacific U36B Dummy, *75 u*	175	225	_____
8575	Milwaukee Road F-3 B Unit, *75 (SSS)*	100	175	_____
8576	Penn Central GP-7, *75 u, 76-77*	125	150	_____
8578	NYC Ballast Tamper, *85, 87*	120	150	_____
8580/8582	Illinois Central F-3 AA set, *85, 87*	400	450	_____
8581	Illinois Central F-3 B Unit, *85, 87*	175	200	_____
8585	Burlington Northern SD-40, *85*	350	400	_____
(8587)	Wabash GP-9 "484", *85 u*	300	375	_____
8600	NYC 4-6-4, *76*	200	250	_____
8601	Rock Island 0-4-0, *76-77*	20	25	_____
8602	D&RGW 2-4-0, *76-78*	25	30	_____
8603	C&O 4-6-4, *76-77*	175	250	_____
8604	Jersey Central 2-4-2, *76 u*	40	45	_____
(8606)	B&A 4-6-4 "784", *86 u*	1100	1400	_____
(8610)	Wabash 4-6-2 "672", *86-87*	500	600	_____
(8615)	L&N 2-8-4 "1970", *86 u*	850	1000	_____
8616	Santa Fe 4-4-2, *86*	65	75	_____
8617	Nickel Plate Road 4-4-2, *86-91*	65	75	_____
8625	Pennsylvania 2-4-0, *86-90*	25	40	_____
(8630)	W&ARR 4-4-0 "3", *86 u*	125	150	_____
8635	Santa Fe 0-4-0, *86 (SSS)*	120	145	_____
8650	Burlington Northern U36B, *76-77*	125	150	_____
8651	Burlington Northern U36B Dummy, *76-77*	90	100	_____
8652	Santa Fe F-3 A Unit, *76-77*	300	400	_____
8653	Santa Fe F-3 A Unit Dummy, *76-77*	175	200	_____
8654	Boston & Maine GP-9, *76-77*	115	150	_____
8655	Boston & Maine GP-9 Dummy, *76-77*	80	100	_____
8656	Canadian National Alco A Unit, *76*	150	200	_____

		Exc	New	Cond/$
8657	Canadian National Alco B Unit, *76*	75	100	_____
8658	Canadian National Alco A Unit Dummy, *76*	100	200	_____
8659	Virginian Rectifier, *76-77*	150	225	_____
8660	CP Rail NW-2, *76-77*	100	125	_____
8661	Southern F-3 B Unit, *76 (SSS)*	200	225	_____
8662	B&O GP-7, *86*	125	140	_____
8664	Amtrak Alco A Unit, *76-77*	100	150	_____
8665	BAR "Jeremiah O'Brien" GP-9 "1776", *76 u*	100	160	_____
8666	Northern Pacific GP-9, *76 (SSS)*	125	150	_____
8667	Amtrak Alco B Unit, *76-77*	75	100	_____
8668	Northern Pacific GP-9 Dummy, *76 (SSS)*	100	125	_____
8669	Illinois Central Gulf U36B, *76-77*	125	150	_____
8670	Chessie System Diesel Switcher, *76*	35	65	_____
8679	Northern Pacific GP-20, *86*	100	125	_____
8687	Jersey Central Trainmaster, *86*	350	400	_____
8690	Lionel Lines Trolley, *86*	125	175	_____
(8701)	W&ARR 4-4-0 "3", *77-79*	175	200	_____
8702	Southern 4-6-4, *77-78*	400	475	_____
8703	Wabash 2-4-2, *77*	25	35	_____
8750	Rock Island GP-7, *77-78*	100	125	_____
8751	Rock Island GP-7 Dummy, *77-78*	50	75	_____
8753	Pennsylvania GG-1, *77 u*	475	550	_____
8754	New Haven Rectifier, *77-78*	175	225	_____
8755	Santa Fe U36B, *77-78*	150	175	_____
8756	Santa Fe U36B Dummy, *77-78*	90	100	_____
8757	Conrail GP-9, *76u, 77-78*	100	165	_____
8758	Southern GP-7 Dummy, *77 u, 78*	80	100	_____
8759	Erie-Lackawanna GP-9, *77-79*	120	150	_____
8760	Erie-Lackawanna GP-9 Dummy, *77-79*	100	125	_____
8761	GTW NW-2, *77-78*	125	175	_____
8762	Great Northern EP-5, *77-78*	225	250	_____
8763	Norfolk & Western GP-9, *76 u, 77-78*	100	125	_____
8764	B&O Budd RDC Passenger, *77 (SSS)*	150	175	_____
8765	B&O Budd RDC Baggage Dummy, *77 (SSS)*	75	100	_____
8766	B&O Budd RDC Baggage, *77 (SSS)*	200	250	_____
8767	B&O Budd RDC Passenger Dummy, *77 (SSS)*	100	125	_____
8768	B&O Budd RDC Passenger Dummy, *77 (SSS)*	100	125	_____
8769	Republic Steel Diesel Switcher, *77-78*	20	40	_____
8770	EMD NW-2, *77-78*	60	75	_____

		Exc	New	Cond/$
8771	Great Northern U36B, *77*	100	120	_____
8772	GM&O GP-20, *77*	100	120	_____
8773	Mickey Mouse U36B, *77-78*	300	400	_____
8774	Southern GP-7, *77 u, 78*	125	150	_____
8775	Lehigh Valley GP-9, *77 u, 78*	125	150	_____
8776	C&NW GP-20, *77 u, 78*	125	150	_____
8777	Santa Fe F-3 B Unit, *77 (SSS)*	200	250	_____
8778	Lehigh Valley GP-9 Dummy, *77 u, 78*	80	100	_____
8779	C&NW GP-20 Dummy, *77 u, 78*	80	100	_____
8800	Lionel Lines 4-4-2, *78-81*	100	125	_____
8801	Blue Comet 4-6-4, *78-80*	400	475	_____
8803	Santa Fe 0-4-0, *78*	15	25	_____
8850	Penn Central GG-1, *78 u, 79*	375	450	_____
8851/8852	New Haven F-3 AA set, *78 u, 79*	300	400	_____
8854	CP Rail GP-9, *78-79*	100	150	_____
8855	Milwaukee Road SD-18, *78*	150	175	_____
8857	Northern Pacific U36B, *78-80*	100	125	_____
8858	Northern Pacific U36B Dummy, *78-80*	55	85	_____
8859	Conrail Recifier, *78-82*	175	225	_____
8860	Rock Island NW-2, *78-79*	100	125	_____
8861	Santa Fe Alco A Unit, *78-79*	75	100	_____
8862	Santa Fe Alco B Unit Dummy, *78-79*	40	50	_____
8864	New Haven F-3 B Unit, *78 (SSS)*	125	175	_____
8866	M&St L GP-9, *78 (SSS)*	100	125	_____
8867	M&St L GP-9 Dummy, *78 (SSS)*	75	100	_____
8868	Amtrak Budd RDC Baggage, *78, 80*	150	200	_____
8869	Amtrak Budd RDC Passenger Dummy, *78, 80*	70	100	_____
8870	Amtrak Budd RDC Passenger Dummy, *78, 80*	70	100	_____
8871	Amtrak Budd RDC Baggage Dummy, *78, 80*	70	100	_____
8872	Santa Fe SD-18, *78 u, 79*	100	150	_____
8873	Santa Fe SD-18 Dummy, *78 u, 79*	75	100	_____
8900	Santa Fe 4-6-4 (FARR #1), *79*	350	425	_____
8902	ACL 2-4-0, *79-82, 86-90*	15	20	_____
8903	D&RGW 2-4-2, *79-81*	20	25	_____
8904	Wabash 2-4-2, *79, 81 u*	35	40	_____
8905	"Smokey Mountain" Dockside 0-4-0, *79*	10	20	_____
8950	Virginian Trainmaster, *79*	375	475	_____
8951	Southern Pacific Trainmaster, *79*	500	600	_____
8952/8953	PRR F-3 AA set, *79*	600	650	_____

MPC MODERN ERA (1970-1986)	Exc	New	Cond/$
8955 Southern U36B, *79*	125	175	_____
8956 Southern U36B Dummy, *79*	100	125	_____
8957 Burlington Northern GP-20, *79*	125	140	_____
[8957] Detroit-Toledo TCA Burlington Northern GP-20, *80 u*		NRS	_____
8958 Burlington Northern GP-20 Dummy, *79*	100	125	_____
[8958] Detroit-Toledo TCA Burlington Northern GP-20 Dummy, *80 u*		NRS	_____
8960 Southern Pacific U36C, *79 u*	100	125	_____
8961 Southern Pacific U36C Dummy, *79 u*	75	100	_____
8962 Reading U36B, *79*	150	175	_____
8970/8971 PRR F-3 AA set, *79 u, 80*	400	500	_____
9001 Conrail Boxcar (O27), *86-87 u, 88-90*	5	10	_____
9010 GN Hopper (O27), *70-71*	6	8	_____
9011 GN Hopper (O27), *70 u, 75-76, 78-83*	6	8	_____
9012 TA&G Hopper (O27), *71-72*	5	7	_____
9013 Canadian National Hopper (O27), *72-76*	5	7	_____
9014 Trailer Train Flatcar (O27), *78-79*		NRS	_____
9015 Reading Hopper (O27), *73-75*	20	25	_____
9016 Chessie System Hopper (O27), *75-79, 87-88*	5	7	_____
[9016] LCCA Chessie System Hopper (O27), *79-80 u*	20	25	_____
9017 Wabash Gondola w/ canisters (O27), *78-82*	4	5	_____
9018 DT&I Hopper (O27), *78-79, 81-82*	5	7	_____
(9019) Unlettered Flatcar (O27), *78*	3	4	_____
9020 Union Pacific Flatcar (O27), *70-78*	4	5	_____
9021 Santa Fe Work Caboose, *70-71, 73-75*	10	15	_____
9022 Santa Fe Bulkhead Flatcar (O27), *70-71, 73-77*	8	15	_____
9023 MKT Bulkhead Flatcar (O27), *73-74*	8	12	_____
9024 C&O Flatcar (O27), *73-75*	4	6	_____
9025 DT&I Work Caboose, *71-74, 77-78*	8	10	_____
9026 Republic Steel Flatcar (O27), *75-82*	6	8	_____
9027 Soo Line Work Caboose, *75-76*	8	10	_____
(9030) "Kickapoo" Gondola (O27), *72, 79*	5	7	_____
9031 NKP Gondola w/ canisters (O27), *73-75, 82-83, 84-91 u*	5	7	_____
9032 Southern Pacific Gondola w/ canisters (O27), *75-78*	3	4	_____
9033 PC Gondola w/ canisters (O27), *76-78, 82, 86 u, 87-90*	3	4	_____

		Exc	New	Cond/$
9034	Lionel Leisure Hopper (O27), *77 u*	30	40	_____
9035	Conrail Boxcar (O27), *78-82*	4	8	_____
9036	Mobilgas 1-D Tank Car (O27), *78-82*	6	12	_____
[9036]	LCCA Mobilgas 1-D Tank Car (O27), *78-79 u*	20	25	_____
9037	Conrail Boxcar (O27), *78 u, 80*	4	8	_____
9038	Chessie System Hopper (O27), *78 u, 80*	15	20	_____
9039	Mobilgas 1-D Tank Car (O27), *78 u, 80*	10	15	_____
9040	General Mills Wheaties Boxcar (O27), *70-72*	7	10	_____
9041	Hershey's Boxcar (O27), *70-71, 73-76*	10	15	_____
9042	Ford Autolite Boxcar (O27), *71u, 72, 74-76*	10	15	_____
9043	Erie-Lackawanna Boxcar (O27), *73-75*	10	15	_____
9044	D&RGW Boxcar (O27), *75-76*	6	8	_____
9045	Toys 'R Us Boxcar (O27), *75 u*	40	50	_____
9046	True Value Boxcar (O27), *76 u*	40	50	_____
9047	Toys 'R Us Boxcar (O27), *76 u*	35	50	_____
9048	Toys 'R Us Boxcar (O27), *76 u*	35	50	_____
(9049)	Toys 'R Us Boxcar (O27), *78 u*		NRS	_____
9050	Sunoco 1-D Tank Car (O27), *70-71*	20	25	_____
9051	Firestone 1-D Tank Car (O27), *74-75, 78*	15	25	_____
9052	Toys 'R Us Boxcar (O27), *77 u*	30	40	_____
9053	True Value Boxcar (O27), *77 u*	35	50	_____
9054	JCPenney Boxcar (O27), *77 u*	35	50	_____
9055	Republic Steel Gondola w/ canisters, *78 u*	10	12	_____
9057	CP Rail SP Caboose, *78-79*	10	15	_____
9058	Lionel Lines SP Caboose, *78-79, 83*	6	8	_____
9059	Lionel Lines SP Caboose, *79 u*	8	10	_____
9060	Nickel Plate Road SP Caboose, *70-72*	6	8	_____
9061	Santa Fe SP Caboose, *70-76*	6	8	_____
9062	Penn Central SP Caboose, *70-72, 74-76*	5	9	_____
9063	GTW SP Caboose, *70, 71-73 u*	15	20	_____
9064	C&O SP Caboose, *71-72, 75-77*	7	10	_____
9065	Canadian National SP Caboose, *71-73 u*	20	25	_____
9066	Southern SP Caboose, *73-76*	8	10	_____
(9067)	Kickapoo Valley Bobber Caboose, *72*	7	10	_____
9068	Reading Bobber Caboose, *73-76*	6	8	_____
[9068]	Gateway TCA Reading Bobber Caboose, *76 u*	—	25	_____
9069	Jersey Central SP Caboose, *73-74, 75-76 u*	6	8	_____
9070	Rock Island SP Caboose, *73-74*	10	15	_____
9071	Santa Fe Bobber Caboose, *74 u, 77-78*	8	10	_____

		Exc	New	Cond/$
9073	Coca-Cola SP Caboose, *74 u, 75*	15	20	_____
9075	Rock Island SP Caboose, *75-76 u*	15	20	_____
9076	"We The People" SP Caboose, *75 u*	20	30	_____
9077	D&RGW SP Caboose, *76-83, 84-91 u*	6	8	_____
9078	Rock Island Bobber Caboose, *76-77*	6	8	_____
9079	GTW Hopper (O27), *77*	20	30	_____
9080	Wabash SP Caboose, *77*	10	12	_____
9085	Santa Fe Work Caboose, *79-82*	5	6	_____
9090	General Mills Mini-Max Car, *71*	35	50	_____
9106	Miller Vat Car, *84-85*	25	35	_____
9107	Dr. Pepper Vat Car, *86-87*	25	30	_____
9110	B&O Quad Hopper, *71*	25	30	_____
9111	N&W Quad Hopper, *72-75*	20	25	_____
9112	D&RGW Covered Quad Hopper, *73-75*	20	25	_____
9113	Norfolk & Western Quad Hopper, *73 (SSS)*	30	35	_____
[9113]	Three Rivers TCA N&W Quad Hopper, *76 u*	30	35	_____
9114	Morton Salt Covered Quad Hopper, *74-76*	20	25	_____
9115	Planter's Covered Quad Hopper, *74-76*	20	25	_____
9116	Domino Sugar Covered Quad Hopper, *74-76*	20	25	
9117	Alaska Covered Quad Hopper, *74 (SSS), 75-76*	25	35	_____
9118	LCCA Corning Covered Quad Hopper, *74 u*	75	100	_____
9119	Detroit & Mackinac Covered Quad Hopper, *75 (SSS)*	25	35	_____
[9119]	Detroit-Toledo TCA Detroit & Mackinac Covered Quad Hopper, *77 u*	25	35	_____
[9119]	North Texas TCA Detroit & Mackinac Covered Quad Hopper, *78 u*	25	35	_____
9120	Northern Pacific Flatcar w/ trailers, *70-71*	35	45	_____
9121	L&N Flatcar w/ bulldozer and scraper, *71-79*	40	50	_____
9122	Northern Pacific Flatcar w/ trailers, *72-75*	35	45	_____
9123	C&O Auto Carrier, *72 u, 73-74*	20	30	_____
(9123)	TCA Dearborn Auto Carrier, *73 u*	30	40	_____
9124	P&LE Flatcar w/ log load, *73-74*	15	20	_____
9125	Norfolk & Western Auto Carrier, *73-77*	25	30	_____
9126	C&O Auto Carrier, *73-75*	20	30	_____
0128	Heinz Vat Car, *73 u, 74-76*	25	35	
9129	N&W Auto Carrier, *75-76*	30	35	_____
9130	B&O Quad Hopper, *70*	20	25	_____
9131	D&RGW Gondola w/ canisters, *73-77*	5	8	_____

	MPC MODERN ERA (1970-1986)	Exc	New	Cond/$
9132	Libby's Vat Car, *75 (SSS), 76-77*	20	25	_____
9133	Burlington Northern Flatcar w/ trailers, *76-77, 80*	35	45	_____
9134	Virginian Covered Quad Hopper, *76-77*	25	30	_____
9135	N&W Covered Quad Hopper, *70 u, 71, 75*	20	25	_____
9136	Republic Steel Gondola w/ canisters, *72-76, 79*	8	10	_____
9138	Sunoco 3-D Tank Car, *78 (SSS)*	50	60	_____
9139	PC Auto Carrier, *76-77*	20	30	_____
9140	Burlington Gondola w/ canisters, *70, 73-82, 87-89*	6	8	_____
9141	Burlington Northern Gondola w/ canisters, *70-72*	8	10	_____
9142	Republic Steel Gondola w/ canisters, *71*	6	8	_____
[9142]	LCCA Republic Steel Gondola w/ canisters, *77-78 u*	15	20	_____
9143	Canadian National Gondola w/ canisters, *71-73 u*	40	50	_____
9144	D&RGW Gondola w/ canisters, *74 (SSS), 75-76*	8	12	_____
9145	ICG Auto Carrier, *77-80*	20	30	_____
9146	Mogen David Vat Car, *77-81*	20	25	_____
9147	Texaco 1-D Tank Car, *77-78*	35	50	_____
9148	Dupont 3-D Tank Car, *77-81*	25	30	_____
9149	CP Rail Flatcar w/ trailers, *77-78*	30	50	_____
9150	Gulf 1-D Tank Car, *70u, 71*	25	30	_____
9151	Shell 1-D Tank Car, *72*	30	35	_____
9152	Shell 1-D Tank Car, *73-76*	25	30	_____
9153	Chevron 1-D Tank Car, *74-76*	20	30	_____
9154	Borden 1-D Tank Car, *75-76*	40	50	_____
9155	LCCA Monsanto 1-D Tank Car, *75 u*	60	70	_____
9156	Mobilgas 1-D Tank Car, *76-77*	35	45	_____
9157	C&O Flatcar w/ crane, *76-78, 81-82*	50	60	_____
9158	PC Flatcar w/ shovel, *76-77, 80*	45	60	_____
9159	Sunoco 1-D Tank Car, *76*	50	60	_____
9160	Illinois Central N5C Caboose, *70-72*	20	30	_____
9161	CN N5C Caboose, *72-74*	15	30	_____
9162	PRR N5C Caboose, *72 (SSS), 73-76*	35	45	_____
9163	Santa Fe N5C Caboose, *73-76*	15	25	_____
9165	Canadian Pacific N5C Caboose, *73 (SSS)*	25	40	_____
9166	D&RGW SP Caboose, *74 (SSS), 75*	20	25	_____
9167	Chessie System N5C Caboose, *74-76*	30	40	_____
9168	Union Pacific N5C Caboose, *75-77*	20	30	_____

		Exc	New	Cond/$
9169	Milwaukee Road SP Caboose, *75 (SSS)*	20	25	_____
(9170)	N&W N5C Caboose "1776", *75*	30	35	_____
9171	Missouri Pacific SP Caboose, *75 u, 76-77*	20	25	_____
9172	Penn Central SP Caboose, *75 u, 76-77*	25	35	_____
9173	Jersey Central SP Caboose, *75 u, 76-77*	20	25	_____
9174	NYC P&E B/W Caboose, *76*	75	90	_____
9175	Virginian N5C Caboose, *76-77*	30	40	_____
9176	BAR N5C Caboose, *76 u*	20	35	_____
9177	Northern Pacific B/W Caboose, *76 (SSS)*	25	35	_____
9178	ICG SP Caboose, *76-77*	20	25	_____
9179	Chessie System Bobber Caboose, *76*	6	10	_____
9180	Rock Island N5C Caboose, *77-78*	20	40	_____
9181	B&M N5C Caboose, *76 u, 77*	30	35	_____
[9181]	NETCA B&M N5C Caboose, *77 u*	25	30	_____
9182	N&W N5C Caboose, *76 u, 77-80*	25	35	_____
9183	Mickey Mouse N5C Caboose, *77-78*	45	75	_____
9184	Erie B/W Caboose, *77-78*	20	30	_____
[9184]	North Texas TCA Erie B/W Caboose, *77 u*	20	25	_____
[9184]	LCOL Erie B/W Caboose, *82 u*	20	25	_____
9185	GTW N5C Caboose, *77*	25	35	_____
9186	Conrail N5C Caboose, *76 u, 77-78*	30	40	_____
[9186]	Atlantic TCA Conrail N5C Caboose, *79 u*	25	35	_____
9187	GM&O SP Caboose, *77*	15	30	_____
9188	GN B/W Caboose, *77*	30	40	_____
9189	Gulf 1-D Tank Car, *77*	50	60	_____
9193	Budweiser Vat Car, *83-84*	125	150	_____
[9193]	Atlantic TCA Budweiser Vat Car, *84 u*	75	100	_____
9200	Illinois Central Boxcar, *70-71*	20	25	_____
9201	Penn Central Boxcar, *70*	20	30	_____
9202	Santa Fe Boxcar, *70*	30	40	_____
9203	Union Pacific Boxcar, *70*	35	45	_____
9204	Northern Pacific Boxcar, *70*	25	30	_____
9205	Norfolk & Western Boxcar, *70*	20	25	_____
9206	Great Northern Boxcar, *70-71*	20	25	_____
9207	Soo Line Boxcar, *71*	15	25	_____
9208	CP Rail Boxcar, *71*	20	25	_____
9209	Burlington Northern Boxcar, *71-72*	20	25	_____
9210	B&O DD Boxcar, *71*	20	30	_____
9211	Penn Central Boxcar, *71*	25	30	_____

MPC MODERN ERA (1970-1986)		Exc	New	Cond/$
9212	LCCA SCL Flatcar w/ trailers, *76 u*	35	40	_____
9213	M&St L Covered Quad Hopper, *78 (SSS)*	25	35	_____
9214	Northern Pacific Boxcar, *71-72*	25	30	_____
9215	Norfolk & Western Boxcar, *71*	25	30	_____
9216	Great Northern Auto Carrier, *78*	25	40	_____
9217	Soo Line Operating Boxcar, *82-84*	30	35	_____
9218	Monon Operating Boxcar, *81*	30	40	_____
9219	Missouri Pacific Operating Boxcar, *83*	30	40	_____
9220	Borden Milk Car, *83-86*	100	125	_____
9221	Poultry Dispatch Operating Chicken Car, *83-85*	65	80	_____
9222	L&N Flatcar w/ trailers, *83-84*	25	40	_____
9223	Reading Operating Boxcar, *84*	30	40	_____
9224	Churchhill Downs Operating Horse Car, *84-86*	125	150	_____
9225	Conrail Operating Barrel Car, *84*	70	85	_____
9226	Delaware & Hudson Flatcar w/ trailers, *84-85*	30	40	_____
9228	Canadian Pacific Operating Boxcar, *86*	20	30	_____
9229	Express Mail Operating Boxcar, *85-86*	30	45	_____
9230	Monon Boxcar, *71 (SSS), 72 u*	15	25	_____
9231	Reading B/W Caboose, *79*	30	40	_____
9232	Allis Chalmers Condenser Car, *80-81*	50	60	_____
9233	Depressed Flatcar w/ transformer, *80*	75	100	_____
9234	Lionel Radioactive Waste Car, *80*	40	60	_____
9235	Union Pacific Derrick Car, *83-84*	15	20	_____
9236	C&NW Derrick Car, *83-85*	25	35	_____
9237	UPS Operating Boxcar, *84*		NM	
9238	Northern Pacific Log Dump Car, *84*	15	20	_____
9239	Lionel Lines N5C Caboose, *83 u*	50	60	_____
9240	NYC Operating Hopper, *86*	40	50	_____
9240	NYC Hopper (O27), *87 u*	20	25	_____
9241	PRR Log Dump Car, *85-86*	15	20	_____
9245	Illinois Central Derrick Car, *85*		NM	
9247	(See 6529)			
9250	Waterpoxy 3-D Tank Car, *70-71*	30	35	_____
X9259	LCCA Southern B/W Caboose, *77 u*	35	40	_____
9260	Reynolds Aluminum Covered Quad Hopper, *75-76*	20	25	_____
9261	Sunmaid Raisins Covered Quad Hopper, *75 u, 76*	20	30	_____
9262	Ralston-Purina Covered Quad Hopper, *75 u, 76*	60	75	_____
9263	PRR Covered Quad Hopper, *75 u, 76-77*	35	50	_____

		Exc	New	Cond/$
9264	Illinois Central Covered Quad Hopper, *75 u, 76-77*	30	35	_____
[9264]	TCA Museum Illinois Central Covered Quad Hopper, *78 u*	25	30	_____
9265	Chessie System Covered Quad Hopper, *75 u, 76-77*	30	35	_____
9266	Southern "Big John" Covered Quad Hopper, *76*	60	75	_____
9267	Alcoa Covered Quad Hopper, *76 (SSS)*	30	40	_____
9268	Northern Pacific B/W Caboose, *77 u*	30	40	_____
9269	Milwaukee Road B/W Caboose, *78*	35	50	_____
9270	Northern Pacific N5C Caboose, *78*	15	25	_____
9271	M&St L B/W Caboose, *78 (SSS), 79*	20	35	_____
9272	New Haven B/W Caboose, *78-80*	20	30	_____
[9272]	Detroit-Toledo TCA New Haven B/W Caboose, *79 u*	25	30	_____
[9272]	METCA New Haven B/W Caboose, *79 u*	25	30	_____
9273	Southern B/W Caboose, *78 u*	40	55	_____
9274	Santa Fe B/W Caboose, *78 u*	60	85	_____
9276	Peabody Quad Hopper, *78*	30	40	_____
9277	Cities Service 1-D Tank Car, *78*	50	60	_____
9278	Lifesavers 1-D Tank Car, *78-79*	125	175	_____
9279	Magnolia 3-D Tank Car, *78*	25	30	_____
9280	Santa Fe Operating Stock Car, *77-81*	25	30	_____
9281	Santa Fe Auto Carrier, *78-80*	20	30	_____
9282	Great Northern Flatcar w/ trailers, *78-79, 81-82*	40	60	_____
9283	Union Pacific Gondola w/ canisters, *77*	15	20	_____
9284	Santa Fe Gondola w/ canisters, *77*	20	25	_____
9285	ICG Flatcar w/ trailers, *77*	50	65	_____
9286	B&LE Covered Quad Hopper, *77*	15	25	_____
9287	Southern N5C Caboose, *77 u, 78*	15	25	_____
[9287]	Southern TCA Southern N5C Caboose, *77 u*	20	25	_____
9288	Lehigh Valley N5C Caboose, *77 u, 78, 80*	20	30	_____
9289	C&NW N5C Caboose, *77 u, 78, 80*	30	50	_____
[9289]	TCA Museum C&NW N5C Caboose, *80 u*	40	50	_____
9290	Union Pacific Operating Barrel Car, *83*	75	95	_____
9300	PC Log Dump Car, *70-75, 77*	15	20	_____
9301	US Mail Operating Boxcar, *73-84*	30	45	_____
[9301]	Sacramento-Sierra TCA US Mail Operating Boxcar, *76 u*	30	45	_____
9302	L&N Searchlight Car, *72 u, 73-78*	15	20	_____
9303	Union Pacific Log Dump Car, *74-78, 80*	10	20	_____

		Exc	New	Cond/$
9304	C&O Coal Dump Car, *74-78*	10	20	_____
9305	Santa Fe Operating Cowboy Car, *80-82*	20	30	_____
9306	Santa Fe Flatcar w/ horses, *80-82*	20	30	_____
9307	Erie Animated Gondola, *80-84*	60	85	_____
9308	Aquarium Car, *81-84*	165	200	_____
9309	TP&W B/W Caboose, *80-81*	25	35	_____
9310	Santa Fe Log Dump Car, *78 u, 79-83*	10	20	_____
9311	Union Pacific Coal Dump Car, *78 u, 79-82*	10	20	_____
9312	Conrail Searchlight Car, *78 u, 79-83*	20	25	_____
9313	Gulf 3-D Tank Car, *79 u*	50	60	_____
9315	Southern Pacific Gondola w/ canisters, *79 u*	20	30	_____
9316	Southern Pacific B/W Caboose, *79 u*	80	100	_____
9317	Santa Fe B/W Caboose, *79*	35	50	_____
9319	TCA Silver Jubilee Mint Car, *79 u*	225	275	_____
9320	Fort Knox Mint Car, *79 u*	200	250	_____
9321	Santa Fe 1-D Tank Car (FARR #1), *79*	40	60	_____
9322	Santa Fe Covered Quad Hopper (FARR #1), *79*	60	80	_____
9323	Santa Fe B/W Caboose (FARR #1), *79*	45	60	_____
9324	Tootsie Roll 1-D Tank Car, *79-81*	50	95	_____
9325	Norfolk & Western Flatcar w/ fences, *79-81 u*	5	10	_____
9325	(See 9363, 9364)			
9326	Burlington Northern B/W Caboose, *79-80*	25	30	_____
[9326]	TTOS Burlington Northern B/W Caboose, *82 u*		NRS	_____
9327	Bakelite 3-D Tank Car, *80*	20	30	_____
9328	Chessie System B/W Caboose, *80*	40	60	_____
9329	Chessie System Crane Car, *80*	60	75	_____
(9330)	"Kickapoo" Dump Car, *72, 79*	3	8	_____
9331	Union 76 1-D Tank Car, *79*	50	60	_____
9332	Reading Crane Car, *79*	50	75	_____
9333	Southern Pacific Flatcar w/ trailers, *79-80*	50	60	_____
9334	Humble 1-D Tank Car, *79*	25	35	_____
9335	B&O Log Dump Car, *86*	15	20	_____
9336	CP Rail Gondola w/ canisters, *79*	25	30	_____
9338	Penn Power Quad Hopper, *79*	60	75	_____
9339	Great Northern Boxcar (O27), *79-83, 85 u, 86*	7	10	_____
9340	Illinois Central Gondola w/ canisters (O27), *79-81, 82 u, 83*	5	10	_____
9341	ACL SP Caboose, *79-82, 86 u, 87-90*	6	8	_____
9344	Citgo 3-D Tank Car, *80*	40	50	_____

No.	Description	Exc	New	Cond/$
9345	Reading Searchlight Car, *84-85*	20	25	_____
9346	Wabash SP Caboose, *79, 81 u*	6	10	_____
9347	TTOS Niagara Falls 3-D Tank Car, *80 u*	40	50	_____
9348	Santa Fe Crane Car (FARR #1), *79 u*	60	75	_____
9349	San Francisco Mint Car, *80*	125	175	_____
9351	PRR Auto Carrier, *80*	20	40	_____
9352	C&NW Flatcar w/ trailers, *80*	75	85	_____
9353	Crystal Line 3-D Tank Car, *80*	20	30	_____
9354	Pennzoil 1-D Tank Car, *80*	40	50	_____
9355	Delaware & Hudson B/W Caboose, *80*	30	40	_____
[9355]	TTOS D&H B/W Caboose, *82 u*		NRS	_____
9356	Lifesavers Stik-O-Pep Tank Car, *80 u*		NM	
9357	Smokey Mountain Bobber Caboose, *79*	8	10	_____
9358	LCCA Sands of Iowa Covered Quad Hopper, *80 u*	30	40	_____
9359	National Basketball Association Boxcar (O27), *79-80 u*	20	25	_____
9360	National Hockey League Boxcar (O27), *79-80 u*	20	25	_____
9361	C&NW B/W Caboose, *80*	55	65	_____
[9361]	TTOS C&NW B/W Caboose, *82 u*		NRS	_____
9362	Major League Baseball Boxcar (O27), *79-80 u*	20	25	_____
(9363)	N&W Dump Car "9325" (O27), *79*	5	8	_____
(9364)	N&W Crane Car "9325" (O27), *79*	8	10	_____
9365	Toys 'R Us Boxcar (O27), *79 u*	40	50	_____
9366	Union Pacific Covered Quad Hopper (FARR #2), *80*	35	45	_____
9367	Union Pacific 1-D Tank Car (FARR #2), *80*	40	50	_____
9368	Union Pacific B/W Caboose (FARR #2), *80*	50	60	_____
9369	Sinclair 1-D Tank Car, *80*	50	60	_____
9370	Seaboard Gondola w/ canisters, *80*	20	25	_____
9371	Lantic Sugar Covered Quad Hopper, *80*	30	45	_____
9372	Seaboard B/W Caboose, *80*	30	45	_____
9373	Getty 1-D Tank Car, *80-81*	40	50	_____
9374	Reading Covered Quad Hopper, *80 81*	60	75	_____
9375	Union Pacific Flatcar w/ fences (O27), *80*		NM	
9376	Soo Line Boxcar (O27), *81 u*		NRS	_____
9376	Texas & Pacific SP Caboose, *80*		NM	
9377	Missouri Pacific Boxcar (O27), *80*		NM	
9378	Lionel Derrick Car, *80-82*	25	30	_____
9379	Santa Fe Gondola w/ canisters, *80-81*	25	35	_____

		Exc	New	Cond/$
9380	NYNH&H SP Caboose, *80-81*	10	12	_____
9381	Chessie System SP Caboose, *80*	8	10	_____
9382	Florida East Coast B/W Caboose, *80*	30	40	_____
[9382]	TTOS Florida East Coast B/W Caboose, *82 u*		NRS	_____
9383	Union Pacific Flatcar w/ trailers (FARR #2), *80 u*	45	60	_____
9384	Great Northern Operating Hopper, *81*	65	80	_____
9385	Alaska Gondola w/ canisters, *81*	50	60	_____
9386	Pure Oil 1-D Tank Car, *81*	45	55	_____
9387	Burlington B/W Caboose, *81*	45	60	_____
9388	Toys 'R Us Boxcar (O27), *81 u*	40	50	_____
9389	Lionel Radioactive Waste Car, *81-82*	35	50	_____
9398	PRR Coal Dump Car, *83-84*	20	25	_____
9399	C&NW Coal Dump Car, *83-85*	15	20	_____
9400	Conrail Boxcar, *78*	15	20	_____
[9400]	NETCA Conrail Boxcar, *78 u*	25	30	_____
9401	Great Northern Boxcar, *78*	15	20	_____
[9401]	Detroit-Toledo TCA GN Boxcar, *78 u*	—	30	_____
9402	Susquehanna Boxcar, *78*	30	35	_____
9403	Seaboard Coast Line Boxcar, *78*	15	20	_____
[9403]	Southern TCA SCL Boxcar, *78 u*	—	30	_____
9404	NKP Boxcar, *78*	30	40	_____
9405	Chattahoochie Boxcar, *78*	15	20	_____
[9405]	Southern TCA Chattahoochie Boxcar, *79 u*	—	30	_____
9406	D&RGW Boxcar, *78-79*	15	20	_____
9407	Union Pacific Stock Car, *78*	30	35	_____
9408	Lionel Lines Circus Stock Car, *78 (SSS)*	40	60	_____
9411	Lackawanna "Phoebe Snow" Boxcar, *78*	50	60	_____
9412	RF&P Boxcar, *79*	20	30	_____
[9412]	WB&A TCA RF&P Boxcar, *79 u*	—	30	_____
9413	Napierville Junction Boxcar, *79*	15	20	_____
[9413]	LCAC Napierville Junction Boxcar, *80 u*		NRS	_____
9414	Cotton Belt Boxcar, *79*	20	25	_____
[9414]	LOTS Cotton Belt Boxcar, *80 u*	—	35	_____
[9414]	Sacramento-Sierra TCA Cotton Belt Boxcar, *80 u*	—	45	_____
9415	Providence & Worcester Boxcar, *79*	15	20	_____
[9415]	NETCA Providence & Worcester Boxcar, *79 u*	25	30	_____
9416	MD&W Boxcar, *79, 81*	15	20	_____
9417	CP Rail Boxcar, *79*	35	45	_____
9418	FARR Boxcar, *79 u*	75	85	_____

		Exc	New	Cond/$
9419	Union Pacific Boxcar (FARR #2), *80*	35	45	_____
9420	B&O "Sentinel" Boxcar, *80*	30	40	_____
9421	Maine Central Boxcar, *80*	12	20	_____
9422	EJ&E Boxcar, *80*	15	25	_____
9423	NYNH&H Boxcar, *80*	15	30	_____
[9423]	NETCA NYNH&H Boxcar, *80 u*	25	30	_____
9424	TP&W Boxcar, *80*	20	25	_____
9425	British Columbia DD Boxcar, *80*	25	35	_____
9426	Chesapeake & Ohio Boxcar, *80*	25	40	_____
9427	Bay Line Boxcar, *80-81*	15	20	_____
[9427]	Sacramento-Sierra TCA Bay Line Boxcar, *81 u*	—	45	_____
9428	TP&W Boxcar, *80-81*	35	50	_____
9429	The Early Years Boxcar, *80*	30	35	_____
9430	The Standard Gauge Years Boxcar, *80*	30	35	_____
9431	The Prewar Years Boxcar, *80*	30	35	_____
9432	The Postwar Years Boxcar, *80*	100	125	_____
9433	The Golden Years Boxcar, *80*	100	125	_____
9434	Joshua Lionel Cowen "The Man" Boxcar, *80 u*	60	75	_____
9435	LCCA Central of Georgia Boxcar, *81 u*	40	55	_____
9436	Burlington Boxcar, *81*	45	60	_____
9437	Northern Pacific Stock Car, *81*	36	60	_____
9438	Ontario Northland Boxcar, *81*	20	30	_____
9439	Ashley Drew & Northern Boxcar, *81*	10	20	_____
9440	Reading Boxcar, *81*	50	70	_____
9441	Pennsylvania Boxcar, *81*	65	85	_____
9442	Canadian Pacific Boxcar, *81*	15	20	_____
9443	Florida East Coast Boxcar, *81*	15	20	_____
[9443]	Southern TCA Florida East Coast Boxcar, *81 u*	—	30	_____
9444	Louisiana Midland Boxcar, *81*	15	20	_____
[9444]	Sacramento-Sierra TCA Louisiana Midland Boxcar, *82 u*	—	45	_____
9445	Vermont Northern Boxcar, *81*	15	20	_____
[9445]	NETCA Vermont Northern Boxcar, *81 u*	25	30	_____
9446	Sabine River & Northern Boxcar, *81*	15	20	_____
9447	Pullman Standard Boxcar, *81*	20	25	_____
9448	Santa Fe Stock Car, *81-82*	50	60	_____
9449	Great Northern Boxcar (FARR #3), *81*	40	50	_____
9450	Great Northern Stock Car (FARR #3), *81 u*	100	125	_____
9451	Southern Boxcar (FARR #4), *83*	40	50	_____

		Exc	New	Cond/$
9452	Western Pacific Boxcar, *82-83*	15	20	_____
[9452]	Sacramento-Sierra TCA WP Boxcar, *83 u*	—	45	_____
9453	MPA Boxcar, *82-83*	15	20	_____
9454	New Hope & Ivyland Boxcar, *82-83*	15	20	_____
9455	Milwaukee Road Boxcar, *82-83*	15	20	_____
9456	PRR DD Boxcar (FARR #5), *84-85*	45	60	_____
9460	LCCA D&TS DD Boxcar, *82 u*	35	60	_____
9461	Norfolk Southern Boxcar, *82*	35	60	_____
9462	Southern Pacific Boxcar, *83-84*	20	25	_____
9463	Texas & Pacific Boxcar, *83-84*	15	20	_____
9464	NC&St L Boxcar, *83-84*	15	20	_____
9465	Santa Fe Boxcar, *83-84*	15	25	_____
9466	Wanamaker Boxcar, *82 u*	80	100	_____
[9466]	Atlantic TCA Wanamaker Boxcar, *83 u*		NRS	_____
9467	Tennessee World's Fair Boxcar, *82 u*	45	60	_____
9468	Union Pacific DD Boxcar, *83*	50	65	_____
9469	NYC "Pacemaker" Boxcar (Std. O), *84-85*	100	125	_____
9470	Chicago Beltline Boxcar, *84*	15	20	_____
9471	Atlantic Coast Line Boxcar, *84*	15	20	_____
[9471]	Southern TCA Atlantic Coast Line Boxcar, *84 u*	—	30	_____
9472	Detroit & Mackinac Boxcar, *84*	20	25	_____
9473	Lehigh Valley Boxcar, *84*	20	25	_____
9474	Erie-Lackawanna Boxcar, *84*	40	50	_____
9475	D&H "I Love NY" Boxcar, *84 u*	25	40	_____
[9475]	LCOL D&H "I Love New York" Boxcar, *85 u*	—	30	_____
9476	PRR Boxcar (FARR #5), *84-85*	50	65	_____
9480	MN&S Boxcar, *85-86*	15	20	_____
9481	Seaboard System Boxcar, *85-86*	15	20	_____
9482	Norfolk Southern Boxcar, *85-86*	15	20	_____
[9482]	Southern TCA Norfolk Southern Boxcar, *85 u*	—	30	_____
9483	Manufacturers Railway Boxcar, *85-86*	15	20	_____
9484	Lionel 85th Anniversary Boxcar, *85*	30	35	_____
9486	GTW "I Love Michigan" Boxcar, *86*	15	25	_____
9486	Artrain GTW "I Love Michigan" Boxcar, *87 u*	—	400	_____
9490	Christmas Boxcar for Lionel Employees, *85 u*	—	1800	_____
9491	Christmas Boxcar, *86 u*	50	75	_____
9492	Lionel Lines Boxcar, *86*	40	45	_____
9500	Milwaukee Road Passenger Car, *73*	40	60	_____
9501	Milwaukee Road Passenger Car, *73 u, 74-76*	30	40	_____

		Exc	New	Cond/$
9502	Milwaukee Road Observation Car, 73	40	60	_____
9503	Milwaukee Road Passenger Car, 73	40	60	_____
9504	Milwaukee Road Passenger Car, 73 u, 74-76	30	40	_____
9505	Milwaukee Road Passenger Car, 73 u, 74-76	30	40	_____
9506	Milwaukee Road Combination Car, 74 u, 75-76	25	40	_____
9507	PRR Passenger Car, 74-75	40	60	_____
9508	PRR Passenger Car, 74-75	40	60	_____
9509	PRR Observation Car, 74-75	50	75	_____
9510	PRR Combination Car, 74u, 75-76	30	40	_____
9511	Milwaukee Road Passenger Car, 74 u	30	50	_____
9512	TTOS Summerdale Junction Passenger Car, 74 u	40	50	_____
9513	PRR Passenger Car, 75-76	30	50	_____
9514	PRR Passenger Car, 75-76	30	50	_____
9515	PRR Passenger Car, 75-76	30	50	_____
9516	B&O Passenger Car, 76	30	50	_____
9517	B&O Passenger Car, 75	50	75	_____
9518	B&O Observation Car, 75	50	75	_____
9519	B&O Combination Car, 75	50	75	_____
9520	TTOS Phoenix Combination Car, 75 u	40	50	_____
9521	PRR Baggage Car, 75 u, 76	100	125	_____
9522	Milwaukee Road Baggage Car, 75 u, 76	100	125	_____
9523	B&O Baggage Car, 75 u, 76	75	100	_____
9524	B&O Passenger Car, 76	40	60	_____
9525	B&O Passenger Car, 76	40	60	_____
9526	TTOS Snowbird Observation Car, 76 u	40	50	_____
(9527)	Milwaukee Road Campaign Observation Car, 76 u	50	60	_____
(9528)	PRR Campaign Observation Car, 76 u	50	60	_____
(9529)	B&O Campaign Observation Car, 76 u	50	60	_____
9530	Southern Baggage Car, 77-78	45	75	_____
9531	Southern Combination Car, 77-78	45	75	_____
9532	Southern Passenger Car, 77-78	45	75	_____
9533	Southern Passenger Car, 77-78	45	75	_____
9534	Southern Observation Car, 77-78	45	75	_____
9535	TTOS Columbus Baggage Car, 77 u	30	40	_____
9536	Blue Comet Baggage Car, 78-80	45	75	_____
9537	Blue Comet Combination Car, 78-80	45	75	_____
9538	Blue Comet Passenger Car, 78-80	45	75	_____
9539	Blue Comet Passenger Car, 78-80	45	75	_____
9540	Blue Comet Observation Car, 78-80	45	75	_____

		Exc	New	Cond/$
9541	Santa Fe Baggage Car, *80-82*	20	30	__
(9544)	TCA Chicago Observation Car "1980", *80 u*	—	75	_____
9545	Union Pacific Baggage Car, *84*	100	125	_____
9546	Union Pacific Combination Car, *84*	100	125	_____
9547	Union Pacific Observation Car, *84*	100	125	_____
(9548)	Union Pacific "Placid Bay" Passenger Car, *84*	100	125	_____
(9549)	Union Pacific "Ocean Sunset" Passenger Car, *84*	100	125	_____
9551	W&ARR Baggage Car, *77 u, 78-80*	45	60	_____
9552	W&ARR Passenger Car, *77u, 78-80*	45	60	_____
9553	W&ARR Flatcar w/ horses, *77u, 78-80*	30	50	_____
(9554)	Chicago & Alton Baggage Car, *81*	50	75	_____
(9555)	Chicago & Alton Combination Car, *81*	50	75	_____
(9556)	Chicago & Alton "Wilson" Passenger Car, *81*	60	90	_____
(9557)	Chicago & Alton "Webster Groves" Passenger Car, *81*	60	90	_____
(9558)	Chicago & Alton Observation Car, *81*	50	75	_____
9559	Rock Island Baggage Car, *81-82*	40	60	_____
9560	Rock Island Passenger Car, *81-82*	40	60	_____
9561	Rock Island Passenger Car, *81-82*	40	60	_____
(9562)	Norfolk & Western Baggage Car "577", *81*	90	125	_____
(9563)	Norfolk & Western Combination Car "578", *81*	90	125	_____
(9564)	Norfolk & Western Passenger Car "579", *81*	110	150	_____
(9565)	Norfolk & Western Passenger Car "580", *81*	110	150	_____
(9566)	Norfolk & Western Observation Car "581", *81*	90	125	_____
(9567)	Norfolk & Western Vista Dome Car "582", *81 u*	350	525	_____
9569	PRR Combination Car, *81 u*	125	150	_____
9570	PRR Baggage Car, *79*	125	150	_____
9571	PRR Passenger Car, *79*	140	175	_____
9572	PRR Passenger Car, *79*	140	175	_____
9573	PRR Vista Dome Car, *79*	125	150	_____
9574	PRR Observation Car, *79*	125	150	_____
9575	PRR Passenger Car, *79-80 u*	135	175	_____
9576	Burlington Baggage Car, *80*	100	125	_____
9577	Burlington Passenger Car, *80*	100	125	_____
9578	Burlington Passenger Car, *80*	100	125	_____
9579	Burlington Vista Dome Car, *80*	100	125	_____
9580	Burlington Observation Car, *80*	100	125	_____
9581	Chessie System Baggage Car, *80*	60	75	_____
9582	Chessie System Combination Car, *80*	60	75	_____

		Exc	New	Cond/$
9583	Chessie System Passenger Car, *80*	60	75	_____
9584	Chessie System Passenger Car, *80*	60	75	_____
9585	Chessie System Observation Car, *80*	60	75	_____
9586	Chessie System Dining Car, *86 u*	100	125	_____
9588	Burlington Vista Dome Car, *80 u*	125	175	_____
(9589)	Southern Pacific Baggage Car, *82-83*	100	125	_____
(9590)	Southern Pacific Combination Car, *82-83*	100	125	_____
(9591)	Southern Pacific "Pullman" Passenger Car, *82-83*	100	125	_____
(9592)	Southern Pacific "Chair" Passenger Car, *82-83*	100	125	_____
(9593)	Southern Pacific Observation Car, *82-83*	100	125	_____
9594	NYC Baggage Car, *83-84*	100	125	_____
9595	NYC Combination Car, *83-84*	100	125	_____
(9596)	NYC "Wayne County" Passenger Car, *83-84*	100	125	_____
(9597)	NYC "Hudson River" Passenger Car, *83-84*	100	125	_____
(9598)	NYC Observation Car, *83-84*	100	125	_____
(9599)	Chicago & Alton Dining Car, *86 u*	90	125	_____
9600	Chessie System Hi-cube Boxcar, *75 u, 76-77*	20	25	_____
9601	ICG Hi-cube Boxcar, *75 u, 76-77*	20	25	_____
[9601]	Gateway TCA ICG Hi-cube Boxcar, *77 u*	—	25	_____
9602	Santa Fe Hi-cube Boxcar, *75 u, 76-77*	20	25	_____
9603	Penn Central Hi-cube Boxcar, *76-77*	20	25	_____
9604	Norfolk & Western Hi-cube Boxcar, *76-77*	20	25	_____
9605	NH Hi-cube Boxcar, *76-77*	20	30	_____
9606	Union Pacific Hi-cube Boxcar, *76 u, 77*	20	25	_____
9607	Southern Pacific Hi-cube Boxcar, *76 u, 77*	20	25	_____
9608	Burlington Northern Hi-cube Boxcar, *76 u, 77*	20	25	_____
9610	Frisco Hi-cube Boxcar, *77*	30	50	_____
9611	TCA Boston Hi-cube Boxcar, *78 u*	35	45	_____
9620	NHL Wales Boxcar, *80*	20	25	_____
9621	NHL Campbell Boxcar, *80*	20	25	_____
9622	NBA Western Boxcar, *80*	20	25	_____
9623	NBA Eastern Boxcar, *80*	20	25	_____
9624	National League Baseball Boxcar, *80*	20	25	_____
9625	American League Baseball Boxcar, *80*	20	25	_____
9626	Santa Fe Hi-cube Boxcar, *82-84*	15	20	_____
9627	Union Pacific Hi-cube Boxcar, *82-83*	15	20	_____
9628	Burlington Northern Hi-cube Boxcar, *82-84*	10	15	_____
9629	Chessie System Hi-cube Boxcar, *83-84*	20	25	_____
9660	Mickey Mouse Hi-cube Boxcar, *77-78*	40	50	_____

|---|---|---|---|
9661 Goofy Hi-cube Boxcar, *77-78*	40	45	_____
9662 Donald Duck Hi-cube Boxcar, *77-78*	40	50	_____
9663 Dumbo Hi-cube Boxcar, *77 u, 78*	40	70	_____
9664 Cinderella Hi-cube Boxcar, *77 u, 78*	55	90	_____
9665 Peter Pan Hi-cube Boxcar, *77 u, 78*	50	90	_____
9666 Pinocchio Hi-cube Boxcar, *78*	125	200	_____
9667 Snow White Hi-cube Boxcar, *78*	350	500	_____
9668 Pluto Hi-cube Boxcar, *78*	150	200	_____
9669 Bambi Hi-cube Boxcar, *78 u*	60	100	_____
9670 Alice In Wonderland Hi-cube Boxcar, *78 u*	50	75	_____
9671 Fantasia Hi-cube Boxcar, *78 u*	50	60	_____
9672 Mickey Mouse 50th Anniversary Hi-cube Boxcar, *78 u*	395	500	_____
9678 TTOS Hollywood Hi-cube Boxcar, *78 u*	25	35	_____
9700 Southern Boxcar, *72-73*	20	25	_____
9700-1976 (See 9779)			
9701 B&O DD Boxcar, *72*	20	25	_____
9701 TCA B&O DD Boxcar, *72 u*	75	100	_____
[9701] LCCA B&O DD Boxcar, *72 u*		NRS	_____
9702 Soo Line Boxcar, *72-73*	20	25	_____
9703 CP Rail Boxcar, *72*	40	50	_____
9704 Norfolk & Western Boxcar, *72*	10	25	_____
9705 D&RGW Boxcar, *72*	12	25	_____
[9705] Sacramento-Sierra TCA D&RGW Boxcar, *75 u*	—	40	_____
9706 C&O Boxcar, *72*	24	25	_____
9707 MKT Stock Car, *72-75*	15	25	_____
9708 US Mail Boxcar, *72-75*	15	25	_____
9708 US Mail Toy Fair Boxcar, *73 u*	100	125	_____
9709 BAR "State of Maine" Boxcar, *72 (SSS), 73-74*	40	45	_____
9710 Rutland Boxcar, *72 (SSS), 73-74*	30	40	_____
9711 Southern Boxcar, *74-75*	20	25	_____
9712 B&O DD Boxcar, *73-74*	30	40	_____
9713 CP Rail Boxcar, *73-74*	20	30	_____
9713 CP Rail Season's Greetings Boxcar, *74 u*	100	125	_____
9714 D&RGW Boxcar, *73-74*	20	25	_____
9715 C&O Boxcar, *73-74*	20	25	_____
9716 Penn Central Boxcar, *73-74*	20	30	_____
9717 Union Pacific Boxcar, *73-74*	20	30	_____
9718 Canadian National Boxcar, *73-74*	20	25	_____

MPC MODERN ERA (1970-1986)

		Exc	New	Cond/$
[9718]	LCAC Canadian National Boxcar, *79 u*		NRS	_____
9719	New Haven DD Boxcar, *73 u*	25	35	_____
9723	Western Pacific Boxcar, *73 (SSS), 74*	30	40	_____
9723	Western Pacific Toy Fair Boxcar, *74 u*	100	125	_____
[9723]	Sacramento-Sierra TCA WP Boxcar, *73 u*		NRS	_____
9724	Missouri Pacific Boxcar, *73 (SSS), 74*	35	40	_____
9725	MKT Stock Car, *73 (SSS), 74-75*	20	25	_____
9726	Erie-Lackawanna Boxcar, *78 (SSS)*	25	30	_____
[9726]	Sacramento-Sierra TCA Erie-Lack. Boxcar, *79 u*	—	45	_____
9727	LCCA TA&G Boxcar, *73 u*	200	250	_____
9728	LCCA Union Pacific Stock Car, *78 u*	35	45	_____
9729	CP Rail Boxcar, *78*	30	40	_____
9730	CP Rail Boxcar, *74-75*	25	30	_____
[9730]	Western Michigan TCA CP Rail Boxcar, *74 u*		NRS	_____
[9730]	Detroit-Toledo TCA CP Rail Boxcar, *76 u*	—	40	_____
[9730]	Sacramento-Sierra TCA CP Rail Boxcar, *77 u*	—	45	_____
9731	Milwaukee Road Boxcar, *74-75*	15	20	_____
9732	Southern Pacific Boxcar, *79 u*	30	40	_____
9733	LCCA Airco Boxcar w/ tank, *79 u*	50	60	_____
9734	Bangor & Aroostook Boxcar, *79*	30	40	_____
9735	Grand Trunk Boxcar, *74-75*	15	20	_____
9737	Central Vermont Boxcar, *74-76*	20	25	_____
9738	Illinois Terminal Boxcar, *82*	50	60	_____
9739	D&RGW Boxcar, *74 (SSS), 75-76*	20	25	_____
[9739]	LCCA D&RGW Boxcar, *78 u*		NRS	_____
[9739]	North Texas TCA D&RGW Boxcar, *76 u*	—	25	_____
9740	Chessie System Boxcar, *74-75*	15	20	_____
[9740]	Great Lakes TCA Chessie System Boxcar, *76 u*	—	25	_____
[9740]	WB&A TCA Chessie System Boxcar, *76 u*	—	30	_____
9742	M&St L Boxcar, *73 u*	25	35	_____
9742	M&St L Season's Greetings Boxcar, *73 u*	100	125	_____
9743	Sprite Boxcar, *74 u, 75*	15	25	_____
9744	Tab Boxcar, *74 u, 75*	15	25	_____
9745	Fanta Boxcar, *74 u, 75*	15	25	_____
9747	Chessie System DD Boxcar, *75-76*	25	30	_____
9748	CP Rail Boxcar, *75-76*	20	25	_____
9749	Penn Central Boxcar, *75-76*	15	25	_____
9750	DT&I Boxcar, *75-76*	10	20	_____
9751	Frisco Boxcar, *75-76*	20	25	_____

		Exc	New	Cond/$
9752	L&N Boxcar, *75-76*	15	20	_____
9753	Maine Central Boxcar, *75-76*	15	25	_____
[9753]	NETCA Maine Central Boxcar, *75 u*	25	30	_____
9754	NYC "Pacemaker" Boxcar, *75 (SSS), 76-77*	30	40	_____
[9754]	METCA NYC "Pacemaker" Boxcar, *76 u*	—	35	_____
9755	Union Pacific Boxcar, *75-76*	20	30	_____
9757	Central of Georgia Boxcar, *74 u*	20	30	_____
9758	Alaska Boxcar, *75 (SSS), 76-77*	30	40	_____
9759	Paul Revere Boxcar, *75 u*	40	50	_____
9760	Liberty Bell Boxcar, *75 u*	40	50	_____
9761	George Washington Boxcar, *75 u*	40	50	_____
(9762)	Toy Fair Boxcar, *75 u*	150	200	_____
9763	D&RGW Stock Car, *76-77*	20	30	_____
9764	GTW DD Boxcar, *76-77*	20	25	_____
9767	Railbox Boxcar, *76-77*	20	25	_____
[9767]	Gateway TCA Railbox Boxcar, *78 u*	—	25	_____
9768	B&M Boxcar, *76-77*	20	25	_____
[9768]	NETCA B&M Boxcar, *76 u*	25	30	_____
9769	B&LE Boxcar, *76-77*	15	20	_____
9770	Northern Pacific Boxcar, *76-77*	15	20	_____
9771	Norfolk & Western Boxcar, *76-77*	15	20	_____
[9771]	LCCA N&W Boxcar, *77 u*		NRS	_____
[9771]	TCA Museum N&W Boxcar, *77 u*	30	40	_____
[9771]	WB&A TCA N&W Boxcar, *78 u*	—	30	_____
9772	Great Northern Boxcar, *76*	75	85	_____
9773	NYC Stock Car, *76*	25	35	_____
9774	TCA Southern Belle Boxcar, *75 u*	30	50	_____
9775	M&St L Boxcar, *76 (SSS)*	25	35	_____
9776	Southern Pacific "Overnight" Boxcar, *76 (SSS)*	50	65	_____
9777	Virginian Boxcar, *76-77*	20	30	_____
9778	Season's Greetings Boxcar, *75 u*	150	200	_____
9779	TCA Philadelphia Boxcar, *76 u*	35	50	_____
9780	Johnny Cash Boxcar, *76 u*	35	45	_____
9781	Delaware & Hudson Boxcar, *77-78*	20	25	_____
9782	Rock Island Boxcar, *77-78*	20	25	_____
9783	B&O "Timesaver" Boxcar, *77-78*	40	50	_____
[9783]	WB&A TCA B&O "Timesaver" Boxcar, *77 u*	—	30	_____
9784	Santa Fe Boxcar, *77-78*	25	35	_____
9785	Conrail Boxcar, *77-78*	20	25	_____

MPC MODERN ERA (1970-1986)	Exc	New	Cond/$
[9785] TCA Museum Conrail Boxcar, *77 u*		NRS	_____
[9785] NETCA Conrail Boxcar, *78 u*	25	30	_____
[9785] Sacramento-Sierra TCA Conrail Boxcar, *78 u*	—	45	_____
9786 C&NW Boxcar, *77-79*	20	35	_____
[9786] TCA Museum C&NW Boxcar, *79 u*		NRS	_____
9787 Jersey Central Boxcar, *77-79*	20	30	_____
9788 Lehigh Valley Boxcar, *77-79*	15	20	_____
[9788] Atlantic TCA Lehigh Valley Boxcar, *78 u*	20	25	_____
9789 Pickens Boxcar, *77*	30	50	_____
9801 B&O "Sentinel" Boxcar (Std. O), *73-75*	50	75	_____
9802 Miller High Life Reefer (Std. O), *73-75*	45	60	_____
9803 Johnson's Wax Boxcar (Std. O), *73-75*	45	60	_____
9805 Grand Trunk Reefer (Std. O), *73-75*	45	60	_____
9806 Rock Island Boxcar (Std. O), *74-75*	100	125	_____
9807 Stroh's Beer Reefer (Std. O), *74-76*	100	150	_____
9808 Union Pacific Boxcar (Std. O), *75-76*	100	125	_____
9809 Clark Reefer (Std. O), *75-76*	45	60	_____
9811 Pacific Fruit Express Reefer (FARR #2), *80*	30	45	_____
9812 Arm & Hammer Reefer, *80*	20	25	_____
9813 Ruffles Reefer, *80*	20	25	_____
9814 Perrier Reefer, *80*	25	35	_____
9815 NYC Reefer (Std. O), *84-85*	75	95	_____
9816 Brach's Candy Reefer, *80*	20	25	_____
9817 Bazooka Gum Reefer, *80*	20	25	_____
9818 Western Maryland Reefer, *80*	30	40	_____
9819 Western Fruit Express Reefer (FARR #3), *81*	30	40	_____
9820 Wabash Gondola w/ coal load (Std. O), *73-74*	50	60	_____
9821 Southern Pacific Gondola w/ coal load (Std. O), *73-75*	50	60	_____
9822 Grand Trunk Gondola w/ coal load (Std. O), *74-75*	50	60	_____
9823 Santa Fe Flatcar w/ crates (Std. O), *75-76*	100	125	_____
9824 NYC Gondola w/ coal load (Std. O), *75-76*	75	100	_____
9825 Schaefer Reefer (Std. O), *76-77*	75	95	_____
9826 P&LE Boxcar (Std. O), *76-77*	100	125	_____
9827 Cutty Sark Reefer, *84*	25	30	_____
9828 J&B Reefer, *84*	25	30	_____
9829 Dewars Reefer, *84*	25	30	_____
9830 Johnny Walker Red Label Reefer, *84*	25	30	_____

MPC MODERN ERA (1970-1986)		Exc	New	Cond/$
9831	Pepsi Cola Reefer, *82*	50	65	_____
9832	Cheerios Reefer, *82*	100	125	_____
9833	Vlasic Pickles Reefer, *82*	20	25	_____
9834	Southern Comfort Reefer, *83-84*	20	30	_____
9835	Jim Beam Reefer, *83-84*	20	30	_____
9836	Old Grand-Dad Reefer, *83-84*	20	30	_____
9837	Wild Turkey Reefer, *83-84*	20	30	_____
9840	Fleischmann's Gin Reefer, *85*	25	30	_____
9841	Calvert Gin Reefer, *85*	25	30	_____
9842	Seagram's Gin Reefer, *85*	25	30	_____
9843	Tanqueray Gin Reefer, *85*	25	30	_____
9844	Sambuca Reefer, *86*	20	25	_____
9845	Bailey's Irish Cream Reefer, *86*	25	30	_____
9846	Seagrams Vodka Reefer, *86*	20	25	_____
9847	Wolfschmidt Vodka Reefer, *86*	20	25	_____
9849	Lionel Lines Reefer, *83 u*	60	75	_____
9850	Budweiser Reefer, *72 u, 73-75*	30	40	_____
9851	Schlitz Reefer, *72 u, 73-75*	25	30	_____
9852	Miller Reefer, *72 u, 73-77*	25	30	_____
9853	Cracker Jack Reefer, caramel, *72 u, 73-75*	30	35	_____
9853	Cracker Jack Reefer, white, *72 u, 73-75*	15	20	_____
9854	Baby Ruth Reefer, *72 u, 73-76*	15	20	_____
9855	Swift Reefer, *72 u, 73-77*	20	30	_____
9856	Old Milwaukee Reefer, *75-76*	20	30	_____
9858	Butterfinger Reefer, *73 u, 74-76*	25	35	_____
9859	Pabst Reefer, *73 u, 74-75*	25	35	_____
9860	Gold Medal Reefer, *73 u, 74-76*	20	25	_____
9861	Tropicana Reefer, *75-77*	35	40	_____
9862	Hamm's Reefer, *75-76*	25	30	_____
9863	REA Reefer, *74 (SSS), 75-76*	30	40	_____
9864	TCA Seattle Reefer, *74 u*	35	45	_____
9866	Coors Reefer, *76-77*	30	40	_____
9867	Hershey's Reefer, *76-77*	40	50	_____
9868	TTOS Oklahoma City Reefer, *80 u*	40	50	_____
9869	Santa Fe Reefer, *76 (SSS)*	40	50	_____
9870	Old Dutch Cleanser Reefer, *77-78, 80*	15	20	_____
9871	Carling's Black Label Reefer, *77-78, 80*	30	35	_____
9872	Pacific Fruit Express Reefer, *77-79*	25	35	_____
[9872]	Midwest TCA PFE Reefer, *79 u*		NRS	_____

		Exc	New	Cond/$
9873	Ralston-Purina Reefer, *78*	30	45	_____
9874	Miller Lite Beer Reefer, *78-79*	30	40	_____
9875	A&P Reefer, *78-79*	25	35	_____
9876	Central Vermont Reefer, *78*	40	50	_____
9877	Gerber Reefer, *79-80*	60	75	_____
9878	Good and Plenty Reefer, *79*	20	25	_____
9879	Hills Brothers Reefer, *79-80*	20	25	_____
9879	Kraft Reefer, *79 u*		NM	
9880	Santa Fe Reefer (FARR #1), *79*	40	50	_____
9881	Rath Packing Reefer, *79 u*	35	45	_____
9882	NYC "Early Bird" Reefer, *79*	35	45	_____
9883	Nabisco Oreo Reefer, *79*	60	75	_____
[9883]	TTOS Phoenix Reefer, *83 u*		NRS	_____
9884	Fritos Reefer, *81-82*	20	25	_____
9885	Lipton Tea Reefer, *81-82*	20	25	_____
9886	Mounds Reefer, *81-82*	20	25	_____
9887	Fruit Growers Express Reefer (FARR #4), *83*	45	60	_____
9888	Green Bay & Western Reefer, *83*	60	75	_____
16800	Lionel Railroader Club Ore Car, *86 u*	80	100	_____
[80948]	LOTS Michigan Central Boxcar, *82 u*	100	175	_____
[86009]	LCAC CN Bunk Car, *86 u*	—	130	_____
97330	(See 9733)			
100408	(See 6567)			
[121315]	LOTS PRR Hi-cube Boxcar, *84 u*	75	100	_____
[830005]	LCAC CN Boxcar, *83 u*		NRS	_____
[840006]	LCAC Canadian Wheat Board Covered Quad Hopper, *84 u*	—	160	_____
79C95204C	Sears Santa Fe Diesel set, *71 u*		NRS	_____
79C97101C	Sears 5-unit set, *71 u*		NRS	_____
79C9715C	Sears 4-unit set, *75 u*		NRS	_____
79C9717C	Sears 7-unit set, *75 u*		NRS	_____
79N9552C	Sears 6-unit set, *72 u*		NRS	_____
79N9553C	Sears 6-unit Diesel set, *72 u*		NRS	_____
79N95223C	Sears 6-unit set, *74 u*		NRS	_____
79N96178C	Sears 4-unit set, *74 u*		NRS	_____
79N97082C	Sears set, *70 u*		NRS	_____
79N97101C	Sears 5-unit set, *75 u*		NRS	_____
79N98765C	Sears Logging Empire set, *78 u*		NRS	_____
UCS	Remote Control Track (O), *70*	5	8	_____

MPC MODERN ERA (1970-1986)	Exc	New	Cond/$
No Number B&A Hudson & Standard O cars set, *86 u*	1900	2200	_____
No Number The Blue Comet set, *78-80, 87 u*	700	800	_____
No Number Burlington "Texas Zephyr" set, *80, 80 u*	1300	1500	_____
No Number Jersey Central set, *86*	425	500	_____
No Number Chessie System Special set, *80, 86 u*	750	950	_____
No Number Chicago & Alton Limited, *81, 86 u*	750	950	_____
No Number Favorite Food Freight set, *81-82*	275	325	_____
No Number The General set, *77-80*	275	300	_____
No Number Great Northern set (FARR #3), *81, 81 u*	800	900	_____
No Number Illinois Central "City of New Orleans" set, *85, 87, 93*	1300	1500	_____
No Number Joshua Lionel Cowen set, *80, 80 u, 82*	700	750	_____
No Number Lionel Lines set, *82-84 u, 86, 86-87 u, 94*	650	800	_____
No Number Mickey Mouse Express set, *77-78, 78 u*	1700	2000	_____
No Number The Mint set, *79 u, 80-83, 84 u, 86 u, 87, 91 u, 93*	1200	1400	_____
No Number NYC "20th Century Limited" set, *83, 83 u*	1300	1500	_____
No Number N&W "Powhattan Arrow" set, *81, 81 u, 82 u, 91 u*	2000	2400	_____
No Number PRR set, *79-80, 79-80 u, 81 u, 83 u*	1500	1700	_____
No Number PRR set (FARR #5), *84-85, 89 u*	750	900	_____
No Number Rock Island & Peoria set, *80-82*	250	325	_____
No Number Santa Fe set (FARR #1), *79, 79 u*	600	750	_____
No Number Southern set (FARR #4), *83, 83 u*	850	1000	_____
No Number Southern Crescent set, *77-78, 87 u*	600	700	_____
No Number Southern Pacific Daylight Diesel set, *82-83, 82-83 u, 90 u*	2800	3000	_____
No Number The Spirit of '76 set, *74-76*	625	700	_____
No Number Toys 'R Us Thunderball Freight set, *75 u*	—	NRS	_____
No Number Union Pacific set (FARR #2), *80, 80 u*	700	800	_____
No Number Union Pacific "Overland Route" set, *84, 92 u*	1000	1400	_____
No Number Wabash set (FF #1), *86, 87*	1000	1200	_____
No Number L.A.S.E.R. Playmat, *81-82*	—	10	_____
No Number Cannonball Freight Playmat, *81-82*	—	10	_____
No Number Station Platform, *83-84*	—	10	_____
No Number Rocky Mountain Platform, *83-84*	—	10	_____
No Number Commando Assault Train Playmat, *83-84*	—	10	_____
No Number Black Cave Flyer Playmat, *82*	—	10	_____

	Exc	New	Cond/$
[No Number] Pacific Northwest TCA F-3 AA, shells only, *74 u*	—	75	____
[No Number] LCCA Lionel Lines Tender only, *76-77 u*	25	30	____
[No Number] Lone Star TCA Texas Special F-3 A Unit, shell only, *81 u*		NRS	____
[No Number] Lone Star TCA Texas Special F-3 B Unit, shell only, *82 u*		NRS	____
[No Number] Sacramento-Sierra TCA Lionel Lines Tender, shell only, *84 u*		NRS	____
[No Number] Atlantic TCA Pennsylvania Reading Seashore Bunk Car, *85 u*	65	80	____

4	(See 18008, 18013)
6	(See 18023)
12	(See 52029)
14	(See 52032)
36	(See 19042)
40	(See 11737)
52	(See 18823)
65-00637	(See 18927)
74	(See 19718)
91	(See 18558)
102	(See 19538)
0121	(See 19717)
125	(See 19724)
150	(See 18817, 18553)
190	(See 17899)
200	(See 18117)
200A	(See 18121)
D200	(See 18512)
D202	(See 18506)
D203	(See 18506)
211	(See 19136)
C217	(See 19715)
D250	(See 18512)
254	(See 18920)
260	(See 19133)
300	(See 17307)
C300	(See 19719)
301	(See 16807, 17308)
351C	(See 11724)
366A	(See 11724)
370B	(See 11724)
371B	(See 18108)
371	(See 18907)
400	(See 18505)

LTI MODERN ERA (1987-1995)

401	(See 18505)
425	(See 19135)
469	(See 19132)
483	(See 18306)
484	(See 18310)
485	(See 18310)
501	(See 17213)
504	(See 18504)
507	(See 19128)
539	(See 16539)
576	(See 19108)
600	(See 18824)
601	(See 19111)
612	(See 18040)
638	(See 18638)
672	(See 8610)
721	(See 18554)
725A	(See 11734)
725B	(See 11734)
736A	(See 11734)
785	(See 18002)
789	(See 19134)
858	(See 18116)
859	(See 18116)
863	(See 18309)
901	(See 19532)
907	(See 18024, 18025)
914	(See 17893)
1017	(See 18921)
1041	(See 16538)
1115	(See 19040)
1116	(See 19041)
1192	(See 19120)
1200	(See 19116)
1201	(See 18022)
1212	(See 19118)
1240	(See 19117)
1289	(See 17875)
1322	(See 19119)

		Exc	New	Cond/$
1458	(See 52031)			
1501	(See 18003)			
1538	(See 18838)			
1552	(See 52007)			
(1602)	Nickel Plate Special set, *86-91*	175	200	_____
(1615)	Cannonball Express set, *86-90*	85	95	_____
(1685)	True Value Freight Flyer set, *86-87 u*		NRS	_____
(1687)	Freight Flyer set, *87-90*	50	60	_____
1752	(See 52035)			
1754	(See 52037)			
1815	(See 18815)			
1818	(See 18931)			
1900	(See 18502)			
1921	(See 52047)			
1947	(See 18830)			
1952	(See 19960)			
1987	(See 16205, 16310, 16311, 16507, 18605)			
[1988]	Midwest TCA IC Boxcar, *88 u*		NRS	_____
1989	(See 16110, 17879, 18614)			
1990	(See 18090, 19708)			
1992	(See 18818)			
1993	(See 16655, 18713, 19927)			
1993X	(See 52008)			
2000	(See 18710, 18711, 18712, 19131)			
2100	(See 18006)			
2101	(See 18011, 18557)			
2110	Graduated Trestle set (22), *70-88*	10	15	_____
2111	Elevated Trestle set (10), *70-88*	10	15	_____
(2113)	Tunnel Portals (2), *84-87*	10	15	_____
(2115)	Dwarf Signal, *84-87*	13	15	_____
(2117)	Block Target Signal, *84-87*	20	25	_____
(2122)	Extension Bridge w/ rock piers, *76-87*	30	40	_____
2126	Whistling Freight Shed, *76-87*	25	30	_____
2127	Diesel Horn Shed, *76-87*	25	30	_____
2154	Automatic Highway Flasher, *70-87*	20	25	_____
2162	Automatic Crossing Gate and Signal, *70-87, 94*		CP	_____
(2170)	Street Lamps (3), *70-87*	15	20	_____
(2180)	Road Signs (16), *77-94*		CP	_____
(2181)	Telephone Poles (10), *77-94*		CP	_____

		Exc	New	Cond/$
2184	(See 17218)			
(2214)	Girder Bridge, *70-71, 72 u, 73-87*	5	10	_____
2283	Die-cast Bumpers (2), *84-94*		CP	_____
2292	Station Platform, *85-87*	6	10	_____
(2300)	Operating Oil Drum Loader, *83-87*	100	150	_____
(2309)	Mechanical Crossing Gate, *82-92*	4	8	_____
(2311)	Mechanical Semaphore, *82-92*	4	8	_____
2320	Flagpole kit, *83-87*	10	15	_____
2321	Operating Sawmill, *84, 86-87*	85	125	_____
2323	Operating Freight Station, *84-87*	80	100	_____
2324	Operating Switch Tower, *84-87*	70	85	_____
2400	(See 18305)			
2401	(See 18304)			
2402	(See 18304)			
2403	(See 18305)			
2487	(See 18833)			
2601	(See 52023)			
2626	(See 18016)			
(2709)	Rico Station kit, *81-94*		CP	_____
(2716)	Short Extension Bridge, *88-94*		CP	_____
(2717)	Short Extension Bridge, *77-87*	3	5	_____
(2719)	Watchman's Shanty kit, *77-87*	3	5	_____
(2720)	Lumber Shed kit, *77-84, 87*	3	5	_____
(2784)	Freight Platform kit, *81-90*	6	9	_____
2848	(See 12848)			
(2900)	Lockon, *70-94*		CP	_____
(2901)	Track Clips (12), *71-94*		CP	_____
2903	(See 18630)			
(2905)	Lockon and Wire, *74-94*		CP	_____
2909	Smoke Fluid, *70-94*		CP	_____
2910	OTC Contactor, *84-86, 88*	4	0	_____
(2927)	Maintenance kit, *70, 78-94*	5	7	_____
2956	(See 19721)			
(2985)	The Lionel Train Book, *86-94*	10	12	_____
3000	(See 18009, 33000)			
3004	(See 33004)			
3005	(See 33005)			
3158	(See 18034)			
3285	(See 16805)			

		Exc	New	Cond/$
3400	(See 19109)			
3500	(See 19110)			
4000	(See 18812, 18825)			
4002	(See 18211)			
4004	(See 18218)			
4023	(See 52030)			
4060	Power Master Transformer, *80-93*	15	25	_____
4060	(See 18831)			
4100	(See 18030)			
4124	(See 18514)			
4136	(See 18819)			
4410	(See 18007)			
4501	(See 18018)			
4574	(See 18306)			
4600	(See 18816)			
4690	MW Transformer, *86-89*	75	95	_____
4851	DC Transformer, *85-91, 94*	3	4	_____
4866	(See 18308)			
(5012)	Curved Track 27", card of 4 (O27), *70-94*		CP	_____
(5014)	Half-Curved Track 27" (O27), *70-94*		CP	_____
(5016)	36" Straight Track (O27), *87-88*	2	3	_____
(5017)	Straight Track, card of 4 (O27), *70-94*		CP	_____
(5019)	Half-Straight Track (O27), *70-94*		CP	_____
5020	90° Crossover (O27), *70-94*		CP	_____
(5021)	Left Manual Switch 27" (O27), *70-94*		CP	_____
(5022)	Right Manual Switch 27" (O27), *70-94*		CP	_____
5023	45° Crossover (O27), *70-94*		CP	_____
(5024)	35" Straight Track (O27), *88-94*		CP	_____
(5033)	Curved Track 27" (O27), *79-94*		CP	_____
(5038)	Straight Track (O27), *79-94*		CP	_____
(5041)	Insulator Pins (12) (O27), *70-94*		CP	_____
(5042)	Steel Pins (12) (O27), *70-94*		CP	_____
(5044)	Curved Track Ballast 42" (O27), *88*		NM	
(5045)	Curved Track Ballast 54" (O27), *87-88*	1	2	_____
(5046)	Curved Track Ballast 27" O27), *87-88*	1	2	_____
(5047)	Straight Track Ballast (O27), *87-88*	1	2	_____
(5049)	Curved Track 42" (O27), *88-94*		CP	_____
5100	(See 18001)			
(5113)	Curved Track 54" (O27), *79-94*		CP	_____

		Exc	New	Cond/$
5121	Left Remote Switch 27" (027), *70-94*		CP	_____
5122	Right Remote Switch 27" (027), *70-94*		CP	_____
5132	Right Remote Switch 31" (0), *80-94*		CP	_____
5133	Left Remote Switch 31" (0), *80-94*		CP	_____
(5149)	Remote Uncoupling Section (027), *70-94*		CP	_____
5165	Right Remote Switch 72" (0), *87-94*		CP	_____
5166	Left Remote Switch 72" (0), *87-94*		CP	_____
5167	Right Remote Switch 42" (027), *88-94*		CP	_____
5168	Left Remote Switch 42" (027), *88-94*		CP	_____
5300	(See 18636)			
5340	(See 18005, 18012)			
5454	(See 18026, 18027)			
(5500)	Straight Track (0), *71-94*		CP	_____
5500	(See 18216)			
(5501)	Curved Track 31" (0), *71-94*		CP	_____
(5504)	Half-Curved Track 31" (0), *83-94*		CP	_____
(5505)	Half-Straight Track (0), *83-94*		CP	_____
(5522)	36" Straight Track (0), *87-88*	3	4	_____
(5523)	40" Straight Track (0), *88-94*		CP	_____
5530	Remote Uncoupling Section (0), *81-94*		CP	_____
5540	90° Crossover (0), *81-94*		CP	_____
(5543)	Insulator Pins (12) (0), *70-94*		CP	_____
5545	45° Crossover (0), *83-94*		CP	_____
(5551)	Steel Pins (12) (0), *70-94*		CP	_____
(5554)	Curved Track 54" (0), *90-94*		CP	_____
(5560)	Curved Track Ballast 72" (0), *87-88*	1	2	_____
(5561)	Curved Track Ballast 31" (0), *87-88*	1	2	_____
(5562)	Straight Track Ballast (0), *87-88*	1	2	_____
(5572)	Curved Track 72" (0), *79-94*		CP	_____
5658	(See 16559)			
[5731]	TCA Museum L&N Reefer, *90 u*	100	150	_____
5800	(See 18836)			
5808	(See 18826)			
6001	(See 18107)			
6002	(See 18107)			
6005	(See 18821)			
6006	(See 18210)			
6007	(See 18217)			
6061	(See 16061)			

		Exc	New	Cond/$
6062	(See 16062)			
6063	(See 16063)			
6064	(See 16064)			
6065	(See 16065)			
6066	(See 16066)			
6067	(See 16067)			
6068	(See 16068)			
6069	(See 16069)			
6070	(See 16070)			
6071	(See 16071)			
6072	(See 16072)			
6073	(See 16073)			
6074	(See 16074)			
6080	(See 16080)			
6081	(See 16081)			
6082	(See 16082)			
6083	(See 16083)			
6086	(See 16086)			
6087	(See 16087)			
6088	(See 16088)			
6089	(See 16089)			
6090	(See 16090)			
6108	(See 16108)			
6137	NKP Hopper (O27), *86-91*	15	20	_____
6150	Santa Fe Hopper (O27), *85-86, 92 u*	15	20	_____
6177	Reading Hopper (O27), *86-90*	20	25	_____
6200	(See 18010)			
6226	(See 16226)			
6254	NKP Gondola w/ canisters, *86-91*	10	12	_____
6258	Santa Fe Gondola w/ canisters (O27), *85-86, 92 u*	—	6	_____
6336	(See 16336)			
6408	(See 16408)			
6430	Santa Fe SP Caboose, *83-89*	6	8	_____
6464	(See 19248, 19249, 19250, 19258, 19269)			
6464-100	(See 19259, 19260)			
6464-125	(See 19267)			
6464-150	(See 19268)			
6464-1895	(See 52058)			
6464-1993	(See 52009)			

LTI MODERN ERA (1987-1995)

		Exc	New	Cond/$
6493	L&C B/W Caboose, *86-87*	25	45	_____
6508	(See 16508)			
6528	(See 16528)			
6576	Santa Fe Flatcar w/ fences (O27), *92 u*	8	12	_____
6585	PRR Flatcar w/ fences (O27), *86-90*	5	10	_____
6602	(See 16053)			
6603	(See 16054)			
6609	(See 16079)			
6616	(See 16052, 16077)			
6620	(See 16050, 16075)			
6630	(See 16051, 16076)			
6919	Nickel Plate Road SP Caboose, *86-91*	5	10	_____
6921	PRR SP Caboose, *86-90*	5	10	_____
7000	(See 51301)			
7200	(See 19415)			
7220	Illinois Central Baggage Car, *85, 87*	100	125	_____
7221	Illinois Central Combination Car, *85, 87*	100	125	_____
7222	Illinois Central Passenger Car, *85, 87*	100	125	_____
7223	Illinois Central Passenger Car, *85, 87*	100	125	_____
7224	Illinois Central Dining Car, *85, 87*	100	125	_____
7225	Illinois Central Observation Car, *85, 87*	100	125	_____
7227	Wabash Dining Car (FF #1), *86-87*	100	125	_____
7228	Wabash Baggage Car (FF #1), *86-87*	100	125	_____
7229	Wabash Combination Car (FF #1), *86-87*	100	125	_____
7230	Wabash Passenger Car (FF #1), *86-87*	100	125	_____
7231	Wabash Passenger Car (FF #1), *86-87*	100	125	_____
7232	Wabash Observation Car (FF #1), *86-87*	100	125	_____
7420	(See 18513)			
7500	(See 18214)			
7613	(See 17613)			
7643	(See 18215)			
7805	(See 16078)			
7890	(See 17303)			
7914	Toys 'R Us Giraffe Car, *85-89 u*	75	100	_____
7925	Erie-Lackawanna Boxcar (O27), *86-90*	8	12	_____
7926	NKP Boxcar (O27), *86-91*	8	11	_____
7930	True Value Boxcar (O27), *86-87 u*	40	60	_____
7932	Kay Bee Toys Boxcar (O27), *86-87 u*	40	50	_____
8004	(See 18004)			

		Exc	New	Cond/$
8014	(See 18014)			
8100	(See 11711)			
8101	(See 11711)			
8102	(See 11711)			
8103	(See 18103)			
8119	(See 18119/18120)			
8120	(See 18119/18120)			
8124	(See 51300)			
8200	(See 18200)			
8201	(See 18201)			
8203	(See 18203)			
8204	(See 18204)			
8206	(See 18206)			
8209	(See 18209)			
8212	(See 18212)			
8213	D&RGW 2-4-2, *82-83, 84-91 u*	60	70	_____
8223	(See 18835)			
8300	(See 18300)			
8301	(See 18301)			
8302	(See 18302)			
8303	(See 18303)			
8311	(See 18311)			
[8389]	NLOE Long Island Boxcar, *89 u*		NRS	_____
[8390]	NLOE Long Island Covered Quad Hopper, *90 u*		NRS	_____
[8391A]	NLOE Long Island Bunk Car, *91 u*		NRS	_____
[8391B]	NLOE Long Island Tool Car, *91 u*		NRS	_____
8392	(See 17893)			
8393	(See 52019, 52020)			
8394	(See 52026)			
8400	(See 18400)			
8404	(See 18404)			
8419	(See 18419)			
8446	(See 18832)			
8459	(See 18202)			
8500	(See 18500, 18550)			
8501	(See 18219, 18501)			
8502	(See 18220)			
8503	(See 18503)			

		Exc	New	Cond/$
8578	NYC Ballast Tamper, *85, 87*	120	150	_____
8580/8582	Illinois Central F-3 AA set, *85, 87*	400	450	_____
8581	Illinois Central F-3 B Unit, *85, 87*	175	200	_____
8586	(See 18208)			
8600	(See 18600)			
8601	(See 18601)			
8602	(See 18602)			
8604	(See 18604)			
8606	(See 18606)			
8607	(See 18607)			
8608	(See 18608)			
8609	(See 18609)			
8610	(See 18610)			
(8610)	Wabash 4-6-2 "672" (FF #1), *86-87*	500	600	_____
8611	(See 18611)			
8612	(See 18612)			
8613	(See 18613)			
8615	(See 18615)			
8616	(See 18616)			
8617	Nickel Plate Road 4-4-2, *86-91*	65	75	_____
8618	(See 18618)			
8620	(See 18620)			
8621	(See 18621)			
8622	(See 18622)			
8623	(See 18623)			
8625	Pennsylvania 2-4-0, *86-90*	25	40	_____
8625	(See 18625, 18635)			
8626	(See 18626)			
8627	(See 18627)			
8628	(See 18628)			
8632	(See 18632)			
8633	(See 18627, 18633, 18637)			
8641	(See 18641)			
8688	(See 18213)			
8689	(See 18207)			
8699	(See 18307)			
8700	(See 18700)			
8702	(See 18702)			
8704	(See 18704)			

		Exc	New	Cond/$
8705	(See 18705)			
8706	(See 18706)			
8707	(See 18707)			
8716	(See 18716)			
8800	(See 18800)			
8801	(See 18801)			
8802	(See 18802)			
8803	(See 18803)			
8804	(See 18804)			
8805	(See 18805, 18890)			
8806	(See 18806)			
8807	(See 18807)			
8808	(See 18808)			
8809	(See 18809, 18551)			
8810	(See 18810)			
8811	(See 18811)			
8813	(See 18813, 18552)			
8814	(See 18814)			
8820	(See 18820)			
8827	(See 18827)			
8834	(See 18834)			
8837	(See 18837)			
8900	(See 18900)			
8901	(See 18901/18902)			
8902	ACL 2-4-0, *79-82, 86-90*	15	20	____
8902	(See 18901/18902)			
8903	(See 18903/18904)			
8904	(See 18903/18904)			
8906	(See 18906)			
8908	(See 18908/18909)			
8909	(See 18908/18909)			
8910	(See 18910)			
8911	(See 18911)			
[8912]	LCAC Canada Southern Operating Hopper, *89 u*	—	125	____
8912	(See 18912)			
8913	(See 18913)			
8915	(See 18915)			
8916	(See 18916)			
8918	(See 18918)			

		Exc	New	Cond/$
8919	(See 18919)			
8922	(See 18922)			
8923	(See 18923)			
8924	(See 18924)			
8925	(See 18925)			
8926	(See 18926)			
8977	(See 18000)			
9001	Conrail Boxcar (O27), *86-87 u, 88-90*	5	10	_____
9011	(See 19011)			
9015	(See 19015)			
9016	Chessie System Hopper (O27), *75-79, 87-88*	5	7	_____
9016	(See 19016)			
9017	(See 19017)			
9018	(See 19018)			
9019	(See 19019)			
9023	(See 19023)			
9024	(See 19024)			
9025	(See 19025)			
9026	(See 19026)			
9027	(See 19027)			
9031	NKP Gondola w/ canisters (O27), *73-75, 82-83, 84-91 u*	5	7	_____
9031	(See 19031)			
9032	(See 19032)			
9033	PC Gondola w/ canisters (O27), *76-78, 82, 86 u, 87-90*	3	4	_____
9033	(See 19033)			
9077	D&RGW SP Caboose, *76-83, 84-91 u*	6	8	_____
9100	(See 18205, 19100)			
9101	(See 19101)			
9102	(See 19102)			
9103	(See 19103)			
9104	(See 19104)			
9105	(See 19105)			
9106	(See 19106)			
9107	Dr. Pepper Vat Car, *86-87*	25	30	_____
9121	(See 19121)			
9129	(See 19129)			
9140	Burlington Gondola w/ canisters, *70, 73-82, 87-89*	6	8	_____

		Exc	New	Cond/$
9146	(See 19821)			
9215	(See 52004)			
9240	NYC Hopper (O27), *87 u*	20	25	_____
9312	(See 18905)			
9405	(See 19716)			
9706	(See 19706)			
9790	(See 19243)			
9791	(See 19244)			
10001	(See 19251)			
10131	(See 16541)			
(11700)	Conrail Limited set, *87*	550	650	_____
(11701)	Rail Blazer set, *87-88*	—	80	_____
(11702)	Black Diamond set, *87*	175	225	_____
(11703)	Iron Horse Freight set, *88-91*	135	140	_____
(11704)	Southern Freight Runner set, *87 (SSS)*	225	300	_____
(11705)	Chessie System Unit Train set, *88*	500	600	_____
(11706)	Dry Gulch Line set, *88 (SSS)*	225	300	_____
(11707)	Silver Spike set, *88-89*	275	300	_____
(11708)	Midnight Shift set, *88u, 89*	80	100	_____
(11710)	CP Rail Freight set, *89*	450	525	_____
(11711)	Santa Fe F-3 ABA set "8100", "8101", "8102", *91*	700	800	_____
(11712)	Great Lakes Express set, *90 (SSS)*	300	325	_____
(11713)	Santa Fe Dash 8-40B set, *90*	500	600	_____
(11714)	Badlands Express set, *90-91*	60	75	_____
(11715)	Lionel 90th Anniversary set, *90*	300	375	_____
(11716)	Lionelville Circus Special set, *90-91*	200	250	_____
(11717)	CSX Freight set, *90*	250	300	_____
(11718)	Norfolk Southern Dash 8-40C Unit Train set, *92*	600	650	_____
(11719)	Coastal Freight set, *91 (SSS)*	275	325	_____
(11720)	Santa Fe Special set, *91*	60	75	_____
(11721)	Mickey's World Tour Train set, *91, 92 u*	100	125	_____
(11722)	Girl's Train set, *91*	400	475	_____
(11723)	Amtrak Maintenance Train set, *91, 92 u*	275	300	_____
(11724)	Great Northern F-3 ABA set "366A", "370B", "351C", *92*	500	575	_____
(11726)	Erie-Lackawanna Freight set, *91 u*	250	300	_____
(11727)	Coastal Limited set, *92*	100	130	_____
(11728)	High Plains Runner set, *92*	150	165	_____

		Exc	New	Cond/$
(11729)	L&N Express set, *92*		NM	
11730	Evergreen Intermodal Container (See 12805)			
11731	Maersk Intermodal Container (See 12805)			
11732	American President Lines Intermodal Container (See 12805)			
(11733)	Feather River set, *92 (SSS)*	300	350	_____
(11734)	Erie Alco ABA set "725A", "725B", "736A" (FF #7), *93*	350	400	_____
(11735)	New York Central Flyer set, *93-94*		CP	_____
(11736)	Union Pacific Express set, *93-94*		CP	_____
(11737)	TCA F-3 ABA set "40", *93 u*	450	550	_____
(11738)	Soo Line set, *93 (SSS)*	300	350	_____
(11739)	Super Chief set, *93-94*		CP	_____
(11740)	Conrail Consolidated set, *93*	275	300	_____
(11741)	Northwest Express set, *93*	150	175	_____
(11742)	Coastal Limited set, *93 u*	100	125	_____
(11743)	Chesapeake & Ohio Freight set, *94*		CP	_____
(11744)	NYC Passenger/Freight set, *94 (SSS)*		CP	_____
(11745)	US Navy set, *94*		CP	_____
(11746)	Seaboard Freight set, *94*		CP	_____
(11750)	McDonald's Nickel Plate Special set, *87 u*		NRS	_____
(11751)	49C95171C Sears Pennsylvania Passenger set, *87 u*	150	200	_____
(11752)	JCPenney Timber Master set, *87 u*	100	150	_____
(11753)	Kay Bee Toys Rail Blazer set, *87 u*	100	125	_____
(11754)	Key America set, *87 u*		NRS	_____
(11755)	Timber Master set, *87 u*		NRS	_____
(11756)	Hawthorne Freight Flyer set, *87-88 u*	100	125	_____
(11757)	Chrysler Mopar Express set, *87 u*	250	300	_____
(11757)	Chrysler Mopar Express set, *88 u*	300	350	_____
(11758)	The Desert King set, *89 (SSS)*	250	300	_____
(11759)	JCPenney Silver Spike set, *88 u*		NRS	_____
(11761)	JCPenney Iron Horse Freight set, *88 u*		NRS	_____
(11761)	True Value Cannonball Express set, *88 u*	100	150	_____
(11762)	True Value Cannonball Express set, *89 u*	100	150	_____
(11763)	United Model Freight Hauler set, *88 u*		NRS	_____
(11704)	49N95178 Sears Iron Horse Freight set, *88 u*	200	250	_____
(11765)	Spiegel Silver Spike set, *88 u*		NRS	_____
(11767)	Shoprite Freight Flyer set, *88 u*	100	150	_____

		Exc	New	Cond/$
(11769)	JCPenney Midnight Shift set, *89 u*		NRS	_____
(11770)	49GY95280 Sears Circus set, *89 u*	200	225	_____
(11771)	K-Mart Microracers set, *89 u*	100	125	_____
(11772)	Macy's Freight Flyer set, *89 u*	150	200	_____
(11773)	49GY95281 Sears NYC Passenger set, *89 u*		NRS	_____
(11774)	Ace Hardware Cannonball Express set, *89 u*	150	175	_____
(11775)	Anheuser-Busch set, *89-92 u*	200	250	_____
(11776)	Pace Iron Horse Freight set, *89 u*	150	175	_____
(11777)	49N95265 Sears Lionelville Circus Special set, *90 u*	225	250	_____
(11778)	49N95264 Sears Badlands Express set, *90 u*	60	75	_____
(11779)	49N95267 Sears CSX Freight set, *90 u*	250	300	_____
(11780)	49N95266 Sears Northern Pacific Passenger set, *90 u*	200	250	_____
(11781)	True Value Cannonball Express set, *90 u*	100	150	_____
(11783)	Toys 'R Us Heavy Iron set, *90-91 u*	200	250	_____
(11784)	Pace Iron Horse Freight set, *90 u*	150	175	_____
(11785)	Costco Union Pacific Express set, *90 u*	175	200	_____
(11789)	Sears Illinois Central Passenger set, *91 u*	200	225	_____
(11793)	Santa Fe set w/ mailer, *91 u*	60	75	_____
(11794)	Mickey's World Tour set w/ mailer, *91 u*	100	125	_____
(11796)	Union Pacific Express set, *91 u*	175	200	_____
(11797)	Sears Coastal Limited set w/ mailer, *92 u*	100	130	_____
(11800)	Toys 'R Us Heavy Iron Thunder Limited set, *92-93 u*	250	300	_____
(11803)	Mall Promotion Nickel Plate Special set, *92 u*		NRS	_____
(11804)	K-Mart Coastal Limited set, *92 u*	100	130	_____
(11810)	Budweiser Modern Era set, *93-94 u*		CP	_____
(11811)	United Auto Workers set, *93 u*	175	225	_____
(11812)	Mall Promotion Coastal Limited set, *93 u*		NRS	_____
(11813)	Crayola Activity Train set, *94 u*		CP	_____
(11814)	Ford Limited Edition set, *94 u*		CP	_____
(11818)	Chrysler Mopar set, *94 u*		CP	_____
12000	(See 52000)			
12046	(See 52046)			
12700	Erie Magnetic Gantry Crane, *87*	175	200	_____
(12701)	Operating Fueling Station, *87*	100	125	_____
(12702)	Control Tower, *87*	80	100	_____
(12703)	Icing Station, *88-89*	80	100	_____

LTI MODERN ERA (1987-1995)

		Exc	New	Cond/$
(12704)	Dwarf Signal, *88-93*	15	20	_____
(12705)	Lumber Shed kit, *88-94*		CP	_____
(12706)	Barrel Loader Building kit, *87-94*		CP	_____
(12707)	Billboards (3), *87-94*		CP	_____
(12708)	Street Lamps (3), *88-93*	10	15	_____
(12709)	Banjo Signal, *87-91*	30	35	_____
(12710)	Engine House kit, *87-91*	25	30	_____
(12711)	Water Tower kit, *87-94*		CP	_____
(12712)	Automatic Ore Loader, *87-88*	25	40	_____
(12713)	Automatic Gateman, *87-88, 94*		CP	_____
(12714)	Automatic Crossing Gate, *87-91, 93-94*		CP	_____
(12715)	Illuminated Bumpers (2), *87-94*		CP	_____
(12716)	Searchlight Tower, *87-89, 91-92*	25	30	_____
(12717)	Non-Illuminated Bumpers (3), *87-94*		CP	_____
(12718)	Barrel Shed kit, *87-94*		CP	_____
(12719)	Animated Refreshment Stand, *88-89*	75	95	_____
12720	Rotary Beacon, *88-89*	40	50	_____
(12721)	Illuminated Extension Bridge w/ rock plers, *89*	30	45	_____
(12722)	Roadside Diner w/ smoke, *88-89*	40	60	_____
(12723)	Microwave Tower, *88-91, 94*		CP	_____
(12724)	Double Signal Bridge, *88-90*	45	60	_____
12725	Lionel Tractor & Trailer, *88-89*	15	20	_____
(12726)	Grain Elevator kit, *88-91, 94*		CP	_____
(12727)	Automatic Operating Semaphore, *89-94*		CP	_____
(12728)	Illuminated Freight Station, *89*	30	40	_____
(12729)	Mail Pick-up set, *88-91*	20	25	_____
(12730)	Girder Bridge, *88-94*		CP	_____
(12731)	Station Platform, *88-94*		CP	_____
(12732)	Coal Bag, *88-94*		CP	_____
(12733)	Watchman Shanty kit, *88-94*		CP	_____
(12734)	Passenger/Freight Station, *89-94*		CP	_____
(12735)	Diesel Horn Shed, *88-91*	30	35	_____
(12736)	Coaling Station kit, *88-91*	20	30	_____
(12737)	Whistling Freight Shed, *88-94*		CP	_____
(12739)	Lionel Gas Company Tractor and Tanker, *89*	15	20	_____
(12740)	Log Package (3), *88-92, 94*		CP	_____
12741	Union Pacific Intermodal Crane, *89*	210	240	_____
(12742)	Gooseneck Street Lamps (2), *89-94*		CP	_____
(12743)	Track Clips (12) (O), *89-94*		CP	_____

		Exc	New	Cond/$
(12744)	Rock Piers (2), *89-92, 94*		CP	____
(12745)	Barrel Pack (6), *89-94*		CP	____
(12746)	Operating/Uncoupling Track (O27), *89-94*		CP	____
(12748)	Illuminated Station Platform, *89-94*		CP	____
(12749)	Rotary Radar Antenna, *89-92*	25	35	____
(12750)	Crane kit, *89-91*	8	10	____
(12751)	Shovel kit, *89-91*	8	10	____
(12752)	History of Lionel Trains videotape (VHS), *89-92, 94*		CP	____
(12753)	Ore Load (2), *89-91*	2	4	____
(12754)	Graduated Trestle set (22), *89-94*		CP	____
(12755)	Elevated Trestle set (10), *89-94*		CP	____
(12756)	The Making of the Scale Hudson			____
	videotape (VHS), *91-94*		CP	
(12759)	Floodlight Tower, *90-94*		CP	____
(12760)	Automatic Highway Flasher, *90-91*	35	40	____
(12761)	Animated Billboard, *90-91, 93*	30	35	____
(12762)	Freight Station			
	w/ train control and sounds, *90-91*		NM	
(12763)	Single Signal Bridge, *90-91, 93*	30	35	____
(12765)	Die-cast Auto Assortment (6), *90*		NM	____
(12767)	Steam Clean and Wheel Grind Shop, *92-93*	250	300	
(12768)	Burning Switch Tower, *90, 93*	100	125	____
(12770)	Arch-Under Bridge, *90-94*		CP	____
(12771)	Mom's Roadside Diner w/ smoke, *90-91*	40	60	____
(12772)	Illuminated Extension Bridge w/ rock piers, *90-94*		CP	____
(12773)	Freight Platform kit, *90-94*		CP	____
(12774)	Lumber Loader kit, *90-94*		CP	____
12777	Chevron Tractor and Tanker, *90-91*	10	15	____
12778	Conrail Tractor and Trailer, *90*	10	15	____
12779	Lionelville Grain Company			
	Tractor and Trailer, *90*	10	15	____
(12780)	RS-1 50 Watt Transformer, *90-93*	100	150	____
12781	N&W Intermodal Crane, *90-91*	210	225	____
(12782)	Lift Bridge, *91-92*	400	500	____
12783	Monon Tractor and Trailer, *91*	15	20	____
(12784)	Intermodal Containers (3), *91*	15	20	____
12785	Lionel Gravel Company Tractor and Trailer, *91*	10	15	____
12786	Lionel Steel Company Tractor and Trailer, *91*	10	15	____
12787	Family Lines Intermodal Container (See 12784)			

		Exc	New	Cond/$
12788	UP Intermodal Container (See 12784)			
12789	B&M Intermodal Container (See 12784)			
(12790)	ZW-II Transformer, *91*		NM	
(12791)	Animated Passenger Station, *91*	75	90	____
(12794)	Lionel Tractor, *91*	10	15	____
(12795)	Cable Reels (2), *91-94*		CP	____
(12797)	Crossing Gate and Signal, *91*		NM	
(12798)	Forklift Loader Station, *92-94*		CP	____
(12800)	Scale Hudson Replacement Pilot Truck, *91 u*	15	20	____
(12802)	"Chat & Chew" Roadside Diner			
	w/ smoke and lights, *92-94*		CP	____
(12804)	Highway Lights (4), *92-94*		CP	____
(12805)	Intermodal Containers (3), *92*	10	15	____
12806	Lionel Lumber Company Tractor and Trailer, *92*	10	15	____
(12807)	Little Caesars Tractor and Trailer, *92*	10	15	____
12808	Mobil Tractor and Tanker, *92*	10	15	____
(12809)	Animated Billboard, *92-93*	30	35	____
(12810)	American Flyer Tractor and Trailer			
	"DX26925", *94*		CP	____
12811	Alka Seltzer Tractor and Trailer, *92*	10	15	____
(12812)	Illuminated Freight Station, *93-94*		CP	____
(12818)	Animated Freight Station, *92, 94*		CP	____
12819	Inland Steel Tractor and Trailer, *92*	10	15	____
(12821)	Lionel Catalog Videotape (VHS), *92*	15	20	____
(12826)	Intermodal Containers (3), *93*	10	15	____
(12827)	CSX Intermodal Container "610584" (See 12826)			
(12828)	NYC Intermodal Container (See 12826)			
(12829)	Great Northern Container (See 12826)			
12831	Rotary Beacon, *93-94*		CP	____
(12832)	Block Target Signal, *93-94*		CP	____
(12833)	RoadRailer Tractor and Trailer, *93*	10	15	____
12834	Pennsylvania Gantry Crane, *93*	135	150	____
(12835)	Operating Fueling Station, *93*	80	100	____
12836	Santa Fe Quantum Tractor and Trailer, *93*	10	15	____
(12837)	Humble Oil Tractor and Tanker, *93*	10	15	____
(12838)	Crate Load, *93-94*		CP	____
(12839)	Grade Crossing (2), *93-94*		CP	____
(12840)	Insulated Straight Track (O), *93-94*		CP	____
(12841)	Insulated Straight Track (O27), *93-94*		CP	____

		Exc	New	Cond/$
(12842)	Dunkin' Donuts Tractor and Trailer, *92 u*	30	40	_____
(12843)	Die-cast Metal Sprung Trucks (2), *93-94*		CP	_____
(12844)	Coil Covers (2) (O), *93-94*		CP	_____
(12847)	Icing Station, *94*		CP	_____
(12848)	Operating Oil Derrick "2848", *94*		CP	_____
(12849)	Lionel Transformer w/ wall pack, *94*		CP	_____
(12852)	Trailer Frame, *94*		CP	_____
(12853)	Coil Covers (2) (Std. O), *94*		CP	_____
(12854)	US Navy Tractor & Tanker, *94*		CP	_____
(12855)	Intermodal Containers (3), *94*		CP	_____
12856	CP Rail Intermodal Container (See 12855)			
12857	Frisco Intermodal Container (See 12855)			
12858	Vermont Railways Intermodal Container (See 12855)			_____
(12860)	Lionel Vistor's Center Tractor and Trailer, *94 u*		CP	_____
(12861)	Lionel Leasing Company Tractor, *94*		CP	_____
(12862)	Oil Drum Loader, *94*		CP	_____
(12864)	Little Caesars Tractor and Trailer, *94*		CP	_____
(12865)	Wisk Tractor and Trailer, *94*		CP	_____
(12866)	PH-1 Powerhouse, *95*		CP	_____
(12867)	PM-1 Powermaster, *95*		CP	_____
(12868)	Cab-1 Remote Controller, *95*		CP	_____
(12869)	Marathon Oil Tractor and Tanker, *94*		CP	_____
(12873)	Operating Sawmill, *95*		CP	_____
(12874)	Street Lamps (3), *94*		CP	_____
(12875)	Lionel Railroader Club Tractor and Trailer, *94 u*		CP	_____
(12877)	Operating Fueling Station, *95*		CP	_____
(12878)	Control Tower, *95*		CP	_____
(12881)	Chrysler Mopar Tractor and Trailer, *94 u*		CP	_____
(12885)	40 Watt Transformer, *95*		CP	_____
(12887)	Lionel Conductor Display, *95*		CP	_____
(12890)	Big Red Switch, *95*		CP	_____
15791	(See 17889)			
15906	RailSounds Trigger Button, *90-94*		CP	_____
16000	PRR Vista Dome Car (O27), *87-88*	25	35	_____
16001	PRR Passenger Car (O27), *87-88*	25	35	_____
16002	PRR Passenger Car (O27), *87-88*	25	35	_____
16003	PRR Observation Car (O27), *87-88*	25	35	_____
16009	PRR Combination Car (O27), *88*	30	35	_____

LTI MODERN ERA (1987-1995)

		Exc	New	Cond/$
16010	Virginia & Truckee Passenger Car, *88 (SSS)*	40	50	_____
16011	Virginia & Truckee Passenger Car, *88 (SSS)*	40	50	_____
16012	Virginia & Truckee Baggage Car, *88 (SSS)*	40	50	_____
16013	Amtrak Combination Car (O27), *88-89*	25	40	_____
16014	Amtrak Vista Dome Car (O27), *88-89*	25	40	_____
16015	Amtrak Observation Car (O27), *88-89*	25	40	_____
16016	NYC Baggage Car (O27), *89*	25	35	_____
16017	NYC Combination Car (O27), *89*	25	35	_____
16018	NYC Passenger Car (O27), *89*	25	35	_____
16019	NYC Vista Dome Car (O27), *89*	25	35	_____
16020	NYC Passenger Car (O27), *89*	25	35	_____
16021	NYC Observation Car (O27), *89*	25	35	_____
16021	(See 17210)			
16022	Pennsylvania Baggage Car (O27), *89*	25	35	_____
16022	(See 17211)			
16023	Amtrak Passenger Car (O27), *89*	25	35	_____
16023	(See 17212)			
16024	NP Dining Car (O27), *92*	40	50	_____
16027	LL Combination Car (O27), *90 (SSS)*	40	50	_____
16028	LL Passenger Car (O27), *90 (SSS)*	40	50	_____
16029	LL Passenger Car (O27), *90 (SSS)*	40	50	_____
16030	LL Observation Car (O27), *90 (SSS)*	40	50	_____
16031	Pennsylvania Dining Car (O27), *90*	35	40	_____
16033	Amtrak Baggage Car (O27), *90*	25	35	_____
16034	NP Baggage Car (O27), *90-91*	20	30	_____
16035	NP Combination Car (O27), *90-91*	20	30	_____
16036	NP Passenger Car (O27), *90-91*	20	30	_____
16037	NP Vista Dome Car (O27), *90-91*	20	30	_____
16038	NP Passenger Car (O27), *90-91*	20	30	_____
16039	NP Observation Car (O27), *90-91*	20	30	_____
16040	Southern Pacific Baggage Car, *90-91*	25	35	_____
16041	NYC Dining Car (O27), *91*	40	50	_____
16042	Illinois Central Baggage Car (O27), *91*	25	35	_____
16043	Illinois Central Combination Car (O27), *91*	25	35	_____
16044	Illinois Central Passenger Car (O27), *91*	25	35	_____
16045	Illinois Central Vista Dome Car (O27), *91*	25	35	_____
16046	Illinois Central Passenger Car (O27), *91*	25	35	_____
16047	Illinois Central Observation Car (O27), *91*	25	35	_____
16048	Amtrak Dining Car (O27), *91-92*	40	50	_____

		Exc	New	Cond/$
16049	Illinois Central Dining Car (O27), *92*	25	35	_____
(16050)	C&NW Baggage Car "6620", *93*	45	55	_____
(16051)	C&NW Combination Car "6630", *93*	45	55	_____
(16052)	C&NW Passenger Car "6616", *93*	45	55	_____
(16053)	C&NW Passenger Car "6602", *93*	45	55	_____
(16054)	C&NW Observation Car "6603", *93*	45	55	_____
16055	Santa Fe Passenger Car (O27), *93-94*		CP	_____
16056	Santa Fe Vista Dome Car (O27), *93-94*		CP	_____
16057	Santa Fe Passenger Car (O27), *93-94*		CP	_____
16058	Santa Fe Combination Car (O27), *93-94*		CP	_____
16059	Santa Fe Vista Dome Car (O27), *93-94*		CP	_____
16060	Santa Fe Observation Car (O27), *93-94*		CP	_____
(16061)	N&W Baggage Car "6061", *94*		CP	_____
(16062)	N&W Combination Car "6062", *94*		CP	_____
(16063)	N&W Passenger Car "6063", *94*		CP	_____
(16064)	N&W Passenger Car "6064", *94*		CP	_____
(16065)	N&W Observation Car "6065", *94*		CP	_____
(16066)	NYC Combination Car "6066", *94 (SSS)*		CP	_____
(16067)	NYC Passenger Car "6067", *94 (SSS)*		CP	_____
(16068)	UP Baggage Car "6068" (O27), *94*		CP	_____
(16069)	UP Combination Car "6069" (O27), *94*		CP	_____
(16070)	UP Passenger Car "6070" (O27), *94*		CP	_____
(16071)	UP Dining Car "6071" (O27), *94*		CP	_____
(16072)	UP Vista Dome Car "6072" (O27), *94*		CP	_____
(16073)	UP Passenger Car "6073" (O27), *94*		CP	_____
(16074)	UP Observation Car "6074" (O27), *94*		CP	_____
(16075)	Missouri Pacific Baggage Car "6620", *95*		CP	_____
(16076)	Missouri Pacific Combination Car "6630", *95*		CP	_____
(16077)	Missouri Pacific Passenger Car "6616", *95*		CP	_____
(16078)	Missouri Pacific Passenger Car "7805", *95*		CP	_____
(16079)	Missouri Pacific Observation Car "6609", *95*		CP	_____
(16080)	New Haven Baggage Car "6080" (O27), *95*		CP	_____
(16081)	New Haven Combination Car "6081" (O27), *95*		CP	_____
(16082)	New Haven Passenger Car "6082" (O27), *95*		CP	_____
(16083)	New Haven Vista Dome Car "6083" (O27), *95*		CP	_____
(16086)	New Haven Observation Car "6086" (O27), *95*		CP	_____
(16087)	NYC Baggage Car "6087", *95 (SSS)*		CP	_____
(16088)	NYC Passenger Car "6088", *95 (SSS)*		CP	_____
(16089)	NYC Dining Car "6089", *95 (SSS)*		CP	_____

LTI MODERN ERA (1987-1995)

		Exc	New	Cond/$
(16090)	NYC Observation Car "6090", *95 (SSS)*		CP	_____
(16091)	NYC Passenger Cars, set of 4, *95 (SSS)*		CP	_____
16102	Southern 3-D Tank Car, *87 (SSS)*	40	50	_____
16103	Lehigh Valley 2-D Tank Car (O27), *88*	25	30	_____
16104	Santa Fe 2-D Tank Car (O27), *89*	20	25	_____
16105	D&RGW 3-D Tank Car, *89 (SSS)*	45	60	_____
(16106)	Mopar Express 3-D Tank Car, *88 u*	75	125	_____
16107	Sunoco 2-D Tank Car (O27), *90*	20	25	_____
(16108)	Racing Fuel 1-D Tank Car "6108", (O27), *89 u, 92 u*	10	15	_____
16109	B&O 1-D Tank Car, *91 (SSS)*	40	50	_____
(16110)	Circus Animals Operating Stock Car "1989", *89 u*	25	35	_____
16111	Alaska 1-D Tank Car (O27), *90-91*	15	20	_____
16112	Dow Chemical 3-D Tank Car, *90*	25	35	_____
16113	Diamond Shamrock 2-D Tank Car (O27), *91*	20	30	_____
16114	Hooker 1-D Tank Car (O27), *91*	15	20	_____
16115	MKT 3-D Tank Car, *92*	20	25	_____
16116	US Army 1-D Tank Car, *91 u*	40	50	_____
16119	MKT 2-D Tank Car (O27), *92, 93 u*	15	20	_____
16121	C&NW Stock Car, *92 (SSS)*	75	90	_____
16123	Union Pacific 3-D Tank Car, *93-94*		CP	_____
16124	Penn Salt 3-D Tank Car, *93*	20	25	_____
16125	Virginian Stock Car, *93*	20	25	_____
16126	Jefferson Lake 3-D Tank Car, *93*	25	30	_____
16127	Mobil 1-D Tank Car, *93*	25	30	_____
16128	Alaska 1-D Tank Car, *94*		CP	_____
16129	Alaska 1-D Tank Car (O27), *93 u, 94*		CP	_____
16130	SP Stock Car (O27), *93 u, 94*		CP	_____
16131	T&P Reefer, *94*		CP	_____
16132	Deep Rock 3-D Tank Car, *94*		CP	_____
16133	Santa Fe Reefer, *94*		CP	_____
16134	Reading Reefer, *94*		CP	_____
16135	C&O Stock Car, *94*		CP	_____
16136	B&O 1-D Tank Car, *94*		CP	_____
16137	Ford 1-D Tank Car, *94 u*		CP	_____
16138	Goodyear 1-D Tank Car, *95*		CP	_____
16140	Domino Sugar 1-D Tank Car, *95*		CP	_____
16200	Rock Island Boxcar (O27), *87-88*	8	12	_____

LTI MODERN ERA (1987-1995)

		Exc	New	Cond/$
16201	Wabash Boxcar (O27), *88-91*	8	12	_____
16203	Key America Boxcar (O27), *87 u*		NRS	_____
16204	Hawthorne Boxcar (O27), *87 u*	60	100	_____
(16205)	Mopar Express Boxcar "1987"			
	(O27), *87-88 u*	50	60	_____
16206	D&RGW Boxcar, *89 (SSS)*	50	60	_____
16207	True Value Boxcar (O27), *88 u*	50	75	_____
16208	PRR Auto Carrier w/ cars, *89*	35	50	_____
16209	Disney Magic Boxcar (O27), *88 u*	75	100	_____
16211	Hawthorne Boxcar (O27), *88 u*	50	75	_____
16213	Shoprite Boxcar (O27), *88 u*	50	75	_____
16214	D&RGW Auto Carrier, *90*	30	35	_____
16215	Conrail Auto Carrier, *90*	30	35	_____
16217	Burlington Northern Auto Carrier, *92*	30	35	_____
16219	True Value Boxcar (O27), *89 u*	50	75	_____
(16220)	Ace Hardware Boxcar (O27), *89 u*	50	75	_____
(16221)	Macy's Boxcar (O27), *89 u*	50	75	_____
16222	Great Northern Boxcar (O27), *90-91*	8	15	_____
(16223)	Budweiser Reefer, *89-92 u*	50	60	_____
16224	True Value "Lawn Chief" Boxcar (O27), *90 u*	50	75	_____
16225	Budweiser Vat Car, *90-91 u*	100	125	_____
(16226)	Union Pacific Boxcar "6226" (O27), *90-91 u*	15	20	_____
16227	Santa Fe Boxcar (O27), *91*	15	20	_____
16228	Union Pacific Auto Carrier, *92*	30	35	_____
16229	Erie-Lackawanna Auto Carrier, *91 u*	60	70	_____
16232	Chessie System Boxcar, *92, 93 u, 94*		CP	_____
16233	MKT DD Boxcar, *92*	20	30	_____
16234	ACY Boxcar, *92 (SSS)*	40	50	_____
16235	Railway Express Agency Reefer, *92*	25	35	_____
16236	NYC "Pacemaker" Boxcar, *92 u*	35	40	_____
16237	Railway Express Agency Boxcar, *92 u*	35	40	_____
16238	NYNH&H Boxcar, *93-94*		CP	_____
16239	Union Pacific Boxcar, *93-94*		CP	_____
16241	Toys 'R Us Boxcar, *92-93 u*	50	65	_____
16242	Grand Trunk Auto Carrier, *93*	35	40	_____
16243	Conrail Boxcar, *93*	30	40	_____
16244	Duluth, South Shore & Atlantic Boxcar, *93*	20	25	_____
16245	Contadina Boxcar, *93*	20	25	_____
16247	ACL Boxcar, *94*		CP	_____

		Exc	New	Cond/$
16247	(See 52046)			
16248	Budweiser Boxcar, *93-94 u*		CP	_____
16249	United Auto Workers Boxcar, *93 u*		NRS	_____
16250	Santa Fe Boxcar (O27), *93 u, 94*		CP	_____
16251	Columbus & Greenville Boxcar, *94*		CP	_____
(16252)	Rapid Strike Attack Force Fleet Boxcar "6106888", *94*		CP	_____
16253	Santa Fe Auto Carrier, *94*		CP	_____
16255	Wabash DD Boxcar, *95*		CP	_____
16256	Ford DD Boxcar, *94 u*		CP	_____
(16257)	Crayola Boxcar, *94 u*		CP	_____
16258	Lehigh Valley Boxcar, *95*		CP	_____
16259	Chrysler Mopar Boxcar, *94 u*		CP	_____
16260	Chrysler Mopar Auto Carrier, *94 u*		CP	_____
16300	Rock Island Flatcar w/ fences (O27), *87-88*	8	10	_____
16301	Lionel Barrel Ramp Car, *87*	20	25	_____
16303	PRR Flatcar w/ trailers, *87*	40	50	_____
16304	Rock Island Gondola w/ cable reels (O27), *87-88*	5	10	_____
16305	Lehigh Valley Ore Car, *87*	75	110	_____
16306	Santa Fe Barrel Ramp Car, *88*	15	20	_____
16307	NKP Flatcar w/ trailers, *88*	30	40	_____
16308	Burlington Northern Flatcar w/ trailer, *88-89*	40	60	_____
16309	Wabash Gondola w/ canisters, *88-91*	10	15	_____
(16310)	Mopar Express Gondola w/ canisters "1987", *87-88 u*	30	40	_____
(16311)	Mopar Express Flatcar w/ trailers "1987", *87-88 u*	100	150	_____
16313	PRR Gondola w/ cable reels (O27), *88 u, 89*	8	10	_____
16314	Wabash Flatcar w/ trailers, *89*	30	40	_____
16315	PRR Flatcar w/ fences (O27), *88 u, 89*	8	10	_____
16317	PRR Barrel Ramp Car, *89*	20	25	_____
16318	Lionel Lines Depressed Flatcar w/ cable reels, *89*	20	25	_____
16320	Great Northern Barrel Ramp Car, *90*	20	25	_____
16321/ 16322	Sealand TTUX Flatcar set w/ trailers, *90*	90	110	_____
16323	Lionel Lines Flatcar w/ trailers, *90*	30	40	_____
16324	PRR Depressed Flatcar w/ cable reels, *90*	20	25	_____
16325	Microracers Exhibition Ramp Car, *89 u*	25	35	_____
16326	Santa Fe Depressed Flatcar w/ cable reels, *91*	20	25	_____

		Exc	New	Cond/$
(16327)	"The Big Top" Circus Gondola			
	w/ canisters, *89 u*	20	25	_____
16328	NKP Gondola w/ cable reels, *90-91*	15	20	_____
16329	SP Flatcar w/ horses (O27), *90-91*	20	25	_____
16330	MKT Flatcar w/ trailers, *91*	25	35	_____
16331	Southern Barrel Ramp Car, *91*		NM	
16332	Lionel Lines Depressed Flatcar			
	w/ transformer, *91*	20	25	_____
16333	Frisco Bulkhead Flatcar w/ wood load, *91*	20	25	_____
(16334)	C&NW TTUX Flatcar set w/ trailers			
	"16337" and "16338" , *91*	70	85	_____
16335	NYC "Pacemaker" Flatcar w/ trailer, *91 (SSS)*	75	95	_____
(16336)	UP Gondola w/ canisters "6336", *90-91 u*	20	25	_____
16337/ 16338	C&NW TTUX Flatcars			
	w/ trailers (See 16334)			
16339	Mickey's World Tour Gondola			
	w/ canisters (O27), *91, 92 u*	20	25	_____
16340	Amtrak Flatcar w/ stakes, *91*		NM	
16341	NYC Depressed Flatcar w/ transformer, *92*	25	30	_____
16342	CSX Gondola w/ coil covers, *92*	20	25	_____
16343	Burlington Gondola w/ coil covers, *92*	20	25	_____
16345/ 16346	SP TTUX Flatcar set w/ trailers, *92*	60	75	_____
16347	Ontario Northland Bulkhead Flatcar			
	w/ pulp load, *92*	30	35	_____
16348	Lionel-Erie Liquified Gas Car, *92*	40	50	_____
16349	Allis Chalmers Condenser Car, *92*	40	50	_____
16350	CP Rail Bulkhead Flatcar w/ wood load, *91 u*	25	35	_____
16351	Lionel Flatcar w/ USN submarine, *92*	50	65	_____
16352	US Military Flatcar w/ cruise missile, *92*	40	50	_____
16353	B&M Gondola w/ coil covers, *91 u*	30	40	_____
16355	Burlington Gondola, *92, 93 u, 94*		CP	_____
16356	MKT Depressed Flatcar w/ cable reels, *92*	20	25	_____
16357	L&N Flatcar w/ trailer, *92*	30	40	_____
16358	L&N Gondola w/ coil covers, *92*	25	35	_____
16359	Pacific Coast Gondola w/ coil covers, *92 (SSS)*	35	40	_____
(16360)	N&W Maxi-Stack Flatcar set			
	w/ containers "16361" and "16362", *93*	70	85	_____
16361/ 16362	N&W Maxi-Stack Flatcars			
	w/ containers (See 16360)			

LTI MODERN ERA (1987-1995)

		Exc	New	Cond/$
(16363)	Southern TTUX Flatcar set w/ trailers "16364" and "16365", *93*	60	75	_____
16364/ 16365	Southern TTUX Flatcars w/ trailers (See 16363)			
16367	Clinchfield Gondola w/ coil covers, *93*	20	25	_____
16368	MKT Liquid Oxygen Car, *93*	25	30	_____
16369	Amtrak Flatcar w/ wheel load, *92 u*	20	30	_____
16370	Amtrak Flatcar w/ rail load, *92 u*	20	30	_____
16371	BN I-Beam Flatcar w/ load, *92 u*	40	50	_____
16372	Southern I-Beam Flatcar w/ load, *92 u*	30	40	_____
16373	Erie-Lackawanna Flatcar w/ stakes, *93*	20	25	_____
16374	D&RGW Flatcar w/ trailer, *93*	30	35	_____
16375	NYC Bulkhead Flatcar, *93-94*		CP	_____
16376	UP Flatcar w/ trailer, *93-94*		CP	_____
16378	Toys 'R Us Flatcar w/ trailer, *92-93 u*	75	125	_____
16379	NP Bulkhead Flatcar w/ pulp load, *93*	25	30	_____
16380	UP I-Beam Flatcar w/ load, *93*	30	35	_____
16381	CSX I-Beam Flatcar w/ load, *93*	30	35	_____
16382	Kansas City Southern Bulkhead Flatcar, *93*	20	25	_____
16383	Conrail Flatcar w/ trailer, *93*	50	60	_____
16384	Soo Line Gondola w/ cable reels, *93*	20	25	_____
16385	Soo Line Ore Car, *93*	60	75	_____
16386	SP Flatcar w/ wood load, *94*		CP	_____
16387	Kansas City Southern Gondola w/ coil covers, *94*		CP	_____
16388	LV Gondola w/ canisters, *94*		CP	_____
16389	PRR Flatcar w/ wheel load, *94*		CP	_____
16390	Lionel Flatcar w/ water tank, *94*		CP	_____
16391	United Auto Workers Gondola, *93 u*		NRS	_____
16392	Wabash Gondola w/ canisters (027), *93 u, 94*		CP	_____
16393	Wisconsin Central Bulkhead Flatcar, *94*		CP	_____
16394	Central Vermont Bulkhead Flatcar, *94*		CP	_____
16395	CP Flatcar w/ rail load, *94*		CP	_____
16396	Alaska Bulkhead Flatcar, *94*		CP	_____
16397	Milwaukee Road I-Beam Flatcar w/ load, *94*		CP	_____
16398	C&O Flatcar w/ trailer, *94*		CP	_____
16399	Western Pacific I-Beam Flatcar w/ load, *94*		CP	_____
16400	PRR Hopper (027), *88 u, 89*	20	25	_____

		Exc	New	Cond/$
16402	Southern Quad Hopper w/ coal load, *87 (SSS)*	35	50	_____
16406	CSX Quad Hopper w/ coal load, *90*	30	40	_____
16407	B&M Covered Quad Hopper, *91 (SSS)*	30	35	_____
(16408)	Union Pacific Hopper "6408" (O27), *90-91 u*	20	25	_____
16410	MKT Hopper (O27), *92, 93 u*	20	25	_____
16411	L&N Quad Hopper w/ coal load, *92*	30	35	_____
16412	C&NW Covered Quad Hopper, *94*		CP	_____
16413	Clinchfield Quad Hopper w/ coal load, *94*		CP	_____
16413	(See 52059)			
16414	CCC&St L Hopper (O27), *94*		CP	_____
16416	D&RGW Quad Hopper w/ coal load, *95*		CP	_____
16417	Wabash Covered Quad Hopper, *95*		CP	_____
16500	Rock Island Bobber Caboose, *87-88*	10	15	_____
16501	Lehigh Valley SP Caboose, *87*	20	25	_____
16503	NYC Transfer Caboose, *87*	15	20	_____
16504	Southern N5C Caboose, *87 (SSS)*	25	45	_____
16505	Wabash SP Caboose, *88-91*	10	15	_____
16506	Santa Fe B/W Caboose, *88*	30	35	_____
(16507)	Mopar Express SP Caboose "1987", *87-88 u*	40	50	_____
(16508)	Lionel Lines SP Caboose "6508", *89 u*	15	20	_____
16509	D&RGW SP Caboose, *89 (SSS)*	25	35	_____
16510	New Haven B/W Caboose, *89*	25	35	_____
16511	PRR Bobber Caboose, *88 u, 89*	10	15	_____
16513	Union Pacific SP Caboose, *89*	15	25	_____
16515	Lionel Lines RailScope SP Caboose, *89*	25	35	_____
16516	Lehigh Valley SP Caboose, *90*	15	25	_____
16517	Atlantic Coast Line B/W Caboose, *90*	20	30	_____
16518	Chessie System B/W Caboose, *90*	35	50	_____
16519	Rock Island Transfer Caboose, *90*	15	25	_____
(16520)	"Welcome To The Show" Circus SP Caboose, *89 u*	15	25	_____
16521	PRR SP Caboose, *90-91*	10	15	_____
16522	"Chills & Thrills" Circus N5C Caboose, *90-91*	10	15	_____
16523	Alaska SP Caboose, *91*	30	40	_____
(16524)	Anheuser-Busch SP Caboose, *89-92 u*	30	40	_____
16525	D&H B/W Caboose, *91 (SSS)*	35	45	_____
16526	Kansas City Southern SP Caboose, *91*	20	25	_____
16527	Western Pacific Work Caboose, *92*		NM	
(16528)	Union Pacific SP Caboose "6528", *90-91 u*	20	25	_____

LTI MODERN ERA (1987-1995)

		Exc	New	Cond/$
(16529)	Santa Fe SP Caboose "16829", *91*	10	15	_____
(16530)	Mickey's World Tour SP Caboose "16830", *91, 92 u*	15	20	_____
16531	Texas & Pacific SP Caboose, *92*	20	25	_____
16533	C&NW B/W Caboose, *92*	25	35	_____
16534	Delaware & Hudson SP Caboose, *92*	20	25	_____
16535	Erie-Lackawanna B/W Caboose, *91 u*	35	45	_____
16536	Chessie System SP Caboose, *92, 93 u, 94*		CP	_____
16537	MKT SP Caboose, *92, 93 u*	20	25	_____
(16538)	L&N B/W Caboose "1041", *92 u*	35	40	_____
16538	L&N/Family Lines Steelside Caboose w/ smoke (Std. O), *92*		NM	
(16539)	WP Steelside Caboose w/ smoke "539" (Std. O), *92 (SSS)*	60	75	_____
(16541)	Montana Rail Link E/V Caboose w/ smoke "10131", *93*	60	75	_____
(16543)	NYC SP Caboose, *93-94*		CP	_____
16544	Union Pacific SP Caboose, *93-94*		CP	_____
16546	Clinchfield SP Caboose, *93*	25	30	_____
16547	Happy Holidays SP Caboose, *93-94*		CP	_____
16548	Conrail SP Caboose, *93*	25	35	_____
16549	Soo Line Work Caboose, *93*	20	30	_____
16550	US Navy Searchlight Caboose, *94*		CP	_____
16551	Budweiser SP Caboose, *93-94 u*		CP	_____
16552	Frisco Searchlight Caboose, *94*		CP	_____
16553	United Auto Workers SP Caboose, *93 u*		NRS	_____
(16554)	GT E/V Caboose w/ smoke "79052", *94*		CP	_____
16555	C&O SP Caboose, *94*		CP	_____
16556	US Navy Gondola, w/ canisters, *94*		CP	_____
16557	Ford SP Caboose, *94 u*		CP	_____
(16558)	Crayola SP Caboose, *94 u*		CP	_____
(16559)	Seaboard Caboose "5658", *95*		CP	_____
16560	Chrysler Mopar Caboose, *94 u*		CP	_____
16600	Illinois Central Coal Dump Car, *88*	15	25	_____
16601	Canadian National Searchlight Car, *88*	20	25	_____
16602	Erie-Lackawanna Coal Dump Car, *87*	15	25	_____
16603	Detroit Zoo Giraffe Car, *87*	40	50	_____
16604	NYC Log Dump Car, *87*	15	25	_____
16605	Bronx Zoo Giraffe Car, *88*	40	45	_____

		Exc	New	Cond/$
16606	Southern Searchlight Car, *87*	15	25	_____
[16606]	Southern TCA Southern Searchlight Car, *88 u*	20	30	_____
16607	Southern Coal Dump Car, *87 (SSS)*	20	30	_____
16608	Lehigh Valley Searchlight Car, *87*	25	35	_____
16609	Lehigh Valley Derrick Car, *87*	25	35	_____
16610	Lionel Track Maintenance Car, *87-88*	15	25	_____
16611	Santa Fe Log Dump Car, *88*	15	25	_____
16612	Soo Line Log Dump Car, *89*	15	25	_____
16613	MKT Coal Dump Car, *89*	15	25	_____
16614	Reading Cop and Hobo Car, *89*	25	35	_____
16615	Lionel Lines Extension Searchlight Car, *89*	20	30	_____
16616	D&RGW Searchlight Car, *89 (SSS)*	25	35	_____
16617	C&NW Boxcar w/ ETD, *89*	20	30	_____
16618	Santa Fe Track Maintenance Car, *89*	15	25	_____
16619	Wabash Coal Dump Car, *90*	15	25	_____
16620	C&O Track Maintenance Car, *90-91*	15	25	_____
16621	Alaska Log Dump Car, *90*	20	30	_____
16622	CSX Boxcar w/ ETD, *90-91*	20	30	_____
16623	MKT DD Boxcar w/ ETD, *91*	20	25	_____
16624	NH Cop and Hobo Car, *90-91*	25	35	_____
16625	NYC Extension Searchlight Car, *90*	20	30	_____
16626	CSX Searchlight Car, *90*	20	30	_____
16627	CSX Log Dump Car, *90*	20	25	_____
16628	"Laughter" Circus Animated Gondola, *90-91*	40	50	_____
16629	"Animal Car" Circus Elephant Car, *90-91*	45	60	_____
16630	SP Operating Cowboy Car, *90-91*	25	30	_____
16631	RI Boxcar w/ Steam RailSounds, *90*	125	150	_____
16632	BN Boxcar w/ Diesel RailSounds, *90*	125	150	_____
16633	Great Northern Cop and Hobo Car, *91*		NM	
16634	WM Coal Dump Car, *91*	20	25	_____
16635	CP Rail Track Maintenance Car, *91*		NM	_____
16636	D&RGW Log Dump Car, *91*	20	25	_____
16637	WP Extension Searchlight Car, *91*	30	35	_____
16638	Lionelville Circus Operating Animal Car, *91*	60	75	_____
16639	B&O Boxcar w/ Steam RailSounds, *91*	125	150	_____
16640	Rutland Boxcar w/ Diesel RailSounds, *91*	125	150	_____
16641	Toys 'R Us Giraffe Car, *90-91 u*	50	75	_____
16642	Mickey's World Tour Goofy Car, *91, 92 u*	40	50	_____
16643	Amtrak Coal Dump Car, *91*		NM	_____

LTI MODERN ERA (1987-1995)

		Exc	New	Cond/$
16644	Amtrak Crane Car, *91, 92 u*	40	50	_____
16645	Amtrak Searchlight Caboose, *91, 92 u*	30	35	_____
16646	Railbox Boxcar w/ ETD, *92*		NM	
16649	Railway Express Agency Boxcar			
	w/ Steam RailSounds, *92*	145	160	_____
16650	NYC "Pacemaker" Boxcar			
	w/ Diesel RailSounds, *92*	145	160	_____
16651	Circus Operating Clown Car, *92*	35	45	_____
16652	Lionel Radar Car, *92*	35	45	_____
16653	Western Pacific Crane Car, *92 (SSS)*	45	60	_____
16654	(See 17214)			
(16655)	Steam Tender w/ RailSounds "1993", *93*	150	175	_____
16656	Burlington Log Dump Car, *92 u*	25	30	_____
16657	Lehigh Valley Coal Dump Car, *92 u*	25	30	_____
16658	Erie-Lackawanna Crane Car, *93*	50	65	_____
16659	Union Pacific Searchlight Car, *93-94*		CP	_____
16660	Lionel Fire Car w/ ladders, *93-94*	55	70	_____
16661	Lionel Flatcar w/ boat, *93*	40	60	_____
16662	Looney Tunes Operating Bugs Bunny			
	and Yosemite Sam Car, *93-94*	35	45	_____
16663	Missouri Pacific Searchlight Car, *93*	25	30	_____
16664	L&N Coal Dump Car, *93*	25	30	_____
16665	Maine Central Log Dump Car, *93*	25	30	_____
16666	Lionel Toxic Waste Car, *93-94*	30	40	_____
16667	Conrail Searchlight Car, *93*	30	35	_____
16668	Ontario Northland Log Dump Car, *93*	25	30	_____
16669	Soo Line Searchlight Car, *93*	25	30	_____
16670	Lionel TV Car, *93-94*	35	40	_____
(16673)	Lionel Lines Tender w/ whistle, *94-95*		CP	_____
16674	Pinkerton Animated Gondola, *94*		CP	_____
16675	Great Northern Log Dump Car, *94*		CP	_____
16676	Burlington Coal Dump Car, *94*		CP	_____
16677	NATO Flatcar w/ Royal Navy submarine, *94*		CP	_____
16678	Rock Island Searchlight Car, *94*		CP	_____
16679	US Mail Operating Boxcar, *94*		CP	_____
16680	Lionel Cherry Picker Car, *94*		CP	_____
16682	Lionelville Farms Operating Stock Car, *94*		CP	_____
16683	Los Angeles Zoo Elephant Car, *94*		CP	_____
16684	US Navy Crane Car, *94*		CP	_____

		Exc	New	Cond/$
16685	Erie Extension Searchlight Car, *95*		CP	
16687	US Mail Operating Boxcar, *94*		CP	
16688	Lionel Fire Car w/ ladders, *94*		CP	
16689	Lionel Toxic Waste Car, *94*		CP	
16690	Looney Tunes Operating Bugs Bunny and			
	Yosemite Sam Car, *94*		CP	
16701	Southern Tool Car, *87 (SSS)*	60	75	
16702	Amtrak Bunk Car, *91, 92 u*	30	35	
16703	NYC Tool Car, *92*	30	35	
16704	Lionel TV Car, *94*		CP	
16800	Lionel Railroader Club Ore Car, *86 u*	80	100	
16801	Lionel Railroader Club Bunk Car, *88 u*	45	60	
16802	Lionel Railroader Club Tool Car, *89 u*	45	60	
16803	Lionel Railroader Club Searchlight Car, *90 u*	40	50	
16804	Lionel Railroader Club B/W Caboose, *91 u*	35	50	
(16805)	Budweiser Malt Nutrine Reefer			
	"3285", *91-92 u*	65	80	
16806	Toys 'R Us Boxcar, *92 u*	40	50	
(16807)	HJ Heinz Reefer "301", *93*	35	40	
16808	Toys 'R Us Boxcar, *93 u*	40	50	
16829	(See 16529)			
16830	(See 16530)			
(16901)	Lionel Catalog Videotape (VHS), *91 u*	20	25	
16903	CP Bulkhead Flatcar w/ pulp load, *94 (SSS)*		CP	
(16904)	NYC "Pacemaker" TTUX Flatcar set			
	w/ trailers "16905" and "16906", *94*		CP	
16905/ 16906	NYC "Pacemaker" TTUX Flatcars			
	w/ trailers (See 16904)			
16907	Lionel Flatcar w/ farm tractors, *94*		CP	
(16908)	US Navy Flatcar "04039" w/ submarine			
	"930", *94*		CP	
(16909)	(See 16556)			
16910	Missouri Pacific Flatcar w/ trailer, *94*		CP	
16911	B&M Flatcar w/ trailer, *94*		CP	
(16912)	CN Maxi-Stack Flatcar set w/ containers			
	"640000" and "640001", *94*		CP	
16915	Lionel Lines Gondola (O27), *93-94 u*		CP	
16916	Ford Flatcar w/ trailer, *94 u*		CP	
(16917)	Crayola Gondola w/ crayons, *94 u*		CP	

LTI MODERN ERA (1987-1995)

		Exc	New	Cond/$
16919	Chrysler Mopar Gondola w/ coil covers, *94 u*		CP	_____
17000	(See 17107)			
17002	Conrail 2-bay ACF Hopper (Std. O), *87*	100	125	_____
17003	Dupont 2-bay ACF Hopper (Std. O), *90*	60	85	_____
17004	MKT 2-bay ACF Hopper (Std. O), *91*	35	45	_____
17005	Cargill 2-bay ACF Hopper (Std. O), *92*	35	45	_____
17006	Soo Line 2-bay ACF Hopper (Std. O), *93 (SSS)*	50	60	_____
(17007)	GN 2-bay ACF Hopper "173872" (Std. O), *94*		CP	_____
17100	Chessie System 3-bay ACF Hopper (Std. O), *88*	50	60	_____
17101	Chessie System 3-bay ACF Hopper (Std. O), *88*	50	60	_____
17102	Chessie System 3-bay ACF Hopper (Std. O), *88*	50	60	_____
17103	Chessie System 3-bay ACF Hopper (Std. O), *88*	50	60	_____
17104	Chessie System 3-bay ACF Hopper (Std. O), *88*	50	60	_____
17107	Sclair 3-bay ACF Hopper (Std. O), *89*	100	125	_____
17108	Santa Fe 3-bay ACF Hopper (Std. O), *90*	60	75	_____
17109	N&W 3-bay ACF Hopper (Std. O), *91*	35	45	_____
17110	Union Pacific Hopper w/ coal load (Std. O), *91*	35	45	_____
17111	Reading Hopper w/ coal load (Std. O), *91*	35	45	_____
17112	Erie-Lack 3-bay ACF Hopper (Std. O), *92*	35	45	_____
17113	LV Hopper w/ coal load (Std. O), *92-93*	35	40	_____
17114	Peabody Hopper w/ coal load (Std. O), *92-93*	50	60	_____
(17118)	Archer Daniels Midland 3-bay ACF Hopper "60029" (Std. O), *93*	35	45	_____
(17120)	CSX Hopper w/ coal load "295110" (Std. O), *94*		CP	_____
(17121)	ICG Hopper w/ coal load "72867" (Std. O), *94*		CP	_____
(17122)	RI 3-bay ACF Hopper "800200" (Std. O), *94*		CP	_____
17200	Canadian Pacific Boxcar (Std. O), *89*	60	75	_____
17201	Conrail Boxcar (Std. O), *87*	60	75	_____
17202	Santa Fe Boxcar w/ Diesel RailSounds (Std. O), *90*	130	150	_____
17203	Cotton Belt DD Boxcar (Std. O), *91*	35	45	_____
17204	Missouri Pacific DD Boxcar (Std. O), *91*	35	45	_____
17207	C&IM DD Boxcar (Std. O), *92*	35	45	_____
17208	Union Pacific DD Boxcar (Std. O), *92*	35	45	_____
(17209)	B&O DD Boxcar "296000" (Std. O), *93*	40	50	_____
(17210)	Chicago & Illinois Midland Boxcar "16021" (Std. O), *92 u*	—	50	_____
(17211)	Chicago & Illinois Midland Boxcar "16022" (Std. O), *92 u*	—	50	_____

LTI MODERN ERA (1987-1995)

		Exc	New	Cond/$
(17212)	Chicago & Illinois Midland Boxcar "16023" (Std. O), *92 u*	—	50	_____
(17213)	Susquehanna Boxcar "501" (Std. O), *93*	35	40	_____
17214	Railbox Boxcar w/ Diesel RailSounds (Std. O), *93*	150	175	_____
(17216)	PRR DD Boxcar "60155" (Std. O), *94*		CP	_____
(17217)	New Haven "State of Maine" Boxcar "45003" (Std. O), *95*		CP	_____
(17218)	BAR "State of Maine" Boxcar "2184" (Std. O), *95*		CP	_____
17300	Canadian Pacific Reefer (Std. O), *89*	60	75	_____
17301	Conrail Reefer (Std. O), *87*	60	75	_____
17302	Santa Fe Reefer w/ ETD (Std. O), *90*	60	75	_____
(17303)	C&O Reefer "7890" (Std. O), *93*	35	45	_____
(17304)	Wabash Reefer "26269" (Std. O), *94*		CP	_____
(17305)	Pacific Fruit Express Reefer "459400" (Std. O), *94*		CP	_____
(17306)	Pacific Fruit Express Reefer "459401" (Std. O), *94*		CP	_____
(17307)	Tropicana Reefer "300" (Std. O), *95*		CP	_____
(17308)	Tropicana Reefer "301" (Std. O), *95*		CP	_____
17400	CP Rail Gondola w/ coal load (Std. O), *89*	50	65	_____
17401	Conrail Gondola w/ coal load (Std. O), *87*	50	65	_____
17402	Santa Fe Gondola w/ coal load (Std. O), *90*	50	65	_____
(17403)	Chessie System Gondola w/ coil covers "371629" (Std. O), *93*	35	45	_____
(17404)	Illinois Central Gulf Gondola w/ coil covers "245998" (Std. O), *93*	35	45	_____
(17405)	Reading Gondola w/ coil covers "24876" (Std. O), *94*		CP	_____
(17406)	PRR Gondola w/ coil covers "385405" (Std. O), *95*		CP	_____
17500	CP Flatcar w/ logs (Std. O), *89*	50	65	_____
17501	Conrail Flatcar w/ stakes (Std. O), *87*	50	65	_____
17502	Santa Fe Flatcar w/ trailer (Std. O), *90*	75	95	_____
17503	NS Flatcar w/ trailer (Std. O), *92*	50	65	_____
17504	NS Flatcar w/ trailer (Std. O), *92*	50	65	_____
17505	NS Flatcar w/ trailer (Std. O), *92*	50	65	_____
17506	NS Flatcar w/ trailer (Std. O), *92*	50	65	_____

LTI MODERN ERA (1987-1995)

		Exc	New	Cond/$
17507	NS Flatcar w/ trailer (Std. 0), *92*	50	65	_____
17508	BN I-Beam Flatcar w/ load (Std. 0), *92*		NM	
17509	Southern I-Beam Flatcar w/ load (Std. 0), *92*		NM	
(17510)	NP Flatcar w/ logs "51200" (Std. 0), *94*		CP	_____
(17511)	WM Flatcars w/ logs, set of 3 (Std. 0), *95*		CP	_____
17512	WM Flatcar w/ logs (Std. 0), *95*		CP	_____
17513	WM Flatcar w/ logs (Std. 0), *95*		CP	_____
17514	WM Flatcar w/ logs (Std. 0), *95*		CP	_____
17600	NYC Woodside Caboose (Std. 0), *87 u*	75	95	_____
17601	Southern Woodside Caboose (Std. 0), *88*	75	95	_____
17602	Conrail Woodside Caboose (Std. 0), *87*	100	125	_____
17603	Rock Island Woodside Caboose (Std. 0), *88*	40	50	_____
17604	Lackawanna Woodside Caboose (Std. 0), *88*	60	75	_____
17605	Reading Woodside Caboose (Std. 0), *89*	50	65	_____
17606	NYC Steelside Caboose w/ smoke (Std. 0), *90*	60	75	_____
17607	Reading Steelside Caboose w/ smoke (Std. 0), *90*	60	75	_____
17608	C&O Steelside Caboose w/ smoke (Std. 0), *91*	60	75	_____
17610	Wabash Steelside Caboose w/ smoke (Std. 0), *91*	60	75	_____
17611	NYC Woodside Caboose (Std. 0), *90 u, 91*	60	75	_____
17612	NKP Steelside Caboose w/ smoke (FF #6) (Std. 0), *92*	60	75	_____
(17613)	Southern Steelside Caboose w/ smoke "7613" (Std. 0), *92*	60	75	_____
17615	Northern Pacific Woodside Caboose w/ smoke (Std. 0), *92*	60	75	_____
17870	LCCA East Camden & Highland Boxcar (Std. 0), *87 u*	75	95	_____
(17871)	TTOS NYC Flatcar w/ Kodak and Xerox trailers "81487", *87 u*	300	400	_____
(17872)	TTOS Anaconda Ore Car "81988", *88 u*	70	100	_____
17873	LCCA Ashland Oil 3-D Tank Car, *88 u*	50	75	_____
(17874)	LOTS MILW Log Dump Car "59629", *88 u*	100	140	_____
(17875)	LOTS PHD Boxcar "1289", *89 u*	75	95	_____
17876	LCCA Columbia Newberry & Laurens Boxcar (Std. 0), *89 u*	60	75	_____
(17877)	TTOS MKT 1-D Tank Car "3739469", *89 u*	60	75	_____

LTI MODERN ERA (1987-1995)

		Exc	New	Cond/$
17878	Gadsden Pacific Magma Ore Car w/ load, 89 u	60	75	_____
(17879)	TCA Valley Forge Dining Car "1989", 89 u	65	85	_____
17880	LCCA D&RGW Woodside Caboose (Std. O), 90 u	65	85	_____
17881	Gadsden Pacific Phelps-Dodge Ore Car w/ load, 90 u	50	60	_____
(17882)	LOTS B&O DD Boxcar w/ ETD "298011", 90 u	90	125	_____
(17883)	TCA New Georgia RR Passenger Car, 90 u	50	60	_____
17884	TTOS Columbus & Dayton Terminal Boxcar (Std. O), 90	50	70	_____
17885	Artrain 1-D Tank Car, 90 u	80	100	_____
17886	Gadsden Pacific Cyprus Ore Car w/ load, 91 u	40	50	_____
17887	LCCA Conrail Flatcar w/ Armstrong Tile Trailer (Std. O), 91 u	60	75	_____
17888	LCCA Conrail Flatcar w/ Ford New Holland Trailer (Std. O), 91 u	75	95	_____
(17889)	TTOS SP Flatcar w/ trailer "15791" (Std. O), 91 u	60	75	_____
(17890)	LOTS CSX Auto Carrier "151161", 91 u	95	110	_____
17891	Artrain Grand Trunk Boxcar, 91 u	80	100	_____
(17892)	LCCA Conrail Flatcars w/ trailers (Std. O) (See 17887, 17888)			
[17893]	LCAC BAOC 1-D Tank Car "914", 91 u	—	100	_____
[17893]	NLOE Long Island 1-D Tank Car "8392", 92 u		NRS	_____
(17894)	TTOS Southern Pacific Tractor, 91 u	20	25	_____
(17895)	LCCA Tractor, 91 u	15	20	_____
(17896)	LCCA Lancaster Lines Tractor, 91 u	25	30	_____
(17898)	TCA Wabash Reefer, 92 u	50	60	_____
(17899)	LCCA NASA Uni-body Tank Car "190" (Std. O), 92 u	75	95	_____
17900	Santa Fe Uni-body Tank Car (Std. O), 90	40	50	_____
17901	Chevron Uni-body Tank Car (Std. O), 90	40	50	_____
17902	NJ Zinc Uni-body Tank Car (Std. O), 91	40	50	_____
17903	Conoco Uni-body Tank Car (Std. O), 91	40	50	_____
17904	Texaco Uni-body Tank Car (Std. O), 92	40	50	_____
17905	Archer Daniels Midland Uni-body Tank Car (Std. O), 92	40	50	_____
(17906)	SCM Uni-body Tank Car "78286" (Std. O), 93	50	60	_____
17908	Marathon Oil Uni-body Tank Car (Std. O), 95		CP	_____
(18000)	PRR 0-6-0 "8977" 89, 91	525	650	_____

LTI MODERN ERA (1987-1995)

		Exc	New	Cond/$
(18001)	Rock Island 4-8-4 "5100", *87*	400	500	_____
(18002)	NYC 4-6-4 "785", *87 u*	800	900	_____
(18003)	Delaware Lackawanna & Western			
	4-8-4 "1501", *88*	450	550	_____
(18004)	Reading 4-6-2 "8004", *89*	350	450	_____
(18005)	NYC 4-6-4 "5340" w/ display case, *90*	1100	1400	_____
(18006)	Reading 4-8-4 "2100", *89 u*	800	900	_____
(18007)	Southern Pacific 4-8-4 "4410", *91*	475	550	_____
(18008)	Disneyland 35th Anniversary			
	4-4-0 "4" w/ display case, *90*	250	300	_____
(18009)	NYC 4-8-2 "3000", *90 u, 91*	850	975	_____
(18010)	Pennsylvania 6-8-6 "6200", *91-92*	1100	1400	_____
(18011)	Chessie System 4-8-4 "2101", *91*	600	775	_____
(18012)	NYC 4-6-4 "5340", *90*	1000	1250	_____
(18013)	Disneyland 35th Anniversary 4-4-0 "4", *90*	200	250	_____
(18014)	Lionel Lines 2-6-4 "8014", *91*	130	180	_____
(18016)	Northern Pacific 4-8-4 "2626", *92*	500	600	_____
(18018)	Southern 2-8-2 "4501", *92*	850	950	_____
(18022)	Pere Marquette 2-8-4 "1201", *93*	600	700	_____
(18023)	Western Maryland Shay "6", *92*	1000	1200	_____
(18024)	Sears T&P 4-8-2 "907"			
	w/ display case, *92 u*	900	1000	_____
(18025)	T&P 4-8-2 "907", *92 u* (See 18024)			_____
(18026)	NYC Smithsonian Dreyfuss Hudson			
	4-6-4 "5454" 2-rail, *92 u*		NRS	_____
(18027)	NYC Dreyfuss Hudson 4-6-4 "5454"			
	3-rail, *93 u*		NRS	_____
(18030)	Frisco 2-8-2 "4100", *93 u*	750	900	_____
(18034)	Santa Fe 2-8-2 "3158", *94*		CP	_____
(18040)	N&W 4-8-4 "612", *95*		CP	_____
(18090)	LCCA D&RGW 4-6-2 "1990", *90 u*	350	425	_____
(18100)	Santa Fe F-3 A Unit "8100" (See 11711)			
(18101)	Santa Fe F-3 B Unit "8101" (See 11711)			
(18102)	Santa Fe F-3 A Unit Dummy "8102"			
	(See 11711)			
(18103)	Santa Fe F-3 B Unit "8103", *91 u*	300	350	_____
(18104)	Great Northern F-3 A Unit "366A" (See 11724)			
(18105)	Great Northern F-3 B Unit "370B" (See 11724)			
(18106)	Great Northern F-3 A Unit Dummy "351C"			

		Exc	New	Cond/$
	(See 11724)			
(18107)	D&RGW Alco PA-1 ABA set			
	"6001" & "6002", 92	750	900	_____
(18108)	Great Northern F-3 B Unit "371B", 93	120	150	_____
(18109)	Erie Alco A Unit "725A" (See 11734)			
(18110)	Erie Alco B Unit "725B" (See 11734)			
(18111)	Erie Alco A Unit Dummy "736A" (See 11734)			
(18112)	TCA F-3 A Unit "40" (See 11737)			
(18113)	TCA F-3 B Unit (See 11737)			
(18114)	TCA F-3 A Unit Dummy "40" (See 11737)			
(18115)	Santa Fe F-3 B Unit, 93	120	150	_____
(18116)	Erie-Lackawanna Alco PA-1 AA set			
	"858" and "859", 93	525	650	_____
(18117/18118)	Santa Fe F-3 AA set "200", 93	350	400	_____
(18119/18120)	UP Alco AA set "8119" & "8120", 94		CP	_____
(18121)	Santa Fe F-3 B Unit "200A", 94		CP	_____
(18200)	Conrail SD-40 "8200", 87	275	325	_____
(18201)	Chessie System SD-40 "8201", 88	275	325	_____
(18202)	Erie-Lackawanna SD-40 Dummy "8459", 89 u	150	175	_____
(18203)	CP Rail SD-40 "8203", 89	225	300	_____
(18204)	Chessie System SD-40 Dummy "8204", 90 u	150	175	_____
(18205)	Union Pacific Dash 8-40C "9100", 89	300	350	_____
(18206)	Santa Fe Dash 8-40B "8206", 90	275	325	_____
(18207)	Norfolk Southern Dash 8-40C "8689", 92	300	350	_____
(18208)	BN SD-40 Dummy "8586", 91 u	150	175	_____
(18209)	CP Rail SD-40 Dummy "8209", 92 u	175	200	_____
(18210)	Illinois Central SD-40 "6006", 93	300	325	_____
(18211)	Susquehanna Dash 8-40B "4002", 93	300	325	_____
(18212)	Santa Fe Dash 8-40B Dummy "8212", 93	175	200	_____
(18213)	Norfolk Southern Dash 8-40C "8688", 94		CP	_____
(18214)	CSX Dash 8-40C "7500", 94		CP	_____
(18215)	CSX Dash 8-40C "7643", 94		CP	_____
(18216)	Conrail SD-60M "5500", 94		CP	_____
(18217)	Illinois Central SD-40 "6007", 94		CP	_____
(18218)	Susquehanna Dash 8-40B "4004", 94		CP	_____
(18219)	C&NW Dash 8-40C "8501", 95		CP	_____
(18220)	C&NW Dash 8-40C "8502", 95		CP	_____
(18300)	PRR GG-1 "8300", 87	425	500	_____
(18301)	Southern Trainmaster "8301", 88	400	425	_____

LTI MODERN ERA (1987-1995)

		Exc	New	Cond/$
(18302)	GN EP-5 "8302" (FF#3), 88	200	275	_____
(18303)	Amtrak GG-1 "8303", 89	400	450	_____
(18304)	Lackawanna MU Car set Powered and Dummy "2401" and "2402", 91	400	450	_____
(18305)	Lackawanna MU Car set, Dummies, "2400" and "2403", 92	300	350	_____
(18306)	PRR MU Car set, Powered and Dummy "4574" and "483", 92	400	475	_____
(18307)	PRR Trainmaster "8699", 94		CP	_____
(18308)	PRR GG-1 "4866", 92	400	475	_____
(18309)	Reading Trainmaster "863", 93	300	350	_____
(18310)	PRR MU Car set, Dummies "484" and "485", 93	300	375	_____
(18311)	Disney EP-5 "8311", 94		CP	_____
(18400)	Santa Fe Vulcan Rotary Snowplow "8400", 87	150	200	_____
(18401)	Handcar, 87-88	40	60	_____
18402	Lionel Lines Burro Crane, 88	90	125	_____
(18403)	Santa Claus Handcar, 88	30	45	_____
(18404)	San Francisco Trolley "8404", 88	100	175	_____
18405	Santa Fe Burro Crane, 89	100	125	_____
18406	Lionel Track Maintenance Car, 89, 91	50	75	_____
(18407)	Snoopy and Woodstock Handcar, 90-91	40	70	_____
(18408)	Santa Claus Handcar, 89	35	50	_____
18410	PRR Burro Crane, 90	125	150	_____
18411	Canadian Pacific Fire Car, 90	125	150	_____
18412	Union Pacific Fire Car, 91		NM	
(18413)	Charlie Brown and Lucy Handcar, 91	30	60	_____
(18416)	Bugs Bunny and Daffy Duck Handcar, 92-93	60	75	_____
18417	Lionel Gang Car, 93	90	110	_____
(18419)	Lionelville Electric Trolley "8419", 94		CP	_____
(18421)	Sylvester and Tweety Handcar, 94		CP	_____
(18422)	Santa and Snowman Handcar, 94		CP	_____
(18500)	Milwaukee Road GP-9 "8500" (FF#2), 87	200	240	_____
(18500)	(See 18550)			
(18501)	WM NW-2 "8501" (FF#4), 89	200	250	_____
(18502)	Lionel Lines 90th Anniversary GP-9 "1900", 90	175	225	_____
(18503)	Southern Pacific NW-2 "8503", 90	225	285	_____
(18504)	Frisco GP-7 "504" (FF#5), 91	200	260	_____

		Exc	New	Cond/$
(18505)	NKP GP-7 Powered and Dummy set "400" and "401" (FF#6), *92*	375	440	_____
(18506)	CN Budd RDC Powered and Dummy set "D202" and "D203", *92*	275	325	_____
(18507)	CN Budd RDC Baggage "D202" (See 18506)			
(18508)	CN Budd RDC Passenger Dummy "D203" (See 18506)			
(18510)	CN Budd RDC Passenger Dummy "D200" (See 18512)			
(18511)	CN Budd RDC Passenger Dummy "D250" (See 18512)			
(18512)	CN Budd RDC Dummies set "D200" and "D250", *93*	250	300	_____
(18513)	NYC GP-7 "7420", *94*		CP	_____
(18514)	Missouri Pacific GP-7 "4124", *95*		CP	_____
(18550)	JCPenney MILW GP-9 "8500" w/ display case, *87 u*		NRS	_____
(18551)	JCPenney Susquehanna RS-3 "8809" w/ display case, *89 u*	200	250	_____
(18552)	JCPenney DM&IR SD-18 "8813" w/ display case, *90 u*	200	250	_____
(18553)	Sears UP GP-9 "150" w/ display case, *91 u*	175	225	_____
(18554)	JCPenney GM&O RS-3 "721" w/ display case, *92-93 u*	175	225	_____
(18555)	Sears C&IM SD-9 "52", *92 u*	175	225	_____
(18556)	Sears Chicago & Illinois Midland Caboose and Freight Car set, *92 u*	150	175	_____
(18557)	Chessie System 4-8-4 "2101" w/ display case for export, *92 u*		NRS	_____
(18558)	JCPenney MKT GP-9 "91" w/ display case, *94 u*		CP	_____
(18600)	ACL 4-4-2 "8600", *87 u*	75	90	_____
(18601)	Great Northern 4-4-2 "8601", *88*	75	90	_____
(18602)	PRR 4-4-2 "8602", *87*	100	125	_____
(18604)	Wabash 4-4-2 "8604", *88-91*	75	90	_____
(18605)	Mopar Express 4-4-2 "1987", *87-88 u*	80	125	_____
(18606)	NYC 2-6-4 "8606", *89*	125	160	_____
(18607)	Union Pacific 2-6-4 "8607", *89*	125	160	_____
(18608)	D&RGW 2-6-4 "8608", *89 (SSS)*	125	160	_____
(18609)	Northern Pacific 2-6-4 "8609" *90*	150	175	_____

LTI MODERN ERA (1987-1995)	Exc	New	Cond/$
(18610) Rock Island 0-4-0 "8610", *90*	175	210	_____
(18611) Lionel Lines 2-6-4 "8611", *90 (SSS)*	160	175	_____
(18612) C&NW 4-4-2 "8612", *89*	75	90	_____
(18613) NYC 4-4-2 "8613", *89 u*	85	110	_____
(18614) Circus Train 4-4-2 "1989", *89 u*	85	110	_____
(18615) GTW 4-4-2 "8615", *90*	75	90	_____
(18616) Northern Pacific 4-4-2 "8616", *90 u*	85	110	_____
(18617) Adolphus III 4-4-2, *89-92 u*	100	125	_____
(18618) B&O 4-4-2 "8618", *91*		NM	
(18620) Illinois Central 2-6-2 "8620", *91*	175	200	_____
(18621) Western Pacific 0-4-0 "8621", *92*		NM	
(18622) Union Pacific 4-4-2 "8622", *90-91 u*	75	95	_____
(18623) Texas & Pacific 4-4-2 "8623", *92*	80	110	_____
(18625) Illinois Central 4-4-2 "8625", *91 u*	80	110	_____
(18626) Delaware & Hudson 2-6-2 "8626", *92*	175	200	_____
(18627) C&O 4-4-2 "8627" or "8633", *92, 93 u, 94*		CP	
(18628) MKT 4-4-2 "8628", *92, 93 u*	75	90	_____
(18630) C&NW 4-6-2 "2903", *93*	300	360	_____
(18632) NYC 4-4-2 "8632", *93-94*		CP	_____
(18633) Union Pacific 4-4-2 "8633", *93-94*		CP	_____
(18633) (See 18627, 18637)			
(18635) Santa Fe 2-6-4 "8625", *93*	200	225	_____
(18636) B&O 4-6-2 "5300", *94*		CP	
(18637) United Auto Workers 4-4-2 "8633", *93 u*		NRS	_____
(18638) Norfolk & Western 2-6-4 "638", *94*		CP	_____
(18641) Ford 4-4-2 "8641", *94 u*		CP	_____
(18689) (See 18207)			
(18700) Rock Island 0-4-0 "8700", *87-88*	40	50	_____
(18702) V&TRR 4-4-0 "8702", *88 (SSS)*	125	150	_____
(18704) Lionel Lines 2-4-0 "8704", *89 u*	40	50	_____
(18705) "Neptune" 0-4-0 "8705", *90-91*	40	50	_____
(18706) Santa Fe 2-4-0 "8706", *91*	40	50	_____
(18707) Mickey's World Tour 2-4-0 "8707", *91, 92 u*	60	75	_____
(18709) Lionel Employee Learning Center "Blue Engine" 0-4-0, *92 u*	—	200	_____
(18710) Southern Pacific 2-4-0 "2000", *93*	35	45	_____
(18711) Southern 2-4-0 "2000", *93*	35	45	_____
(18712) Jersey Central 2-4-0 "2000", *93*	35	45	_____
(18713) Chessie System 2-4-0 "1993", *94*		CP	_____

		Exc	New	Cond/$
(18716)	Lionelville Circus 4-4-0 "8716", *90-91*	100	125	_____
(18800)	Lehigh Valley GP-9 "8800", *87*	110	130	_____
(18801)	Santa Fe U36B "8801", *87*	110	130	_____
(18802)	Southern GP-9 "8802", *87 (SSS)*	125	150	_____
(18803)	Santa Fe RS-3 "8803", *88*	100	120	_____
(18804)	Soo Line RS-3 "8804", *88*	100	120	_____
(18805)	Union Pacific RS-3 "8805", *89*	100	120	_____
(18806)	New Haven SD-18 "8806", *89*	100	120	_____
(18807)	Lehigh Valley RS-3 "8807", *90*	100	125	_____
(18808)	ACL SD-18 "8808", *90*	100	125	_____
(18809)	Susquehanna RS-3 "8809", *89 u* (See 18551)			
(18810)	CSX SD-18 "8810", *90*	100	135	_____
(18811)	Alaska SD-9 "8811", *91*	125	175	_____
(18812)	Kansas City Southern GP-38 "4000", *91*	100	135	_____
(18813)	DM&IR SD-18 "8813", *90 u* (See 18552)			
(18814)	D&H RS-3 "8814", *91 (SSS)*	100	125	_____
(18815)	Amtrak RS-3 "1815", *91, 92 u*	100	135	_____
(18816)	C&NW GP-38-2 "4600", *92*	125	150	_____
(18817)	UP GP-9 "150", *91 u* (See 18553)			
(18818)	Lionel Railroader Club GP-38-2 "1992", *92 u*	125	150	_____
(18819)	L&N GP-38-2 "4136", *92*	125	160	_____
(18820)	WP GP-9 "8820", *92 (SSS)*	125	160	_____
(18821)	Clinchfield GP-38-2 "6005", *93*	125	160	_____
(18823)	Chicago & Illinois Midland SD-9 "52", *92 u* (See 18555)			
(18824)	Montana Rail Link SD-9 "600", *93*	135	165	_____
(18825)	Soo Line GP-38-2 "4000", *93 (SSS)*	135	165	_____
(18826)	Conrail GP-7 "5808", *93*	135	165	_____
(18827)	Happy Holidays RS-3 "8827", *93*	150	175	_____
(18830)	Budweiser GP-9 "1947", *93-94 u*		CP	_____
(18831)	SP GP-20 "4060", *94*		CP	_____
(18832)	PRR RSD-4 "8446", *95*		CP	_____
(18833)	Milwaukee Road RS-3 "2487", *94*		CP	_____
(18834)	C&O SD-28 "8834", *94*		CP	_____
(18835)	NYC RS-3 "8223", *94 (SSS)*		CP	_____
(18836)	Grand Trunk GP-38-2 "5800", *94*		CP	_____
(18837)	Happy Holidays RS-3 "8837", *94*		CP	_____
(18838)	Seaboard RSC-3 "1538", *95*		CP	_____
(18890)	LOTS UP RS-3 "8805", *89 u*	125	150	_____

LTI MODERN ERA (1987-1995)

		Exc	New	Cond/$
(18900) PRR Diesel Switcher "8900", *88 u, 89*		30	40	_____
(18901)/(18902) PRR Alco AA set				
"8901" and "8902", *88*		125	150	_____
(18903)/(18904) Amtrak Alco AA set				
"8903" and "8904", *88-89*		100	150	_____
(18905) PRR 44-tonner "9312", *92*		125	150	_____
(18906) Erie-Lackawanna RS-3 "8906", *91 u*		150	175	_____
(18907) Rock Island 44-tonner "371", *93*		130	160	_____
(18908)/(18909) NYC Alco AA set "8908" and "8909", *93*		100	125	_____
(18910) CSX Diesel Switcher "8910", *93*		30	40	_____
(18911) UP Diesel Switcher "8911", *93*		30	40	_____
(18912) Amtrak Diesel Switcher "8912", *93*		30	40	_____
(18913) Santa Fe Alco A Unit "8913", *93-94*			CP	_____
(18915) WM Alco A Unit "8915", *93*		55	70	_____
(18916) WM Alco A Unit Dummy "8916", *93*		35	40	_____
18917 Soo Line NW-2, *93*		75	95	_____
(18918) B&M NW-2 "8918", *93*		75	95	_____
(18919) Santa Fe Alco A Unit Dummy "8919", *93-94*			CP	_____
(18920) Frisco NW-2 "254", *94*			CP	_____
(18921) C&NW NW-2 "1017", *94*			CP	_____
(18922) New Haven Alco A Unit "8922", *94*			CP	_____
(18923) New Haven Alco A Unit Dummy "8923", *94*			CP	_____
(18924) Illinois Central Diesel Switcher "8924", *94*			CP	_____
(18925) D&RGW Diesel Switcher "8925", *94*			CP	_____
(18926) Reading Diesel Switcher "8926", *94*			CP	_____
(18927) US Navy NW-2 "65-00637", *94*			CP	_____
(18928) C&NW Switcher Calf Unit, *95*			CP	_____
(18929) B&M Switcher Calf Unit, *95*			CP	_____
(18930) Crayola Diesel Switcher, *94 u*			CP	_____
(18931) Chrysler Mopar NW-2 "1818", *94 u*			CP	_____
19000 Blue Comet Dining Car, *87 u*		75	100	_____
19001 Southern Dining Car, *87 u*		75	100	_____
19002 Pennsylvania Dining Car, *88 u*		45	60	_____
19003 Milwaukee Road Dining Car, *88 u*		45	60	_____
19010 B&O Dining Car, *89 u*		50	60	_____
(19011) Lionel Lines Baggage Car "9011", *93*		200	250	_____
(19015) Lionel Lines Passenger Car "9015", *91*		100	125	_____
(19016) Lionel Lines Passenger Car "9016", *91*		100	125	_____
(19017) Lionel Lines Passenger Car "9017", *91*		100	125	_____

LTI MODERN ERA (1987-1995)

		Exc	New	Cond/$
(19018)	Lionel Lines Observation Car "9018", *91*	100	125	_____
(19019)	SP Baggage Car "9019", *93*	125	175	_____
(19023)	SP Passenger Car "9023", *92*	110	130	_____
(19024)	SP Passenger Car "9024", *92*	110	130	_____
(19025)	SP Passenger Car "9025", *92*	110	130	_____
(19026)	SP Observation Car "9026", *92*	110	130	_____
(19027)	Reading Baggage Car "9027", *92*		NM	
(19031)	Reading Passenger Car "9031", *92*		NM	
(19032)	Reading Passenger Car "9032", *92*		NM	
(19033)	Reading Observation Car "9033", *92*		NM	
(19038)	Adolphus Busch Observation Car, *92-93 u*	—	90	_____
(19039)	Pere Marquette Baggage Car, *93*	—	100	_____
(19040)	Pere Marquette Passenger Car "1115", *93*	—	100	_____
(19041)	Pere Marquette Passenger Car "1116", *93*	—	100	_____
(19042)	Pere Marquette Observation Car "36", *93*	—	100	_____
(19100)	Amtrak Baggage Car "9100", *89*	90	110	_____
(19101)	Amtrak Combination Car "9101", *89*	90	110	_____
(19102)	Amtrak Passenger Car "9102", *89*	90	110	_____
(19103)	Amtrak Vista Dome Car "9103", *89*	90	110	_____
(19104)	Amtrak Dining Car "9104", *89*	90	110	_____
(19105)	Amtrak Full Vista Dome Car "9105", *89 u*	100	125	_____
(19106)	Amtrak Observation Car "9106", *89*	90	110	_____
(19107)	SP Full Vista Dome Car, *90 u*	100	125	_____
(19108)	N&W Full Vista Dome Car "576", *91 u*	110	125	_____
(19109)	Santa Fe Baggage Car "3400", *91*	110	125	_____
(19110)	Santa Fe Combination Car "3500", *91*	110	125	_____
(19111)	Santa Fe Dining Car "601", *91*	110	125	_____
(19112)	Santa Fe Passenger Car, *91*	110	125	_____
(19113)	Santa Fe Vista Dome Observation Car, *91*	110	125	_____
(19116)	Great Northern Baggage Car "1200", *92*	95	110	_____
(19117)	Great Northern Combination Car "1240", *92*	95	110	_____
(19118)	Great Northern Passenger Car "1212", *92*	95	110	_____
(19119)	Great Northern Vista Dome Car "1322", *92*	95	110	_____
(19120)	Great Northern Observation Car "1192", *92*	95	110	_____
(19121)	Union Pacific Vista Dome Car "9121", *92 u*	100	125	_____
(19122)	D&RGW California Zephyr Baggage Car, *93*	100	125	_____
(19123)	D&RGW California Zephyr "Silver Bronco" Vista Dome Car, *93*	100	125	_____
(19124)	D&RGW California Zephyr			_____

		Exc	New	Cond/$
	"Silver Colt" Vista Dome Car, *93*	100	125	_____
(19125)	D&RGW California Zephyr "Silver Mustang" Vista Dome Car, *93*	100	125	_____
(19126)	D&RGW California Zephyr "Silver Pony" Vista Dome Car, *93*	100	125	_____
(19127)	D&RGW California Zephyr Vista Dome Observation Car, *93*	100	125	_____
(19128)	Santa Fe Full Vista Dome Car "507", *92 u*	165	200	_____
(19129)	Illinois Central Full Vista Dome Car "9129", *93*	100	125	_____
(19130)	Lackawanna Passenger Cars, set of 4, *94*		CP	_____
(19131)	Lackawanna Baggage Car "2000", *94*		CP	_____
(19132)	Lackawanna Dining Car "469", *94*		CP	_____
(19133)	Lackawanna Passenger Car "260", *94*		CP	_____
(19134)	Lackawanna Observation Car "789", *94*		CP	_____
(19135)	Lackawanna Combination Car "425", *94*		CP	_____
(19136)	Lackawanna Passenger Car "211", *94*		CP	_____
19200	Tidewater Southern Boxcar, *87*	10	20	_____
19201	Lancaster & Chester Boxcar, *87*	60	75	_____
19202	PRR Boxcar, *87*	35	45	_____
19203	D&TS Boxcar, *87*	10	20	_____
19204	Milwaukee Road Boxcar (FF #2), *87*	25	35	_____
19205	Great Northern DD Boxcar (FF #3), *88*	25	35	_____
19206	Seaboard System Boxcar, *88*	15	20	_____
19207	CP Rail DD Boxcar, *88*	15	20	_____
19208	Southern DD Boxcar, *88*	15	20	_____
19209	Florida East Coast Boxcar, *88*	15	20	_____
19210	Soo Line Boxcar, *89*	15	20	_____
19211	Vermont Railway Boxcar, *89*	15	20	_____
19212	PRR Boxcar, *89*	20	25	_____
19213	SP&S DD Boxcar, *89*	15	20	_____
19214	Western Maryland Boxcar (FF #4), *89*	30	35	_____
19215	Union Pacific DD Boxcar, *90*	15	20	_____
19216	Santa Fe Boxcar, *90*	15	20	_____
19217	Burlington Boxcar, *90*	15	20	_____
19218	New Haven Boxcar, *90*	15	20	_____
19219	Lionel Lines 1900-1906 Boxcar w/ Diesel RailSounds, *90*	140	175	_____
19220	Lionel Lines 1926-1934 Boxcar, *90*	30	40	_____
19221	Lionel Lines 1935-1937 Boxcar, *90*	30	40	_____

		Exc	New	Cond/$
19222	Lionel Lines 1948-1950 Boxcar, *90*	30	40	_____
19223	Lionel Lines 1979-1989 Boxcar, *90*	30	40	_____
19228	Cotton Belt Boxcar, *91*	15	20	_____
19229	Frisco Boxcar			
	w/ Diesel RailSounds (FF #5), *91*	130	150	_____
19230	Frisco DD Boxcar (FF #5), *91*	30	40	_____
19231	TA&G DD Boxcar, *91*	15	20	_____
19232	Rock Island DD Boxcar, *91*	15	20	_____
19233	Southern Pacific Boxcar, *91*	15	20	_____
19234	NYC Boxcar, *91*	60	75	_____
19235	MKT Boxcar, *91*	60	75	_____
19236	NKP DD Boxcar (FF #6), *92*	25	35	_____
19237	C&IM Boxcar, *92*	15	20	_____
19238	Kansas City Southern Boxcar, *92*	15	20	_____
19239	Toronto, Hamilton & Buffalo DD Boxcar, *92*	15	20	_____
19240	Great Northern DD Boxcar, *92*	15	20	_____
19241	Mickey Mouse 60th Anniversary			
	Hi-cube Boxcar, *91 u*	125	150	_____
19242	Donald Duck 50th Anniversary			
	Hi-cube Boxcar, *91 u*	125	150	_____
(19243)	Clinchfield Boxcar "9790", *91 u*	40	50	_____
(19244)	L&N Boxcar "9791", *92*	30	40	_____
19245	Mickey's World Tour Hi-cube Boxcar, *92 u*	60	75	_____
19246	Disney World 20th Anniversary			
	Hi-cube Boxcar, *92 u*	60	75	_____
(19247)	6464 Series Boxcars, 1st Edition, set of 3, *93*	150	175	_____
(19248)	Western Pacific Boxcar "6464", *93*	50	60	_____
(19249)	Great Northern Boxcar "6464", *93*	50	60	_____
(19250)	M&St L Boxcar "6464", *93*	50	60	_____
(19251)	Montana Rail Link DD Boxcar "10001", *93*	20	25	_____
19254	Erie Boxcar (FF #7), *93*	30	35	_____
19255	Erie DD Boxcar (FF #7), *93*	30	35	_____
19256	Goofy Hi-cube Boxcar, *93*	50	60	_____
(19257)	6464 Series Boxcars, 2nd Edition, set of 3, *94*		CP	_____
(19258)	Rock Island Boxcar "6464", *94*		CP	_____
(19259)	Western Pacific Boxcar "6464100", *94*		CP	_____
(19260)	Western Pacific Boxcar "6464100", *94*		CP	_____
19261	Perils of Mickey Hi-cube Boxcar I, *93*	50	60	_____
19262	Perils of Mickey Hi-cube Boxcar II, *93*	50	60	_____

LTI MODERN ERA (1987-1995)

		Exc	New	Cond/$
19263	NYC DD Boxcar, *94 (SSS)*		CP	_____
19264	Perils of Mickey Hi-cube Boxcar III, *94*		CP	_____
(19265)	Mickey Mouse 65th Anniversary Hi-cube Boxcar, *94*		CP	_____
(19266)	6464 Series Boxcars, 3rd Edition, set of 3, *95*		CP	_____
(19267)	NYC "Pacemaker" Boxcar "6464125", *95*		CP	_____
(19268)	Missouri Pacific Boxcar "6464150", *95*		CP	_____
(19269)	Rock Island Boxcar "6464", *95*		CP	_____
19300	PRR Ore Car, *87*	20	25	_____
19301	Milwaukee Road Ore Car, *87*	15	20	_____
19302	Milwaukee Road Quad Hopper w/ coal load (FF #2), *87*	25	35	_____
19303	Lionel Lines Quad Hopper w/ coal load, *87 u*	25	35	_____
19304	GN Covered Quad Hopper (FF #3), *88*	35	40	_____
19305	Chessie System Ore Car, *88*	15	20	_____
19307	B&LE Ore Car w/ load, *89*	15	20	_____
19308	GN Ore Car w/ load, *89*	15	20	_____
19309	Seaboard Covered Quad Hopper, *89*	15	20	_____
19310	L&C Quad Hopper w/ coal load, *89*	25	30	_____
19311	SP Covered Quad Hopper, *90*	15	20	_____
19312	Reading Quad Hopper w/ coal load, *90*	30	40	_____
19313	B&O Ore Car w/ load, *90-91*	15	20	_____
19315	Amtrak Ore Car w/ load, *91*	20	25	_____
19316	Wabash Covered Quad Hopper, *91*	20	25	_____
19317	Lehigh Valley Quad Hopper w/ coal load, *91*	60	75	_____
19318	NKP Quad Hopper w/ coal load (FF #6), *92*	30	35	_____
19319	Union Pacific Covered Quad Hopper, *92*	20	25	_____
19320	PRR Ore Car w/ load, *92*	20	25	_____
19321	B&LE Ore Car w/ load, *92*	20	25	_____
19322	C&NW Ore Car w/ load, *93*	25	30	_____
19323	Detroit & Mackinac Ore Car w/ load, *93*	25	30	_____
19324	Erie Quad Hopper w/ coal load (FF #7), *93*	30	35	_____
19400	Milwaukee Road Gondola w/ cable reels (FF #2), *87*	25	35	_____
19400	(See 51701)			
19401	GN Gondola w/ coal load (FF #3), *88*	25	35	_____
19402	GN Crane Car (FF #3), *88*	45	65	
19403	WM Gondola w/ coal load (FF #4), *89*	25	35	_____
19404	Trailer Train Flatcar w/ WM trailers (FF #4), *89*	40	50	_____

		Exc	New	Cond/$
19405	Southern Crane Car, *91*	50	75	_____
19406	West Point Mint Car, *91 u*	50	70	_____
19408	Frisco Gondola w/ coil covers (FF #5), *91*	40	50	_____
19409	Southern Flatcar w/ stakes, *91*	25	35	_____
19410	NYC Gondola w/ canisters, *91*	50	60	_____
19411	NKP Flatcar w/ Sears trailer (FF #6), *92*	60	80	_____
19412	Frisco Crane Car, *92*	50	65	_____
19413	Frisco Flatcar w/ stakes, *92*	25	30	_____
19414	Union Pacific Flatcar w/ stakes, *92 (SSS)*	25	30	_____
(19415)	Erie Flatcar w/ trailer "7200" (FF #7), *93*	30	40	_____
(19416)	ICG TTUX Flatcar set w/ trailers			
	"19417" and "19418", *93 (SSS)*	75	95	_____
19417/19418	ICG TTUX Flatcars w/ trailers			
	(See 19416)			
19419	Charlotte Mint Car, *93*	40	50	_____
19420	Lionel Lines Vat Car, *94*		CP	_____
19500	Milwaukee Road Reefer (FF #2), *87*	35	45	_____
19502	C&NW Reefer, *87*	35	45	_____
19503	Bangor & Aroostook Reefer, *87*	35	40	_____
19504	Northern Pacific Reefer, *87*	30	35	_____
19505	Great Northern Reefer (FF #3), *88*	40	55	_____
19506	Thomas Newcomen Reefer, *88*	25	30	_____
19507	Thomas Edison Reefer, *88*	25	30	_____
19508	Leonardo Da Vinci Reefer, *89*	25	30	_____
19509	Alexander Graham Bell Reefer, *89*	25	30	_____
19510	PRR Stock Car (FARR #5), *89 u*	35	40	_____
19511	WM Reefer (FF #4), *89*	30	35	_____
19512	Wright Brothers Reefer, *90*	25	30	_____
19513	Ben Franklin Reefer, *90*	25	30	_____
19515	Milwaukee Road Stock Car (FF #2), *90 u*	30	35	_____
19516	George Washington Reefer, *89 u, 91*	15	20	_____
19517	Civil War Reefer, *89 u, 91*	15	20	_____
19518	Man on the Moon Reefer, *89 u, 91*	15	20	_____
19519	Frisco Stock Car (FF #5), *91*	35	40	_____
19520	CSX Reefer, *91*	25	30	_____
19522	Guglielmo Marconi Reefer, *91*	25	30	_____
19523	Dr. Robert Goddard Reefer, *91*	25	30	_____
19524	Delaware & Hudson Reefer, *91 (SSS)*	30	35	_____
19525	Speedy Alka Seltzer Reefer, *91 u*	40	50	_____

LTI MODERN ERA (1987-1995)

		Exc	New	Cond/$
19526	Jolly Green Giant Reefer, *91 u*	30	40	_____
19527	Nickel Plate Road Reefer (FF #6), *92*	30	40	_____
19528	Joshua L. Cowen Reefer, *92*	30	40	_____
19529	A.C. Gilbert Reefer, *92*	30	40	_____
19530	Rock Island Stock Car, *92 u*	35	40	_____
19531	Rice Krispies Reefer, *92 u*	40	50	_____
(19532)	Hormel Reefer "901", *92 u*	35	45	_____
19535	Erie Reefer (FF #7), *93*	30	35	_____
19536	Soo Line REA Reefer, *93 (SSS)*	30	35	_____
19537	Kellogg's Corn Flakes Reefer, *93*		NM	
(19538)	Hormel Reefer "102", *94*		CP	_____
19539	Heinz Reefer, *94*		CP	_____
(19599)	Old Glory Reefers, set of 3, *89 u, 91*	40	45	_____
19600	Milwaukee Road 1-D Tank Car (FF # 2), *87*	50	60	_____
19601	North American 1-D Tank Car (FF #4), *89*	50	60	_____
19602	Johnson 1-D Tank Car (FF #5), *91*	40	50	_____
19603	GATX 1-D Tank Car (FF #6), *92*	40	50	_____
19604	Goodyear 1-D Tank Car, *93 (SSS)*	40	50	_____
19605	Hudson's Bay 1-D Tank Car, *94 (SSS)*		CP	_____
19651	Santa Fe Tool Car, *87*	25	30	_____
19652	Jersey Central Bunk Car, *88*	20	25	_____
19653	Jersey Central Tool Car, *88*	20	25	_____
19654	Amtrak Bunk Car, *89*	25	30	_____
19655	Amtrak Tool Car, *90-91*	25	30	_____
19656	Milwaukee Road Bunk Car w/ smoke, *90*	45	55	_____
19657	Wabash Bunk Car w/ smoke, *91-92*	50	60	_____
19658	Norfolk & Western Tool Car, *91*	25	30	_____
19700	Chessie System E/V Caboose, *88*	55	75	_____
19701	Milwaukee Road N5C Caboose (FF #2), *87*	40	50	_____
19702	PRR N5C Caboose, *87*	50	60	_____
19703	Great Northern E/V Caboose (FF #3), *88*	50	60	_____
19704	WM E/V Caboose w/ smoke (FF #4), *89*	60	75	_____
19705	CP Rail E/V Caboose w/ smoke, *89*	60	75	_____
(19706)	UP E/V Caboose w/ smoke "9706", *89*	60	75	_____
19707	SP Work Caboose w/ searchlight and smoke, *90*	75	100	_____
(19708)	Lionel Lines B/W Caboose "1990", *90*	60	75	_____
19709	PRR Work Caboose w/ smoke, *89, 91*	60	80	_____
19710	Frisco E/V Caboose w/ smoke (FF #5), *91*	60	75	_____
19711	Norfolk Southern E/V Caboose w/ smoke, *92*	60	75	_____

LTI MODERN ERA (1987-1995)

		Exc	New	Cond/$
19712	PRR N5C Caboose, *91*	60	75	_____
19714	NYC Work Caboose w/ searchlight and smoke, *92*	75	100	_____
(19715)	DM&IR E/V Caboose "C-217", *92 u*	60	75	_____
(19716)	Illinois Central E/V Caboose			
	w/ smoke "9405", *93*	60	75	_____
(19717)	Susquehanna B/W Caboose "0121", *93*	50	60	_____
(19718)	Chicago & Illinois Midland			
	E/V Caboose "74", *92 u*	—	65	_____
(19719)	Erie B/W Caboose "C-300" (FF #7), *93*	50	60	_____
19720	Soo Line E/V Caboose, *93 (SSS)*	50	65	_____
(19721)	GM&O E/V Caboose "2956", *93 u*	60	75	_____
19723	Disney E/V Caboose, *94*		CP	_____
(19724)	MKT E/V Caboose "125", *94 u*		CP	_____
19800	Circle L Ranch Operating Cattle Car, *88*	100	140	_____
19801	Poultry Dispatch Chicken Car, *87*	40	50	_____
19802	Carnation Milk Car, *87*	100	135	_____
19803	Reading Ice Car, *87*	50	60	_____
19804	Wabash Operating Hopper, *87*	30	40	_____
19805	Santa Fe Operating Boxcar, *87*	30	40	_____
19806	PRR Operating Hopper, *88*	35	45	_____
19807	PRR E/V Caboose w/ smoke, *88*	55	65	_____
19808	NYC Ice Car, *88*	50	60	_____
19809	Erie-Lackawanna Operating Boxcar, *88*	30	40	_____
19810	Bosco Milk Car, *88*	100	125	_____
19811	Monon Brakeman Car, *90*	50	65	_____
19813	Northern Pacific Ice Car, *89 u*	45	60	_____
19815	Delaware & Hudson Brakeman Car, *92*	50	65	_____
19816	Madison Hardware Operating Boxcar			
	"190991", *91 u*	125	150	_____
19817	Virginian Ice Car, *94*		CP	_____
(19818)	Dairymen's League Milk Car "789", *94*		CP	_____
19819	Poultry Dispatch Operating			
	Chicken Car, *94 (SSS)*		CP	_____
(19820)	Diecast Metal Tender w/ RailSounds II, *95*		CP	_____
(19821)	UP Operating Boxcar "9146", *95*		CP	_____
19822	Operating Pork Dispatch Car, *95*		CP	_____
19900	Toy Fair Boxcar, *87 u*	100	125	_____
19901	I Love Virginia Boxcar, *87*	25	35	_____
19902	Toy Fair Boxcar, *88 u*	100	125	_____

LTI MODERN ERA (1987-1995)

No.	Description	Exc	New	Cond/$
19903	Christmas Boxcar, *87 u*	40	50	_____
19904	Christmas Boxcar, *88 u*	45	60	_____
19905	I Love California Boxcar, *88*	20	25	_____
19906	I Love Pennsylvania Boxcar, *89*	20	25	_____
19907	Toy Fair Boxcar, *89 u*	100	125	_____
19908	Christmas Boxcar, *89 u*	35	45	_____
19909	I Love New Jersey Boxcar, *90*	20	25	_____
19910	Christmas Boxcar, *90 u*	30	35	_____
19911	Toy Fair Boxcar, *90 u*	100	125	_____
19912	I Love Ohio Boxcar, *91*	20	25	_____
19913	Christmas Boxcar, *91 u*	40	50	_____
19913	Christmas Boxcar For Lionel Employees, *91 u*	250	300	_____
19914	Toy Fair Boxcar, *91 u*	100	125	_____
19915	I Love Texas Boxcar, *92*	20	25	_____
19916	Christmas Boxcar For Lionel Employees, *92 u*	300	400	_____
19917	Toy Fair Boxcar, *92 u*	125	150	_____
19918	Christmas Boxcar, *92 u*	60	75	_____
19919	I Love Minnesota Boxcar, *93*	25	30	_____
(19920)	Lionel Visitor's Center Boxcar, *92 u*	30	40	_____
19921	Christmas Boxcar For Lionel Employees, *93 u*	250	300	_____
19922	Christmas Boxcar, *93*	40	50	_____
19923	Toy Fair Boxcar, *93 u*	100	150	_____
19924	Lionel Railroader Club Boxcar, *93 u*	30	40	_____
19925	Learning Center Boxcar For Lionel Employees, *93 u*	300	350	_____
19926	I Love Nevada Boxcar, *94*		CP	_____
(19927)	Lionel Visitor's Center Boxcar "1993", *93 u*	30	40	_____
19928	Christmas Boxcar For Lionel Employees, *94 u*		CP	_____
19929	Christmas Boxcar, *94*		CP	_____
19930	Lionel Railroader Club Quad Hopper w/ coal load, *94 u*		CP	_____
19931	Toy Fair Boxcar, *94 u*		CP	_____
19932	Lionel Visitor's Center Boxcar, *94 u*		CP	_____
19933	I Love Illinois Boxcar, *95*		CP	_____
(19960)	LOTS Western Pacific Boxcar "1952" (Std. O), *92 u*	75	95	_____
19961	Gadsden Pacific Inspiration Consolidated Copper Company Ore Car w/ load, *92 u*	40	50	_____
(19962)	Southwest TTOS SP 3-bay ACF			

		Exc	New	Cond/$
	Hopper "496035" (Std. O), *92 u*	70	85	_____
(19963)	TTOS Union Equity 3-bay ACF Hopper "86892" (Std. O), *92 u*	65	75	_____
(19964)	US JCI Senate Boxcar, *92 u*	75	100	_____
(23001)	Operating Base Smithsonian NYC Hudson, *92 u*		CP	_____
(23002)	Operating Base NYC Hudson, *92 u, 93-94*		CP	_____
(23003)	Operating Base PRR B-6 Switcher, *92 u, 93-94*		CP	_____
(23004)	Operating Base NP 4-8-4, *92 u, 93-94*		CP	_____
(23005)	Operating Base Reading T-1, *92 u, 93-94*		CP	_____
(23006)	Operating Base Chessie System T-1, *92- u, 93-94*		CP	_____
(23007)	Operating Base SP Daylight, *92 u, 93-94*		CP	_____
(23008)	Operating Base NYC L-3 Mohawk, *92 u, 93-94*		CP	_____
(23009)	Operating Base PRR S-2 Turbine, *92 u, 93-94*		CP	_____
(23012)	Operating Base F-3 ABA Diesels, *92 u, 93-94*		CP	_____
24876	(See 17405)			
26269	(See 17304)			
DX26925	(See 12810)			
(33000)	Lionel Lines RailScope GP-9 "3000", *88-90*	175	225	_____
(33002)	RailScope B&W TV, *88-90*	50	75	_____
(33004)	NYC RailScope GP-9 "3004", *90*		NM	
(33005)	Union Pacific RailScope GP-9 "3005", *90*		NM	
[38356]	LOTS Dow Chemical 3-D Tank Car, *87*	75	100	_____
45003	(See 17217)			
51200	(See 17510)			
(51300)	Shell Semi-Scale 1-D Tank Car "8124", *91*	—	120	_____
(51301)	Lackawanna Semi-Scale Reefer "7000", *92*	—	135	_____
(51401)	PRR Semi-Scale Boxcar "100800", *91*	—	120	_____
(51402)	C&O Semi-Scale Stock Car "95250", *92*	—	135	_____
(51501)	B&O Semi-Scale Hopper "532000", *91*	—	120	_____
(51701)	NYC Semi-Scale Caboose "19400", *91*	—	140	_____
(51702)	PRR N-8 Caboose "478039", *91-92*	—	265	_____
52000	Detroit-Toledo TCA Flatcar w/ trailer, *92 u*	80	100	_____
52001	NETCA B&M Quad Hopper w/ coal load, *92 u*	50	60	_____
52003	Ozark TCA "Meet Me in St. Louis" Flatcar w/ trailer, *92 u*		NRS	_____
[52004]	LCAC Algoma Central Gondola w/ coil covers "9215", *92 u*		CP	_____
[52005]	LCAC Canadian National F-3 B Unit, *93 u*		CP	_____
[52006]	LCAC CP Boxcar "930016" (Std. O), *93 u*		CP	_____

		Exc	New
[52007]	NLOE Long Island RS-3 "1552", *92 u*		NRS ___
(52008)	TCA Bucyrus Erie Crane Car "1993X", *93 u*	60	75 ___
(52009)	Sacramento Valley TTOS Western Pacific Boxcar "64641993", *93 u*	65	80 ___
(52010)	TTOS Weyerhaeuser DD Boxcar "838593" (Std. O), *93 u*	55	70 ___
52011	Tucson, Cornelia & Gila Bend Ore Car w/ load, *93 u*	30	40 ___
52013	Artrain Norfolk Southern Flatcar w/ trailer (Std. O), *92 u*	200	250 ___
(52014)	LOTS BN TTUX Flatcar set w/ N&W trailers "637500A" & "637500B", *93 u*	125	150 ___
52016	NETCA B&M Gondola w/ coil covers, *93 u*	50	60 ___
52018	Lakes & Pines TCA 3-M Boxcar, *93 u*		NRS ___
[52019]	NLOE Long Island Boxcar "8393", *93 u*		NRS ___
[52020]	NLOE Long Island B/W Caboose "8393", *93 u*		NRS ___
(52021)	TTOS Weyerhaeuser Tractor & Trailer, *93 u*	20	25 ___
52022	TTOS Union Pacific Boxcar, *93 u*		NRS ___
(52023)	LCCA D&TS 2-bay ACF Hopper "2601" (Std. O), *93 u*	60	75 ___
52024	Artrain Conrail Auto Carrier, *93 u*	85	100 ___
(52025)	LCCA Madison Hardware Tractor & Trailer, *93 u*	25	30 ___
[52026]	NLOE Flatcar w/ Grumman trailer "8394", *94 u*		CP ___
52027	Gadsden Pacific Pinto Valley Mine Ore Car w/ load, *94 u*		CP ___
(52028)	TTOS Ford Cars, set of 3, *94 u*		CP ___
(52029)	TTOS Ford 1-D Tank Car "12" (O27), *94 u*		CP ___
(52030)	TTOS Ford Gondola "4023", *94 u*		CP ___
(52031)	TTOS Ford Hopper "1458" (O27), *94 u*		CP ___
(52032)	TTOS Ford 1-D Tank Car "14" w/ Kughn inscription (O27), *94 u*		CP ___
(52035)	TCA Yorkrail GP-9 "1752", shell only, *94 u*		CP ___
(52036)	TCA 40th Anniversary B/W Caboose, *94 u*		CP ___
(52037)	TCA Yorkrail GP-9 "1754", *94 u*		CP ___
(52038)	LCCA Southern Hopper w/ coal load "360794" (Std. O), *94 u*		CP ___
(52039)	LCCA "Track 29" Bumper, *94 u*		CP ___
52040	Wolverine TTOS GTW Flatcar w/ Lionel Lines Tractor & Trailer, *95 u*		CP ___

		Exc	New	Cond/$
1)	LOTS BN TTUX Flatcar set w/ Conrail trailers "637500D" and "637500E", *94 u*		CP	_____
2042)	LOTS BN TTUX Flatcar w/ CN trailer "637500C", *94 u*		CP	_____
[52043]	NETCA LL Bean Boxcar, *94 u*		CP	_____
52044	Eastwood Vat Car, *94 u*		CP	_____
(52046)	TTOS ACL Boxcar "16247", *94 u*		CP	_____
(52047)	Southwest TTOS Cotton Belt Woodside Caboose w/ smoke "1921" (Std. O), *93-94 u*		CP	_____
(52048)	LOTS CN Tractor and Trailer, *94 u*		CP	_____
52049	Artrain BN Gondola w/ coil covers, *94 u*		CP	_____
52053	TTOS Carail Boxcar, *94 u*		CP	_____
52054	Carail Boxcar, *94 u*		CP	_____
(52055)	LCCA SOVEX Tractor and Trailer, *94 u*		CP	_____
(52056)	LCCA Southern Tractor and Trailer, *94 u*		CP	_____
(52058)	Central California TTOS Santa Fe Boxcar "64641895", *95 u*		CP	_____
(52059)	Eastern TCA Clinchfield Quad Hopper w/ coal load "16413", *94 u*		CP	_____
[52061]	NLOE Stern's Pickle Products Vat Car, *95 u*		CP	_____
59629	(See 17874)			
60029	(See 17118)			
60155	(See 17216)			
72867	(See 17121)			
78286	(See 17906)			
79052	(See 16554)			
81487	(See 17871)			
81988	(See 17872)			
86892	(See 19963)			
[87010]	LCAC CN Express Reefer, *87 u*		NRS	_____
[88011]	LCAC CN Woodside Caboose (Std. O), *88 u*		NRS	_____
95250	(See 51402)			
100800	(See 51401)			
151161	(See 17890)			
173872	(See 17007)			
190991	(See 19816)			
245998	(See 17404)			
295110	(See 17120)			
296000	(See 17209)			
298011	(See 17882)			

		Exc	New	Cond/$
360794	(See 52038)			
371629	(See 17403)			
385405	(See 17406)			
459400	(See 17305)			
459401	(See 17306)			
478039	(See 51702)			
496035	(See 19962)			
532000	(See 51501)			
610584	(See 12827)			
637500A/B	(See 52014)			
637500D/E	(See 52041)			
637500C	(See 52042)			
640000	(See 16912)			
640001	(See 16912)			
800200	(See 17122)			
838593	(See 52010)			
[900013]	LCAC CN Flatcar w/ trailers, *90 u*		NRS	___
[930016]	(See 52006)			
3739469	(See 17877)			
6106888	(See 16252)			
No Number	Amtrak Passenger set, *89, 89 u*	800	1000	___
No Number	C&NW Passenger set, *93*	500	600	___
No Number	D&RGW "California Zephyr" set, *92, 93*	1400	1600	___
No Number	Erie-Lackawanna Passenger set, *93, 94*		CP	___
No Number	Erie set (FF #7), *93*	500	600	___
No Number	Frisco set (FF #5), *91*	500	550	___
No Number	Great Northern "Empire Builder" set, *92*	950	1100	___
No Number	Great Northern set (FF #3), *88*	450	500	___
No Number	Illinois Central "City of New Orleans" set, *85, 87*	1300	1500	___
No Number	Illinois Central set, *91-92*	300	325	___
No Number	Madison Car set, *91, 93*	600	700	___
No Number	The Mint set, *79 u, 80-83, 84 u, 86 u, 87, 91 u, 93*	1200	1400	___
No Number	Milwaukee Road set (FF #2), *87, 90 u*	450	500	___
No Number	Missouri Pacific set, *95*		CP	___
No Number	Norfolk & Western Passenger set, *94*		CP	___
No Number	Nickel Plate Road set (FF #6), *92*	500	600	___
No Number	New Haven set, *94, 95*		CP	___

LTI MODERN ERA (1987-1995)

		Exc	New	Cond/$
No Number	Northern Pacific set, *90-92*	250	325	_____
No Number	New York Central set, *89, 91*	300	350	_____
No Number	Pennsylvania set, *87-90*	300	350	_____
No Number	Pere Marquette set, *93*	900	1000	_____
No Number	SP Daylight Steam set, *90, 92, 93*	1000	1200	_____
No Number	Union Pacific set, *94*		CP	_____
No Number	Wabash set (FF #1), *86, 87*	1000	1200	_____
No Number	Western Maryland set (FF #4), *89*	450	525	_____

O GAUGE CLASSICS

		Exc	New	Cond/$
1-263E	Lionel Lines "Blue Comet" 2-4-2 (See 51004)			
44E	(See 51100)			
350E	Lionel Lines "Hiawatha" 4-4-2 (See 51000)			
882	Lionel Lines Combination Car (See 51000)			
883	Lionel Lines Passenger Car (See 51000)			
884	Lionel Lines Observation Car (See 51000)			
892	(See 51202)			
893	(See 51203)			
894	(See 51204)			
895	(See 51205)			
1612	Lionel Lines Passenger Car (See 51004)			
1613	Lionel Lines Passenger Car (See 51004)			
1614	Lionel Lines Baggage Car (See 51004)			
1615	Lionel Lines Observation Car (See 51004)			
8814	(See 51400)			
8816	(See 51500)			
8817	(See 51700)			
8820	(See 51800)			
(51000)	Milwaukee Road Hiawatha set, *88 u*	—	750	_____
(51001)	Lionel #44 Freight Special set, *89*	—	500	_____
(51004)	Blue Comet set, *91*	—	1000	_____
(51100)	Lionel Lines Electric "44E", *89* (See 51001)			
(51201)	Rail Chief Passenger Cars, set of 4, *90*	—	700	_____
(51202)	Lionel Lines Combination Car "892" (See 51201)			
(51203)	Lionel Lines Passenger Car "893" (See 51201)			
(51204)	Lionel Lines Passenger Car "894" (See 51201)			
(51205)	Lionel Lines Observation Car "895" (See 51201)			
(51400)	Lionel Lines Boxcar "8814", *89* (See 51001)			

LTI MODERN ERA (1987-1995)

(51500) Lionel Lines Hopper "8816", *89* (See 51001)
(51700) Lionel Lines Caboose "8817", *89* (See 51001)
(51800) Lionel Lines Searchlight Car "8820", *89* (See 51001)

STANDARD GAUGE CLASSICS

1-44 (See 13805)
1-214 (See 13605)
1-215 (See 13303)
1-318E Lionel Lines Electric (See 13001)
1-381E (See 13102)
1-384E (See 13101)
1-390E (See 13100)
1-400E (See 13103)
1-408E (See 13107)
1-4390 American Flyer "West Point" Baggage Car (See 13003)
1-4391 American Flyer "Academy" Passenger Car (See 13003)
1-4392 American Flyer "Army Navy" Observation Car (See 13003)
1-4689 (Sec 13109)
2-390E (See 13106)
2-400E (See 13108)
7E (See 13104)
8 (See 13803)
9 (See 13803)
126 (See 13801)
183 (See 13413)
184 (See 13414)
185 (See 13415)
200 (See 13900)
201 (See 13901)
323 (See 13400)
324 (See 13401)
325 (See 13402)
326 (See 13416)
327 (See 13417)
328 (See 13418)
437 (See 13804)
1115 (See 13800)
1217 (See 13702)

LTI MODERN ERA (1987-1995)		Exc	New	Cond/$
1412	(See 13404)			
1413	(See 13405)			
1414	(See 13407)			
1416	(See 13406)			
1420	(See 13409)			
1421	(See 13410)			
1422	(See 13411)			
1423	(See 13425)			
1512	(See 13300)			
1513	(See 13600)			
1517	(See 13700)			
1520	(See 13200)			
2412	(See 13421)			
2413	(See 13422)			
2414	(See 13423)			
2416	(See 13424)			
4400C	(See 51900)			
5130	Lionel Lines Flatcar w/ lumber (See 13001)			
5140	Lionel Lines Reefer (See 13001)			
5150	Lionel Lines "Shell" Tank Car (See 13001)			
5160	Lionel Lines Caboose (See 13001)			
(13001)	1-318E Freight Express Train set, *90-91*	—	900	___
(13002)	Fireball Express set, *90 u*	—	1100	___
(13003)	American Flyer "Mayflower" Passenger Car set, *92*	—	1500	___
(13100)	Lionel Lines 2-4-2 "1-390E", *88 u*	—	550	___
(13101)	Lionel Lines 2-4-0 "1-384E", *89 u*	—	590	___
(13102)	Lionel Lines Electric "1-381E", *89 u*	—	800	___
(13103)	Lionel Lines "Blue Comet" 4-4-4 "1-400E", *90*	—	1100	___
(13104)	Lionel Lines "Old #7" 4-4-0 "7E", *90*	—	800	___
(13106)	Lionel Lines "Fireball Express" 2-4-2 "2-390E" (See 13002)			
(13107)	Lionel Lines Electric "1-408E" , *91*	—	800	___
(13108)	Lionel Lines 4-4-4 "2-400E" *91*	—	1030	___
(13109)	American Flyer "Mayflower" Electric "1-4689", *92*	—	1100	___
(13200)	Lionel Lines Searchlight Car "1520", *89 u*	—	145	___
(13300)	Lionel Lines Gondola "1512", *89 u*	—	102	___
(13303)	Lionel Lines "Sunoco" Tank Car "1-215", *92*	—	200	___
(13400)	Lionel Lines Baggage Car "323", *88 u*	—	200	___

LTI MODERN ERA (1987-1995)

		Exc	New	Cond/$
(13401)	Lionel Lines Passenger Car "324", 88 u	—	200	___
(13402)	Lionel Lines Observation Car "325", 88 u	—	200	___
(13403)	Lionel Lines State Passenger Car set, 89 u	—	1500	___
(13404)	Lionel Lines "California" Passenger Car "1412" (See 13403)			
(13405)	Lionel Lines "Colorado" Passenger Car "1413" (See 13403)			
(13406)	Lionel Lines "New York" Observation Car "1416" (See 13403)			
(13407)	Lionel Lines "Illinois" Passenger Car "1414", 90 u	—	575	___
(13408)	Lionel Lines "Blue Comet" Passenger Car set, 90	—	1375	___
(13409)	Lionel Lines "Faye" Passenger Car "1420" (See 13408)			
(13410)	Lionel Lines "Westphal" Passenger Car "1421" (See 13408)			
(13411)	Lionel Lines "Tempel" Observation Car "1422" (See 13408)			
(13412)	Lionel Lines "Old #7" Passenger Car set, 90	—	800	___
(13413)	Lionel Lines Combination Car "183" (See 13412)			
(13414)	Lionel Lines Passenger Car "184" (See 13412)			
(13415)	Lionel Lines Observation Car "185" (See 13412)			
(13416)	Lionel Lines "New Jersey" Baggage Car "326" (See 13002)			
(13417)	Lionel Lines "Connecticut" Passenger Car "327" (See 13002)			
(13418)	Lionel Lines "New York" Observation Car "328" (See 13002)			
(13420)	Lionel Lines State Passenger Car set, 91	—	1800	___
(13421)	Lionel Lines "California" Passenger Car "2412" (See 13420)			
(13422)	Lionel Lines "Colorado" Passenger Car "2413" (See 13420)			
(13423)	Lionel Lines "Illinois" Passenger Car "2414", 92 u	—	500	___
(13424)	Lionel Lines "New York" Observation Car "2416" (See 13420)			
(13425)	Lionel Lines "Barnard" Passenger Car "1423", 91 u	—	600	___
(13600)	Lionel Lines Cattle Car "1513", 89 u	—	120	___

LTI MODERN ERA (1987-1995)

		Exc	New	Cond/$
13601	Season's Greetings Boxcar, *89 u*	—	125	_____
13602	Season's Greetings Boxcar, *90 u*	—	125	_____
13604	Season's Greetings Boxcar, *91 u*	—	150	_____
(13605)	Lionel Lines Boxcar "1-214", *92*	—	200	_____
(13700)	Lionel Lines Caboose "1517", *89 u*	—	138	_____
(13702)	Lionel Lines Caboose "1217", *91*	—	170	_____
(13800)	Lionelville Passenger Station "1115", *88 u*	200	250	_____
(13801)	Lionelville Station "126", *89 u*	—	155	_____
(13802)	Lionel Runabout Boat, *90*	—	470	_____
(13803)	Lionel Racing Automobiles "8" & "9", *91*	—	640	_____
(13804)	Lionelville Switch Tower "437", *91*	—	250	_____
(13805)	Lionel Racing Boat "1-44", *91*	—	475	_____
(13807)	Racing Automobiles Straight Track, *91 u*		NRS	_____
(13808)	Racing Automobiles Inner Radius Curve Track, *91 u*		NRS	_____
(13809)	Racing Automobiles Outer Radius Curve Track, *91 u*		NRS	_____
(13900)	Electric Rapid Transit Trolley "200", *89 u*	—	250	_____
(13901)	Electric Rapid Transit Trolley Trailer "201", *89 u*	—	180	_____
(51900)	Signal Bridge and Control Panel "4400C", *89 u*	—	280	_____

ARTRAIN

____	**9486**	GTW "I Love Michigan" Boxcar, *87*
____	**17885**	Artrain 1-D Tank Car, *90*
____	**17891**	Artrain Grand Trunk Boxcar, *91*
____	**52013**	Artrain Norfolk Southern Flatcar w/ trailer (Std. O), *92*
____	**52024**	Artrain Conrail Auto Carrier, *93*
____	**52049**	Artrain Burlington Northern Gondola w/ coil covers, *94*

INLAND EMPIRE TRAIN COLLECTORS ASSOC. (IETCA)

____	**[1979]**	IETCA Boxcar, *79*
____	**[1980]**	IETCA SP Caboose, *80*
____	**[1981]**	IETCA Quad Hopper, *81*
____	**[1982]**	IETCA 3-D Tank Car, *82*
____	**[1983]**	IETCA Reefer, *83*
____	**[7522]**	IETCA Carson City Mint Car, *84*
____	**[1986]**	IETCA Bunk Car, *86*

LIONEL CENTRAL OPERATING LINES (LCOL)

____	**[1981]**	LCOL Boxcar, *81*
____	**[9184]**	Erie B/W Caboose, *82*
____	**[6508]**	Canadian Pacific Crane Car, *83*
____	**[5724]**	Pennsylvania Bunk Car, *84*
____	**[9475]**	D&H "I Love NY" Boxcar, *85*
____	**[1986]**	LCOL Work Caboose, shell only, *86*

LIONEL COLLECTORS ASSOC. OF CANADA (LCAC)

____	**[9718]**	Canadian National Boxcar, *79*
____	**[9413]**	Napierville Junction Boxcar, *80*
____	**[8103]**	Toronto, Hamilton & Buffalo Boxcar, *81*
____	**[8204]**	Algoma Central Boxcar, *82*
____	**[6100]**	Ontario Northland Covered Quad Hopper, *82*
____	**[830005]**	Canadian National Boxcar, *83*
____	**[5710]**	Canadian Pacific Reefer, *83*
____	**[840006]**	Canadian Wheat Board Covered Quad Hopper, *84*
____	**[8507/8508]**	Canadian National F-3 AA, shells only, *85*
____	**[5714]**	Michigan Central Reefer, *85*
____	**[86009]**	Canadian National Bunk Car, *86*

UNCATALOGED CLUB CARS AND SPECIAL PRODUCTION

____	**[87010]**	Canadian National Express Reefer, *87*
____	**[88011]**	Canadian National Woodside Caboose (Std. O), *88*
____	**[8912]**	Canada Southern Operating Hopper, *89*
____	**[900013]**	Canadian National Flatcar w/ trailers, *90*
____	**[17893]**	BAOC 1-D Tank Car "914", *91*
____	**[52004]**	Algoma Central Gondola w/ coil covers "9215", *92*
____	**[52005]**	Canadian National F-3 B Unit, *93*
____	**[52006]**	Canadian Pacific Boxcar "930016" (Std. O), *93*

LIONEL COLLECTORS CLUB OF AMERICA (LCCA)

____	**[9701]**	Baltimore & Ohio DD Boxcar, *72*
____	**9727**	TA&G Boxcar, *73*
____	**9118**	Corning Covered Quad Hopper, *74*
____	**9155**	Monsanto 1-D Tank Car, *75*
____	**9212**	Seaboard Coast Line Flatcar w/ trailers, *76*
____	**X9259**	Southern B/W Caboose, *77*
____	**9728**	Union Pacific Stock Car, *78*
____	**9733**	Airco Boxcar w/ tank, *79*
____	**9358**	Sands of Iowa Covered Quad Hopper, *80*
____	**(8068)**	Rock Island GP-20 Diesel "1980", *80*
____	**9435**	Central of Georgia Boxcar, *81*
____	**9460**	D&TS DD Boxcar, *82*
____	**6112**	Commonwealth Edison Quad Hopper w/ coal load, *83*
____	**7403**	LNAC Boxcar, *84*
____	**(6567)**	Illinois Central Gulf Crane Car "100408", *85*
____	**6323**	Virginia Chemicals 1-D Tank Car, *86*
____	**17870**	East Camden & Highland Boxcar (Std. O), *87*
____	**17873**	Ashland Oil 3-D Tank Car, *88*
____	**17876**	Columbia, Newberry & Laurens Boxcar (Std. O), *89*
____	**17880**	D&RGW Woodside Caboose (Std. O), *90*
____	**(18090)**	D&RGW 4-6-2 "1990", *90*
____	**17887**	Conrail Flatcar w/ Armstrong Tile trailer (Std. O), *91*
____	**17888**	Conrail Flatcar w/ Ford New Holland trailer (Std. O), *91*
____	**(17899)**	NASA Uni-body Tank Car "190" (Std. O), *92*
____	**(52023)**	D&TS 2-bay ACF Hopper "2601" (Std. O), *93*
____	**(52038)**	Southern Hopper w/ coal load "360794" (Std. O), *94*

LCCA Meet Specials

____	**[6014-900]**	Frisco Boxcar (O27), *75-76*
____	**[No Number]**	Lionel Lines Tender only, *76-77*
____	**[9142]**	Republic Steel Gondola w/ canisters, *77-78*
____	**[9036]**	Mobilgas 1-D Tank Car (O27), *78-79*

UNCATALOGED CLUB CARS AND SPECIAL PRODUCTION

____	[9016]	Chessie System Hopper (027), *79-80*
____	6483	Jersey Central SP Caboose, *82*

Other LCCA Production

____	[9771]	Norfolk & Western Boxcar, *77*
____	[9739]	D&RGW Boxcar, *78*
____	(17895)	LCCA Tractor, *91*
____	(17896)	Lancaster Lines Tractor, *91*
____	(52025)	Madison Hardware Tractor & Trailer, *93*
____	(52039)	"Track 29" Bumper, *94*
____	(52055)	SOVEX Tractor & Trailer, *94*
____	(52056)	Southern Tractor & Trailer, *94*

LIONEL OPERATING TRAIN SOCIETY (LOTS)

____	[9414]	Cotton Belt Boxcar, *80*
____	[3764]	Kahn Boxcar, *81*
____	[80948]	Michigan Central Boxcar, *82*
____	[6111]	L&N Covered Quad Hopper, *83*
____	[121315]	Pennsylvania Hi-cube Boxcar, *84*
____	[303]	Stauffer Chemical 1-D Tank Car, *85*
____	[6211]	C&O Gondola w/ canisters, *86*
____	[38356]	Dow Chemical 3-D Tank Car, *87*
____	(17874)	Milwaukee Road Log Dump Car "59629", *88*
____	(17875)	PHD Boxcar "1289", *89*
____	(17882)	B&O DD Boxcar w/ ETD "298011", *90*
____	(18890)	Union Pacific RS-3 "8805", *90*
____	(17890)	CSX Auto Carrier "151161", *91*
____	(19960)	Western Pacific Boxcar "1952" (Std. O), *92*
____	(52014)	BN TTUX Flatcar set w/ N&W Trailers "637500A/B", *93*
____	(52041)	BN TTUX Flatcar set w/ Conrail Trailers "637500D/E", *94*

Other LOTS Production:

____	[1223]	Seattle & North Coast Hi-cube Boxcar, *86*
____	(52042)	BN TTUX Flatcar w/ Canadian National Trailer "637500C", *94*
____	(52048)	Canadian National Tractor and Trailer, *94*

LIONEL RAILROADER CLUB (LRRC)

____	0780	LRRC Boxcar, *82*
____	0781	LRRC Flatcar w/ trailers, *83*
____	0784	LRRC Covered Quad Hopper, *84*

UNCATALOGED CLUB CARS AND SPECIAL PRODUCTION

____ **0782**   LRRC 1-D Tank Car, *85*
____ **16800**   LRRC Ore Car, *86*
____ **16801**   LRRC Bunk Car, *88*
____ **16802**   LRRC Tool Car, *89*
____ **16803**   LRRC Searchlight Car, *90*
____ **16804**   LRRC B/W Caboose, *91*
____ **(18818)**   LRRC GP-38-2 "1992", *92*
____ **19924**   LRRC Boxcar, *93*
____ **19930**   LRRC Quad Hopper w/ coal load, *94*
____ **(12875)**   LRRC Tractor and Trailer, *94*

NASSAU LIONEL OPERATING ENGINEERS (NLOE)

____ **[8389]**   Long Island Boxcar, *89*
____ **[8390]**   Long Island Covered Quad Hopper, *90*
____ **[8391A]**   Long Island Bunk Car, *91*
____ **[8391B]**   Long Island Tool Car, *91*
____ **[17893]**   Long Island 1-D Tank Car "8392", *92*
____ **[52007]**   Long Island RS-3 "1552", *93*
____ **[52019]**   Long Island Boxcar "8393", *93*
____ **[52020]**   Long Island B/W Caboose "8393", *93*
____ **[52026]**   NLOE Flatcar w/ Grumman trailer "8394", *94*
____ **[52061]**   Stern's Pickle Products Vat Car "8395", *95*

TRAIN COLLECTORS ASSOCIATION (TCA)

TCA National Convention Cars

____ **6464-1970**   TCA Chicago Boxcar, *70*
____ **6464-1971**   TCA Disneyland Boxcar, *71*
____ **6315**   TCA Pittsburgh 1-D Tank Car, *72*
____ **(9123)**   TCA Dearborn Auto Carrier, *73*
____ **9864**   TCA Seattle Reefer, *74*
____ **9774**   TCA Southern Belle Boxcar, *75*
____ **9779**   TCA Philadelphia Boxcar, *76*
____ **7812**   TCA Houston Stock Car, *77*
____ **9611**   TCA Boston Hi-cube Boxcar, *78*
____ **9319**   TCA Silver Jubilee Mint Car, *79*
____ **(9544)**   TCA Chicago Observation Car "1980", *80*
____ **(0511)**   TCA St. Louis Baggage Car "1981", *81*
____ **(7205)**   TCA Denver Combination Car "1982", *82*
____ **(7206)**   TCA Louisville Passenger Car "1983", *83*
____ **(7212)**   TCA Pittsburgh Passenger Car "1984", *84*
____ **5734-85**   TCA REA Reefer, *85*

UNCATALOGED CLUB CARS AND SPECIAL PRODUCTION

____	**5484**	TCA 4-6-4, *85*
____	**6926**	TCA New Orleans E/V Caboose, *86*
____	**(17879)**	TCA Valley Forge Dining Car "1989", *89*
____	**(17883)**	New Georgia Railroad Passenger Car, *90*
____	**(17898)**	Wabash Reefer, *92*
____	**(52008)**	Bucyrus Erie Crane Car "1993X", *93*
____	**(11737)**	TCA 40th Anniversary F-3 ABA set "40", *93*
____	**(52035)**	Yorkrail GP-9 "1752", shell only, *94*
____	**(52036)**	TCA 40th Anniversary B/W Caboose, *94*
____	**(52037)**	Yorkraii GP-9 "1754", *94*

TCA Museum-Related Cars

____	**[9771]**	Norfolk & Western Boxcar, *77*
____	**[9785]**	Conrail Boxcar, *77*
____	**[9264]**	Illinois Central Gulf Covered Quad Hopper, *78*
____	**[9786]**	Chicago & North Western Boxcar, *79*
____	**[1018-1979]**	Mortgage Burning Hi-cube Boxcar, *79*
____	**[9289]**	Chicago & North Western N5C Caboose, *80*
____	**[7780]**	TCA Museum Boxcar, *80*
____	**[7781]**	Hafner Boxcar, *81*
____	**[7782]**	Carlisle & Finch Boxcar, *82*
____	**[7783]**	Ives Boxcar, *83*
____	**[7784]**	Voltamp Boxcar, *84*
____	**[7785]**	Hoge Boxcar, *85*
____	**[5731]**	L&N Reefer, *90*

Atlantic Division TCA

____	**[9788]**	Lehigh Valley Boxcar, *78*
____	**[9186]**	Conrail N5C Caboose, *79*
____	**[1980]**	Atlantic Division Flatcar w/ trailers, *80*
____	**[6101]**	Burlington Northern Covered Quad Hopper, *82*
____	**[9466]**	Wanamaker Boxcar, *83*
____	**[9193]**	Budweiser Vat Car, *84*
____	**[No Number]**	Pennsylvania Reading Seashore Bunk Car, *85*

Eastern Division TCA

____	**(52059)**	Clinchfield Quad Hopper w/ coal load "16413", *94*

Eastern Division TCA - Washington, Baltimore and Annapolis Chapter

____	**[9740]**	Chessie System Boxcar, *76*
____	**[9783]**	B&O "Timesaver" Boxcar, *77*

ALOGED CLUB CARS AND SPECIAL PRODUCTION

_ [9771]   Norfolk & Western Boxcar, *78*

__ [9412]   Richmond, Fredericksburg, & Potomac Boxcar, *79*

Ft. Pitt Division TCA

_____ [1984-30X] Heinz Ketchup Boxcar, *84*

_____ [1984]   Iron City Beer Reefer, *84*

_____ [1984]   Iron City Beer Boxcar, *84*

_____ [1984]   Heinz Pickles Boxcar, *84*

Great Lakes Division TCA

____ [9740]   Chessie System Boxcar, *76*

____ [1983]   Churchill Downs Boxcar, *83*

____ [1983]   Churchill Downs Reefer, *83*

Great Lakes Division TCA - Detroit & Toledo Chapter

____ [9730]   CP Rail Boxcar, *76*

____ [9119]   Detroit & Mackinac Covered Quad Hopper, *77*

____ [9401]   Great Northern Boxcar, *78*

____ [9272]   New Haven B/W Caboose, *79*

____ [8957]   Burlington Northern GP-20, *80*

____ [8958]   Burlington Northern GP-20 Dummy, *80*

____ 52000   Detroit-Toledo Flatcar w/ trailer, *92*

Great Lakes Division TCA - Three Rivers Chapter

____ [9113]   Norfolk & Western Quad Hopper, *76*

Great Lakes Division TCA - Western Michigan Chapter

____ [9730]   CP Rail Boxcar, *74*

Lake & Pines Division TCA

_____ 52018   3-M Boxcar, 93

Lone Star Division TCA

_____ [7522]   New Orleans Mint Car w/ coin, *86*

Lone Star Division TCA - North Texas Chapter

____ [9739]   D&RGW Boxcar, *76*

____ [9184]   Erie B/W Caboose, *77*

UNCATALOGED CLUB CARS AND SPECIAL PRODUCTION

_____ **[9119]**   Detroit & Mackinac Covered Quad Hopper, *78*
_____ **[No Number]** Texas Special F-3 A Unit, shell only, *81*
_____ **[No Number]** Texas Special F-3 B Unit, shell only, *82*

METCA

_____ **[10]**   Jersey Central F-3 A Unit, shell only, *71*
_____ **[9754]**   New York Central "Pacemaker" Boxcar, *76*
_____ **[9272]**   New Haven B/W Caboose, *79*

Midwest Division TCA

_____ **[00002]** Midwest TCA Stock Car, *75*
_____ **[7600]**   Frisco "Spirit of '76" N5C Caboose "00003", *76*
_____ **[4]**   C&NW F-3 A Unit, shell only, *77*
_____ **[00005]** Midwest TCA Covered Quad Hopper, *78*
_____ **[9872]**   PFE Reefer "00006", *79*
_____ **[1287]**   C&NW Reefer, *84*
_____ **[1988]**   Illinois Central Boxcar, *88*

NETCA

_____ **[1203]**   Boston & Maine NW-2, shell only, *72*
_____ **[9753]**   Maine Central Boxcar, *75*
_____ **[9768]**   Boston & Maine Boxcar, *76*
_____ **[9181]**   Boston & Maine N5C Caboose, *77*
_____ **[9400]**   Conrail Boxcar, *78*
_____ **[9785]**   Conrail Boxcar, *78*
_____ **[9415]**   Providence & Worcester Boxcar, *79*
_____ **[9423]**   NYNH&H Boxcar, *80*
_____ **[9445]**   Vermont Northern Boxcar, *81*
_____ **[5710]**   Canadian Pacific Reefer, *82*
_____ **[5716]**   Vermont Central Reefer, *83*
_____ **[6124]**   Delaware & Hudson Covered Quad Hopper, *84*
_____ **[8051]**   Hood's Milk Boxcar, *86*
_____ **52001**   Boston & Maine Quad Hopper w/ coal load, *92*
_____ **52016**   Boston & Maine Gondola w/ coil covers, *93*
_____ **[52043]** LL Bean Boxcar, *94*

Ozark Division TCA - Gateway Chapter

_____ **[9068]**   Reading Bobber Caboose, *76*
_____ **[9601]**   Illinois Central Gulf Hi-cube Boxcar, *77*
_____ **[9767]**   Railbox Boxcar, *78*

UNCATALOGED CLUB CARS AND SPECIAL PRODUCTION

_____ [5700]   Oppenheimer Reefer, *81*
_____ 52003   St. Louis Flatcar w/ trailer, *92*

Pacific Northwest Division TCA

_____ [No Number] Pacific Northwest Division F-3 AA, shells only, *74*

Rocky Mountain Division TCA

_____ 1971-1976 Rocky Mountain Division Reefer, *76*

Sacramento - Sierra Chapter TCA

_____ [9723]   Western Pacific Boxcar, *73*
_____ [9705]   D&RGW Boxcar, *75*
_____ [9301]   US Mail Operating Boxcar, *76*
_____ [9730]   CP Rail Boxcar, *77*
_____ [9785]   Conrail Boxcar, *78*
_____ [9726]   Erie-Lackawanna Boxcar, *79*
_____ [9414]   Cotton Belt Boxcar, *80*
_____ [9427]   Bay Line Boxcar, *81*
_____ [9444]   Louisiana Midland Boxcar, *82*
_____ [9452]   Western Pacific Boxcar, *83*
_____ [6401]   Virginian B/W Caboose, *84*
_____ [No Number] Lionel Lines Tender, shell only, *84*

Southern Division TCA

_____ [1976]   Florida East Coast F-3 ABA, shells only, 76
_____ [9287]   Southern N5C Caboose, 77
_____ [9403]   Seaboard Coast Line Boxcar, 78
_____ [9405]   Chattahoochie Boxcar, 79
_____ [9443]   Florida East Coast Boxcar, 81
_____ [6111]   L&N Covered Quad Hopper, 83
_____ [9471]   ACL Boxcar, 84
_____ [9482]   Norfolk Southern Boxcar, 85
_____ [1986]   Southern Bunk Car, 86
_____ [16606]   Southern Searchlight Car, 88

TCA Bicentennial Special Set

_____ 1973   TCA Bicentennial Observation Car, *76*
_____ 1974   TCA Bicentennial Passenger Car, *76*
_____ 1975   TCA Bicentennial Passenger Car, *76*
_____ 1976   TCA Bicentennial U36B, *76*

TOY TRAIN OPERATING SOCIETY (TTOS)

_____	**6076**	Santa Fe Hopper (O27), _70_
_____	**9512**	TTOS Summerdale Junction Passenger Car, _74_
_____	**9520**	TTOS Phoenix Combination Car, _75_
_____	**9526**	TTOS Snowbird Observation Car, _76_
_____	**9535**	TTOS Columbus Baggage Car, _77_
_____	**9678**	TTOS Hollywood Hi-cube Boxcar, _78_
_____	**9347**	TTOS Niagara Falls 3-D Tank Car, _79_
_____	**9868**	TTOS Oklahoma City Reefer, _80_
_____	**[9326]**	Burlington Northern B/W Caboose, _82_
_____	**[9355]**	Delaware & Hudson B/W Caboose, _82_
_____	**[9361]**	Chicago & North Western B/W Caboose, _82_
_____	**[9382]**	Florida East Coast B/W Caboose, _82_
_____	**[9883]**	TTOS Phoenix Reefer, _83_
_____	**[1984]**	TTOS Sacramento Northern Boxcar, _84_
_____	**[1985]**	TTOS Snowbird Covered Quad Hopper, _85_
_____	**6582**	TTOS Portland Flatcar w/ wood load, _86_
_____	**(17871)**	NYC Flatcar w/ Kodak and Xerox trailers "81487", _87_
_____	**(17872)**	Anaconda Ore Car "81988", _88_
_____	**(17877)**	MKT 3-D Tank Car "3739469", _89_
_____	**17884**	Columbus & Dayton Terminal Boxcar (Std. O), _90_
_____	**(17889)**	Southern Pacific Flatcar w/ trailer "15791" (Std. O), _91_
_____	**(19963)**	Union Equity 3-bay ACF Hopper "86892" (Std. O), _92_
_____	**(52010)**	Weyerhaeuser DD Boxcar "838593" (Std. O), _93_
_____	**(52029)**	Ford 1-D Tank Car "12" (O27), _94_
_____	**(52030)**	Ford Gondola "4023", _94_
_____	**(52031)**	Ford Hopper "1458" (O27), _94_

TTOS Gadsden-Pacific Ore Cars

_____	**17878**	Magma Ore Car w/ load, _89_
_____	**17881**	Phelps-Dodge Ore Car w/ load, _90_
_____	**17886**	Cyprus Ore Car w/ load, _91_
_____	**19961**	Inspiration Consolidated Copper Co. Ore Car w/ load, _92_
_____	**52011**	Tucson, Cornelia & Gila Bend Ore Car w/ load, _93_
_____	**52027**	Pinto Valley Mine Ore Car w/ load, _94_

Other TTOS Production

_____	**[1983]**	TTOS Phoenix 3-D Tank Car, _83_
_____	**(17894)**	Southern Pacific Tractor, _91_
_____	**(19962)**	Southwest TTOS Southern Pacific 3-bay ACF Hopper "496035" (Std. O), _92_

52009)	Sacramento Valley TTOS Western Pacfic Boxcar "64641993", *93*
(52021)	Weyerhaeuser Tractor and Trailer, *93*
52022	Union Pacific Boxcar, *93*
(52047)	Southwest TTOS Cotton Belt Woodside Caboose w/ smoke "1921" (Std. O), *93-94*
(52032)	Ford 1-D Tank Car w/ Kughn inscription "14" (O27), *94*
(52046)	ACL Boxcar "16247", *94*
(52053)	TTOS Carail Boxcar, *94*
(52040)	Wolverine TTOS GTW Flatcar w/ LL Tractor & Trailer, *95*
(52058)	Central California TTOS Santa Fe Boxcar "64641895", *95*

VIRGINIA TRAIN COLLECTORS (VTC)

[7679]	VTC Boxcar, *79*
[7681]	VTC N5C Caboose, *81*
[7682]	VTC Covered Quad Hopper, *82*
[7683]	Virginia Fruit Express Reefer, *83*
[7684]	Vitraco 3-D Tank Car, *84*
[7685]	VTC Boxcar, *85*
[7686]	VTC GP-7, *86*

SECTION 6
LARGE SCALE

1	(See 85120)
3	(See 85115)
5	(See 85121)
100	(See 85100)
101	(See 85101)
112	(See 85112)
400	(See 87400)
401	(See 87401)
404	(See 87404)
485	(See 85006)
486	(See 85007)
700	(See 87700)
701	(See 87701)
709	(See 87709)
712	(See 87712)
2003	(See 85003)
2004	(See 85005)
5000	(See 55000, 85000)
5001	(See 85001)
5102	(See 85102)
5103	(See 85103)
5104	(See 85104)
5105	(See 85105)
5106	(See 85106)
5107	(See 85107)
5108	(See 85108)
5109	(See 85109)
5110	(See 85110)
5111	(See 85111)
5113	(See 85113)
5114	(See 85114)
6000	(See 86000)
6001	(See 86001)
6002	(See 86002)
6003	(See 86003)
6004	(See 86004)

		Exc	New	Cond/$
6005	(See 86005)			
7402	(See 87402)			
7403	(See 87403)			
7405	(See 87405)			
7406	(See 87406)			
7407	(See 87407)			
7500	(See 87500)			
7501	(See 87501)			
7502	(See 87502)			
7503	(See 87503)			
7504	(See 87504)			
7508	(See 87508)			
7702	(See 87702)			
7703	(See 87703)			
7704	(See 87704)			
7705	(See 87705)			
7706	(See 87706)			
7707	(See 87707)			
7708	(See 87708)			
7711	(See 87711)			
7713	(See 87713)			
7716	(See 87716)			
7800	(See 87800)			
7806	(See 87806)			
(55000)	Lionel Lines RailScope 0-4-0T "5000", *88-90*	—	225	_____
(81000)	Gold Rush Special set, *87-90*	—	190	_____
(81001)	Thunder Mountain Express set, *88-89*	—	200	_____
(81002)	Frontier Freight set, *88-89*	—	175	_____
(81003)	Great Northern set, *90*		NM	
(81004)	North Pole Railroad set, *89-91*	—	165	_____
(81006)	Union Pacific Limited set, *90-91*	—	220	_____
(81007)	Disney Magic Express set, *90*	—	250	_____
(81008)	Walt Disney World set, *91*		NM	
(81011)	Thomas the Tank Engine set, *93 u*	150	175	_____
(81014)	James & Troublesome Trucks set, *94*		CP	_____
(81016)	Thomas the Tank Engine Deluxe Train set, *94*		CP	_____
(81017)	The Ornament Express set, *94*		CP	_____
(81050)	Gold Rush Special set w/ mailer, *87 u*		NRS	_____
(81051)	Spiegel PRR set, *87 u*		NRS	_____

		Exc	New Cond/$
(81054)	Gold Rush Special set w/o transformer, *90 u*		NRS _____
(81057)	North Pole Railroad set w/ mailer, *90 u*		NRS _____
(81059)	JCPenney Thomas the Tank Engine set, *94 u*		CP _____
(82000)	Straight Track, *87-94*		CP _____
(82001)	Curved Track 4.3', *87-94*		CP _____
(82002)	Straight Track, box of 4, *87-94*		CP _____
(82003)	Curved Track 4.3', box of 4, *87-94*		CP _____
(82004)	Curved Track 5.3', *88-94*		CP _____
(82006)	35" Straight Track, *88-94*		CP _____
(82007)	Right Remote Switch, *89-94*		CP _____
(82008)	Left Remote Switch, *89-94*		CP _____
(82010)	Thomas Track Pack, *94*		CP _____
(82011)	Thomas Left Manual Switch, *94*		CP _____
(82012)	Thomas Right Manual Switch, *94*		CP _____
(82013)	Thomas Curved Track 4.3', box of 4, *94*		CP _____
(82014)	Thomas Straight Track, box of 4, *94*		CP _____
(82101)	Lockon w/ wires, *88-94*		CP _____
(82102)	Conversion Rail Joiners (6), *88-94*		CP _____
(82103)	Conversion Knuckle Couplers (2), *88-91*	—	5 _____
(82104)	Water Tower kit, *88-89*	—	50 _____
(82105)	Engine House kit, *88-89*	—	125 _____
(82106)	Watchman Shanty kit, *88-89*	—	65 _____
(82107)	Passenger & Freight Station kit, *88-89*	—	100 _____
(82108)	Manual Uncoupler, *88-94*		CP _____
(82109)	Brass Pins (12), *88-94*		CP _____
(82110)	Lumber Shed kit, *89*	—	65 _____
(82111)	Freight Platform kit, *89*	—	90 _____
(82112)	Figure set (6), *89-94*		CP _____
(82115)	RailSounds Control Box, *90-94*		CP _____
(82115)	Wooden Vehicle Assortment, *89*		NM
(82116)	DC Converter Box, *91 u, 92-94*		CP _____
(82116)	1936 Ford Pickup, *89*		NM
(82117)	Crossing Gate and Signal, *91*		NM
(82117)	1928 Ford Model A Coupe, *89*		NM
(82118)	1936 Ford "Woody" Station Wagon, *89*		NM _____
(82120)	Thomas Sound System, *94*		CP _____
(82121)	Thomas Play Pack, *94*		CP _____
(82122)	Thomas Building Pack, *94*		CP _____
(85000)	Seaboard System GP-9 "5000", *90-91*	—	350 _____

		Exc	New	Cond/$
(85001)	Conrail GP-7 "5001", *90-91*	—	350	_____
(85003)	BN GP-20 "2003", *91 u, 92-94*		CP	_____
(85005)	BN GP-20 Dummy "2004", *92-94*		CP	_____
(85006)	Union Pacific GP-20 "485", *93-94*		CP	_____
(85007)	Union Pacific GP-20 Dummy "486", *93-94*		CP	_____
(85100)	Pennsylvania 0-6-0T "100", *87*	—	110	_____
(85101)	D&RG 0-6-0T "101", *87-90*	—	100	_____
(85102)	New York Central 4-4-2 "5102", *88*	—	200	_____
(85103)	Santa Fe 4-4-2 "5103", *88*	—	200	_____
(85104)	Santa Fe 0-4-0T "5104", *88-89*	—	90	_____
(85105)	Pennsylvania 0-4-0T "5105", *88-89*	—	90	_____
(85106)	Chessie System 4-4-2 "5106", *89*	—	200	_____
(85107)	Great Northern 4-4-2 "5107", *89*	—	200	_____
(85108)	B&O 0-4-0T "5108", *89*	—	95	_____
(85109)	Canadian Pacific 0-6-0T "5109", *89*	—	100	_____
(85110)	PRR 4-4-2 "5110", *90, 94*		CP	_____
(85111)	Great Northern 0-4-0T "5111", *90*		NM	
(85112)	RI&P 0-6-0T "112", *90*		NM	
(85113)	Union Pacific 0-4-0T "5113", *90-91*	—	100	_____
(85114)	North Pole Railroad 0-4-0T "5114", *89-91*	—	105	_____
(85115)	Disneyland 0-6-0T "3", *90*	—	110	_____
(85120)	Thomas the Tank Engine 0-6-0T "1", *93 u, 94*		CP	_____
(85121)	James the Red Engine 2-6-0 "5", *94*		CP	_____
(86000)	PRR Passenger Car "6000", *88-89*	—	65	_____
(86001)	PRR Observation Car "6001", *88-89*	—	65	_____
(86002)	Union Pacific Passenger Car "6002", *90-91*	—	65	_____
(86003)	Union Pacific Observation Car "6003", *90-91*	—	65	_____
(86004)	Disney World Passenger Car "6004", *91*		NM	
(86005)	Disney World Observation Car "6005", *91*		NM	
(86006)	"Annie" Passenger Car, *93 u, 94*		CP	_____
(86007)	"Clarabel" Passenger Car, *93 u, 94*		CP	_____
87000	New York Central Boxcar, *89*	—	45	_____
87001	Pennsylvania Boxcar, *88*	—	45	_____
87002	Santa Fe Boxcar, *88*	—	45	_____
87003	Great Northern Boxcar, *89*	—	45	_____
87004	Southern Boxcar, *90*	—	50	_____
87005	Northern Pacific Boxcar, *90*	—	50	_____
87006	Season's Greetings Boxcar, *89 u*	—	80	_____
87007	Season's Greetings Boxcar, *90 u*	—	85	_____

Number	Description	Exc	New	Cond/$
87009	Western Pacific Boxcar, *91*	—	50	_____
87100	Union Pacific PFE Reefer, *88*	—	50	_____
87101	Pennsylvania Reefer, *88*	—	50	_____
87102	Chesapeake & Ohio Reefer, *89*	—	50	_____
87103	Tropicana Reefer, *90*	—	60	_____
87104	Gerber Reefer, *90*	—	60	_____
87105	Seaboard Reefer, *89*	—	50	_____
87107	A&P Reefer, *91*	—	65	_____
87200	Lionel Handcar, *89-90*	—	70	_____
87201	Milwaukee Road Ore Car, *89*	—	35	_____
87202	Chessie System Ore Car, *89*	—	35	_____
87203	Santa & Snowman Handcar, *90*	—	90	_____
87204	Northern Pacific Ore Car, *90*	—	40	_____
87205	Pennsylvania Ore Car, *90*	—	40	_____
87207	Mickey & Donald Handcar, *91*	—	150	_____
87208	Wile E. Coyote & Roadrunner Handcar, *92*	—	100	_____
(87400)	PRR Gondola "400", *87*	—	35	_____
(87401)	D&RG Gondola "401", *87-90*	—	30	_____
(87402)	Santa Fe Gondola "7402", *88*	—	35	_____
(87403)	New York Central Gondola "7403", *88*	—	35	_____
(87404)	Disneyland Gondola "404", *90*	—	40	_____
(87405)	Chessie System Gondola "7405", *89*	—	35	_____
(87406)	Southern Gondola "7406", *89*	—	35	_____
(87407)	MKT Gondola "7407", *90*	—	40	_____
(87411)	"Troublesome Trucks" Gondola, *94*		CP	_____
(87500)	D&RG Flatcar "7500", *88*	—	35	_____
(87501)	Pennsylvania Flatcar "7501", *88*	—	35	_____
(87502)	Santa Fe Flatcar "7502", *88-89*	—	30	_____
(87503)	ICG Flatcar "7503", *89*	—	30	_____
(87504)	Union Pacific Flatcar "7504", *89*	—	30	_____
87505	Soo Line Flatcar w/ logs, *90*	—	45	_____
(87508)	Merry Christmas Lines Flatcar "7508", *89-91*	—	35	_____
87600	Alaska Tank Car, *89*	—	55	_____
87601	Santa Fe Tank Car, *89*	—	50	_____
87602	Gulf Tank Car, *90*	—	55	_____
87603	Borden Tank Car, *90*	—	55	_____
87604	Shell Tank Car, *91*	—	65	_____
(87700)	Pennsylvania Caboose "700", *87*	—	50	_____
(87701)	D&RG Caboose "701", *87-90*	—	50	_____

		Exc	New	Cond/$
(87702)	Santa Fe Caboose "7702", *88*	—	45	_____
(87703)	New York Central Caboose "7703", *88*	—	45	_____
(87704)	Santa Fe Bobber Caboose "7704", *88-89*	—	40	_____
(87705)	Great Northern Caboose "7705", *89*	—	50	_____
(87706)	Chessie System Caboose "7706", *89*	—	50	_____
(87707)	B&O Bobber Caboose "7707", *89*	—	40	_____
(87708)	Canadian Pacific Bobber Caboose "7708", *89*	—	45	_____
(87709)	Disneyland Caboose "709", *90*	—	50	_____
(87711)	Great Northern Bobber Caboose "7711", *90*		NM	
(87712)	RI&P Caboose "712", *90*		NM	_____
(87713)	Pennsylvania Caboose "7713", *90*	—	50	_____
(87716)	North Pole Railroad Bobber Caboose "7716", *89-91*	—	45	_____
(87800)	NYC Searchlight Car "7800", *89-90*	—	85	_____
87802	Conrail Boxcar w/ ETD, *90-91*	—	70	_____
87803	Seaboard Boxcar w/ ETD, *90-91*	—	70	_____
(87806)	REA Boxcar w/ Steam RailSounds "7806", *91*		NM	

				Exc	New
1945	Consumer Catalog	8-1/2" x 11"	4 pages		NRS
1946	Consumer Catalog	8-3/8" x 11-1/4"	20 pages	35	60
1947	Consumer Catalog	11-1/4" x 7-5/8"	32 pages	30	45
1948	Consumer Catalog	11-1/4" x 8"	36 pages	25	40
1949	Consumer Catalog	11-1/4" x 8"	40 pages	75	100
1950	Consumer Catalog	11-1/4" x 8"	44 pages	35	60
1951	Consumer Catalog	11-1/4" x 7-3/4"	36 pages	25	45
1952	Consumer Catalog	11-1/4" x 7-3/4"	36 pages	20	30
1953	Consumer Catalog	11-1/4" x 7-5/8"	40 pages	20	30
1954	Consumer Catalog	11-1/4" x 7-5/8"	44 pages	15	25
1955	Consumer Catalog	11-1/4" x 7-5/8"	44 pages	12	20
1956	Consumer Catalog	11-1/4" x 7-5/8"	40 pages	12	20
1957	Consumer Catalog	11-1/4" x 7-1/2"	52 pages	10	15
1958	Consumer Catalog	11-1/4" x 7-5/8"	56 pages	8	12
1959	Consumer Catalog	11" x 8-1/2"	56 pages	10	15
1960	Consumer Catalog	11" x 8-3/8"	56 pages	6	10
1961	Consumer Catalog	8-1/2" x 11"	72 pages	6	10
1962	Consumer Catalog	8-1/2" x 11"	100 pages	8	12
1963	Consumer Catalog	8-3/8" x 10-7/8"	56 pages	4	6
1964	Consumer Catalog	8-3/8" x 10-7/8"	24 pages	4	6
1965	Consumer Catalog	8-1/2" x 10-7/8"	40 pages	4	6
1966	Consumer Catalog	10-7/8" x 8-3/8"	40 pages	4	6
1967	Same Catalog as 1966				
1968	Consumer Catalog	8-1/2" x 11"	8 pages	4	6
1969	Consumer Catalog	11" x 8-1/2"	8 pages	3	5
1970	Consumer Catalog w/ foldout poster	8-1/2" x 11"	8 pages	3	5
1971	Consumer Catalog	8-1/2" x 11"	12 pages	3	5
1972	Consumer Catalog	8-1/2" x 11"	16 pages	2	4
1973	Consumer Catalog	8-1/2" x 11"	16 pages	2	4
1974	Consumer Catalog	8-1/2" x 11"	20 pages	2	4
1975	Consumer Catalog	8-1/2" x 11"	24 pages	2	4
1976	Consumer Catalog	8-1/2" x 11"	24 pages	2	4
1977	Consumer Catalog	8-1/2" x 11"	24 pages	2	4
1978	Consumer Catalog	8-1/2" x 11"	24 pages	2	4
1979	Consumer Catalog	8-1/2" x 11"	24 pages	2	4
1980	Consumer Catalog	8-1/2" x 11"	28 pages	2	4
1981	Consumer Catalog	5-1/2" x 7"	32 pages	1	2
1982	Traditional Series Consumer Catalog	8-1/2" x 11"	20 pages	2	4
1982	Collector Series Consumer Catalog	8-1/2" x 11"	12 pages	2	4
1983	Traditional Series Consumer Catalog	8-1/2" x 11"	20 pages	2	3

Year	Description	Size	Pages	Exc	New
1983	Collector Series Consumer Catalog	8-1/2" x 11"	16 pages	2	3
1984	Traditional Series Consumer Catalog	8-1/2" x 11"	20 pages	2	3
1984	Collector Series Consumer Catalog	8-1/2" x 11"	16 pages	2	3
1985	Traditional Series Consumer Catalog	8-1/2" x 11"	20 pages	2	3
1985	Collector Series Consumer Catalog	8-1/2" x 11"	12 pages	2	3
1986	Traditional Series Consumer Catalog	8-1/2" x 11"	16 pages	2	3
1986	Collector Series Consumer Catalog	8-1/2" x 11"	16 pages	2	3
1986	Stocking Stuffers Brochure	8-1/2" x 11"	4 pages	2	3
1987	Consumer Catalog	8-1/2" x 11"	40 pages	2	3
1987	Large Scale Brochure	11" x 8-1/2"	6 pages	1	2
1987	Stocking Stuffers Brochure	8-1/2" x 11"	4 pages	2	3
1988	Consumer Catalog	8-1/2" x 11"	40 pages	2	3
1988	Large Scale Catalog	8-1/2" x 11"	16 pages	1	2
1988	Classics Brochure	8-1/2" x 11"	4 pages	1	2
1988	Hiawatha Brochure	8-1/2" x 11"	4 pages	2	3
1988	Stocking Stuffers Flyer	8-1/2" x 11"	1 page	2	3
1989	Pre-Toy Fair Consumer Catalog	8-1/2" x 11"	20 pages	2	3
1989	Toy Fair Consumer Catalog	8-1/2" x 11"	28 pages	2	3
1989	Pre-Toy Fair Classics Brochure	8-1/2" x 11"	4 pages	1	2
1989	Toy Fair Classics Brochure	8-1/2" x 11"	4 pages	1	2
1989	Large Scale Catalog	8-1/2" x 11"	20 pages	1	2
1989	Stocking Stuffers Brochure	8-1/2" x 11"	4 pages	2	3
1990	Book 1 Consumer Catalog	8-1/2" x 11"	20 pages	2	4
1990	Book 2 Consumer Catalog	8-1/2" x 11"	36 pages	2	3
1990	Large Scale Catalog	8-1/2" x 11"	16 pages	1	2
1990	Stocking Stuffers Brochure	8-1/2" x 11"	6 pages	2	3
1991	Book 1 Consumer Catalog	8-1/2" x 11"	24 pages	2	4
1991	Book 2 Consumer Catalog	8-1/2" x 11"	60 pages	2	3
1991	Stocking Stuffers Brochure	8-1/2" x 11"	6 pages	2	3
1992	Book 1 Consumer Catalog	8-1/2" x 11"	32 pages	2	4
1992	Book 2 Consumer Catalog	8-1/2" x 11"	48 pages	2	3
1992	Stocking Stuffers Brochure	8-1/2" x 11"	8 pages	2	3
1993	Book 1 Consumer Catalog	8-1/2" x 11"	32 pages	2	4
1993	Book 2 Consumer Catalog	8-1/2" x 11"	52 pages	2	3
1993	Stocking Stuffers/1994 Spring Releases Catalog	8-1/2" x 11"	28 pages	2	3
1994	Consumer Catalog	8-1/2" x 11"	64 pages		CP
1994	Thomas the Tank Engine Catalog	8-1/2" x 11"	8 pages		CP
1994	Trainmaster Transformer Catalog	8-1/2" x 11"	8 pages		CP
1994	Stocking Stuffers/1995 Spring Releases Catalog	8-1/2" x 11"	32 pages		CP

ABBREVIATIONS
Pocket Guide Descriptions

A—diesel A unit
AA—two diesel A units
AAR—Association of American Railroads (truck type)
AC—alternating current
acc.—accessory
ACF—hopper type
Alco—diesel type
Alco A—diesel type
Alco FA-2A —diesel type
Alco FA-2B—diesel type
Anniv.—Anniversary
appro.—approaches
auto.—automatic
B—diesel B unit
Bag.—baggage
Bldg.—building
Blvd.—boulevard
Box.—boxcar
b/w—black and white
B/W—bay window
bump.—bumper(s)
Cab.—caboose
cata.—catalog
cent.—central
chem.—chemical
con.—connection
cont.—control
Conv.—conversion
CP—current production
C.V.—Commodore Vanderbilt
Dash-8—diesel type
DC—direct current
DD—double-door
dep.—depressed
d.p.d.t.—double-pole, double-throw switches
dir.—direct
dum.—dummy
dz.—dozen
elec.—electric
electr.—electronic
EP-5—electric type locomotive
TD—end-of-train device

Exp.—express
ext.—extended
E/V—extended vision
F-3—diesel type
F.A.O.S.—F A O Schwarz
FARR—Famous American Railroad Series
FF—Fallen Flag Series
Flat.—flatcar
FM—Fairbanks-Morse
GG-1—electric type locomotive
GE—switcher type
Gen.—general, steam type
Gon.—gondola
GP-7—diesel type
GP-9—diesel type
GP-20—diesel type
GP-35—diesel type
GP-38-2—diesel type
Hi-cube—boxcar type
Hop.—hopper
HS—heat-stamped
illum.—illuminated
ins.—insulated, insulator
lett.—lettering
litho.—lithographed
low-cup.—low-cupola
maint.—maintenance
man.—manual
MB—multi-block door
mech.—mechanical
merch.—merchandise
MU—multiple unit (commuter cars)
N5C—caboose type
N8—caboose type
NBA—National Basketball Assoc.
NHL—National Hockey League
NM—not manufactured
NW-2—diesel type
O—Lionel Gauge (1-1/4" between outside rails)
OO—Lionel Gauge (3/4" between outside rails)
Obs.—observation

—operating
—orange
ss.—passenger
c(s).—piece(s)
port.—porthole
pow.—power, powered
pr.—pair
Pull.—Pullman
Quad—quad hopper
Rad.—radius
R.C.—remote control
RDC—diesel-powered passenger
  unit
rect.—rectifier
rectifier—electric type locomotive
Reefer—refrigerator car
Refrig.—refrigerator
rem.—remote
rnd.—round
RS—rubber-stamped
RS-3—diesel type
RSC-3—diesel type
RSD-4—diesel type
SB—single-block door
SD-9—diesel type
SD-18—diesel type
SD-28—diesel type
SD-40—diesel type
SD-60M—diesel type

sec.—section
SP—caboose type
spec.—special
SSS—Service Station Special
St.—state
Sta.—station
Std.—Standard Gauge (2-1/8"
  between outside rails
Steam—steam engine
str.—straight
Sup.—super
S/W—square window
Switch.—switcher
Tdr.—tender
TOFC—flatcar type
TT—TruTrack
TTUX—flatcar type
Trk.—track
Trans.—transformer
u or uncat.—uncataloged
U36B—diesel type
U36C—diesel type
V. D.—Vista Dome
w/—with
w/o—without
whl.—wheel
1-D—one dome
2-D—two dome
3-D—three dome

Railroad Name Abbreviations

ACL—Atlantic Coast Line
ACY—Akron, Canton and
  Youngstown
ALASK—Alaska Railroad
AT&SF (ATSF)—Atchison, Topeka,
  and Santa Fe
B&A—Boston & Albany
BAOC—British American Oil Co.
BAR—Bangor and Aroostook
B&LE—Bessemer and Lake Erie
B&M—Boston and Maine

BN—Burlington Northern
B&O—Baltimore and Ohio
C&A—Chicago and Alton
C&IM—Chicago & Illinois Midland
CB&Q (CBQ)—Chicago, Burlington,
  and Quincy
CN—Canadian National
CNJ—Central of New Jersey
C&NW (CNW)—Chicago and North
  Western
C&O—Chesapeake and Ohio

CP—Canadian Pacific
CRI&P—Chicago, Rock Island, and Pacific
D&H—Delaware and Hudson
DL&W—Delaware, Lackawanna, and Western
DM&IR—Duluth, Missabe, and Iron Range
D&RG—Denver and Rio Grande
D&RGW—Denver and Rio Grande Western
DT&I—Detroit, Toledo, and Ironton
D&TS—Detroit and Toledo Shore Line
EJ&E—Elgin, Joliet, and Eastern
EMD—Electro-Motive Division
Erie-Lack.—Erie-Lackawanna
FEC—Florida East Coast
GM&O—Gulf, Mobile, and Ohio
GN—Great Northern
GTW—Grand Trunk Western
IC—Illinois Central
ICG—Illinois Central Gulf
IETCA—Inland Empire Train Collectors Association
L&C—Lancaster and Chester
Lack—Lackawanna
LCAC—Lionel Collectors Association of Canada
LCCA—Lionel Collectors Club of America
LCOL—Lionel Central Operating Lines
LL—Lionel Lines
L&N—Louisville and Nashville
LNAC—Louisville, New Albany, and Corydon
LOTS—Lionel Operating Train Society
LRRC—Lionel Railroader Club
LV—Lehigh Valley
MD&W—Minnesota, Dakota, and Western
NETCA—New York Metropolitan Division TCA

MKT—Missouri, Kansas, Texas (KATY)
MNS (MN&S)—Minneapolis, Northfield, and Southern
MP (MoPac)—Missouri Pacific
MPA—Maryland and Pennsylvania (Ma and Pa)
MILW—Milwaukee Road
M&St L—Minneapolis and St. Louis
NC&St L—Nashville, Chattanooga, and St. Louis
NETCA—New England Division Train Collectors Association
NH—New Haven
NKP—Nickel Plate Road
NLOE—Nassau Lionel Operating Engineers
NP—Northern Pacific
N&W—Norfolk and Western
NYC—New York Central
NYNH&H—New York, New Haven, and Hartford
ON—Ontario Northland
PC—Penn Central
P&E—Peoria and Eastern
PFE—Pacific Fruit Express
PHD—Port Huron and Detroit
P&LE—Pittsburgh and Lake Erie
PRR—Pennsylvania Railroad
REA—Railway Express Agency
RF&P—Richmond, Fredericksburg, and Potomac
RI—Rock Island
SCL—Seaboard Coast Line
SP—Southern Pacific
SP&S—Spokane, Portland, and Seattle
SUNX—Sunoco
TA&G—Tennessee, Alabama, and Georgia
TCA—Train Collectors Association
T&P—Texas and Pacific
TP&W—Toledo, Peoria, and Western
TTOS—Toy Train Operating Society

NOTES

NOTES

NOTES

NOTES

NOTES

NOTES